MW00810282

A
VETTER COMMUNICATIONS
COMPANY, INC.
IMPRINT

Hail to the Dragon Slayer

ARTHUR A. LEMANN III

HAIL TO THE DRAGON SLAYER

VCCI

 Published by VCCI, an imprint of Pontalba Press, 4417 Dryades Street, New Orleans, Louisiana, 70115.

First Edition

Designed by Stephanie Stephens
Cover and Author Photograph by Philip Gould

Lemann, Arthur Anthony, 1942-
Hail to the dragon slayer / Arthur A. Lemann III
—1st ed.
p. cm.
ISBN: 0-9653145-6-1

1. Lemann, Arthur Anthony, 1942- 2. Lawyers–Louisiana–Biography. 3. Trials–Louisiana I. Title.

KF373.L46A3 1998 340'.092[B]
QBI98-616

To all the poor souls in Angola
who made this book possible.

ACKNOWLEDGMENTS

I owe much to many: Sheila Bosworth, Ann Goette, and Nancy Lemann, my literary friends, who reviewed an early manuscript and offered many helpful hints; Elizabeth Neilson and Myra Peak, who tended the King's English; Cyril Vetter, my agent and life-long friend, who kept faith in the project although I betrayed him once in our youth; and foremost, to my dear wife, Roberta, who has earned a place in heaven for putting up with me all these long years—thank you.

Table of Contents

PROLOGUE

The Birth of a Dragon Slayer

I am born on Tobacco Road near Augusta. Born in Georgia, but mind you I'm not from Georgia. I'm from Louisiana. In fact, all Lemanns are from Louisiana. My father just happened to be at Fort Gordon during the beginning of World War II, and my mother had followed him there before he was shipped overseas. After the war, my father returned to Louisiana, where he belonged.

My upbringing was privileged. I grew up on a sugar cane plantation, Palo Alto, which has been in my family since before the Civil War. My father, Arthur, or "Bubs" as he liked to be called, was a squire and very much "boss" of the plantation. My mother, Camille Ker, on the other hand, was a romantic. It was from her that I inherited my love for errantry. She would sit me on the potty and give me books about King Arthur, Sir Lancelot, Sir Galahad, and knights in shining armor on white steeds rescuing distressed damsels from fire-breathing dragons.

Palo Alto is located three miles south of Donaldsonville, where Bayou Lafourche meets the Mississippi River. Legend has it that the pirate, Jean Lafitte, used Bayou Lafourche as a secret route to transport his plunder from the Gulf of Mexico to the Mississippi River and then to New Orleans. Palo Alto faces Bayou Lafourche and La. 1, the highway that runs along the bayou from the Gulf to the Mississippi River at Donaldsonville.

The house at Palo Alto was built in the 1840s by my great, great, great grandfather, Mathias Rodriguez, an Islenos from the Canary Islands. Mathias built the home as a wedding gift for his daughter, Rosalee, who married Oscar Ayraud. Shortly before the Civil War, my great great grandfather, Oscar, mortgaged Palo Alto to Jacob Lemann, another great great grandfather, who foreclosed on the property after the War. Obviously, the Ayrauds didn't think much of the Lemanns, that is, until 1914, when Jacob's grandson married Oscar's granddaughter.

Jacob was the first Lemann to come to this country, coming as a stowaway from Germany in the 1820s. A Jewish peddler, he soon amassed a fortune, owning at one time thirteen sugar cane plantations. And so we Lemanns are from the South, but yet, we aren't Southerners. In the 1850s, Jacob moved the family to New York City, but mind you, we aren't Yankees either. With property in the South and North, the Lemanns moved to Paris to wait out the war. After the South lost, Jacob moved back to Louisiana to take economic advantage of the freed slaves. Thus, my sense of commerce, what little there is, comes from my father's side.

My chivalry, on the other hand, comes from my mother's side. She and her sister, my Aunt Delta, trace their heritage back to Shakespeare's *Henry IV* and to Sir Walter Scott's *Lay of the Last Minstrel*. It seems the Percys and the Kers hated one another, but like the Lemanns and the Ayrauds, they eventually intermarried in this country. Mother and Aunt Delta are still researching the family tree, and Sir Walter Scott is an important clue. I'm quite certain that sooner or later they will trace my lineage back to Ivanhoe.

Aunt Delta has been widowed longer than married. Her husband died some fifty years ago, but still she dresses in black, wearing a black hood and veil at all times and for all occasions. She also claims that, as a child, she had to sleep with goats for warmth. Like Scarlett O'Hara, Aunt Delta has known hard times.

My mother's family were Scottish free-thinkers. In South Louisiana, when you cross a Scottish free-thinker with a Jew, you beget a Roman Catholic. And so I was raised as a Roman Catholic. We were taught by nuns and terrified by priests. The dominance of the Church was total and unchallenged. A Catholic education in Donaldsonville during the 1940s and 1950s was much the same as it had been in France during the 1640s and 1650s—Voltaire had not arrived. For example, we were taught never to twirl a rosary because it would turn into a snake . . . this was the word of the Lord.

The first words out of my mouth each morning were, "MiMi, MaMa, MoMo." This signaled my mother and grandmothers to tend to my every whim. A shrink once said that this morning ritual was at the root of my inability to view women separately. As the theory goes, I must have confused the Holy Trinity with "MiMi, MaMa, MoMo." This illness is known as my 3-M syndrome.

Most people stop doing something three times a day to eat. At Palo Alto, we stopped eating three times a day to do something else, mostly to get ready for the next meal. The main meal, if one must be favored over another, was at noon and usually set for at least thirteen, counting the siblings, parents, great grandfather, and city cousins who had a habit of "passing by" on any given day around noon. Rice and gravy, red beans, round steak smothered with turnips, fresh Creole tomatoes, succotash, hot buttered biscuits, fig preserves, apple pie from a window sill, and gallons of minted iced tea for most of us, and then perhaps red Kool-Aid for brother David because he didn't like iced tea; pink Kool-Aid for sister

Kathleen because she didn't like iced tea or red Kool-Aid; green Kool-Aid for brother Robert because he didn't like iced tea, red or pink Kool-Aid; chicken for brother Peter because the round steak "squeaked"; corn and carrots separated from the succotash for sister Sue because she didn't like butter beans; butter beans for sister Becky because she didn't like corn and carrots; and all three separated for sister Zabette, not because she didn't like them mixed up, but just because she was Zabette.

Lunch, or dinner as we called it, started in the kitchen about seven o'clock, right after breakfast. Ceola, the cook, would begin browning the meat before making the roux, after which commenced the process of adding "just enough of 'dis" and "just enough of 'dat" to one of her glorious gravies. Of course, at the same time, crawfish heads had to be cleaned and tails peeled for the bisque that was for dinner day after tomorrow. Two ovens at full blast in August before air-conditioning produced a heat so ferocious that Ceola used to say she saw monkeys "dancin'" on the fence across the backyard, and my mother once claimed to have seen a cobra staring her down from behind the stove. But no matter how powerful the heat, and no matter how much starch went into the seersucker suits and button-down shirts drenched with perspiration and incense from a Sunday morning mass, nothing could overcome the gusto of a meal devoured on that twenty-foot cypress table in that majestic room where Lemanns ate a hundred years ago and no doubt will eat a hundred years from now.

Early on, I identified with the underdog. My childhood friends, Sonny and Boo-Boo, were children of plantation workers. Like them, I held my father in awe and showed him respect but deep down, I was sympathetic to their outlook—and, after all, he was the boss. So I sided with them. For instance, we would pick blackberries on the plantation and divide them into three piles: Sonny would take one pile home to his mother; Boo-Boo would take another pile home to his mother; and we sold the remaining pile to my mother, splitting the proceeds equally. This seemed perfectly fair to me. It was also my first lesson in fee splitting.

Besides heaven, the greatest invention of the Catholic Church is confession. No other religion offers such a handy redemption. That was especially true once I learned the ropes. It was the custom in Donaldsonville for all school children to go to confession on Friday and communion on Sunday. Not to receive communion on Sunday resulted in instant public castigation. The problem, of course, was that Friday and Saturday nights were traditional nights of sin. I still remember the great agony of trying to make it from Friday's confession to Sunday's communion. But I soon learned how to beat the system. By confessing on Friday to uncommitted sins and throwing in one whopper to cover the scam, I could march up to the rail on Sunday mornings under the watchful eye of parents and priests with a clear conscience. Again, I sided with the sinners. It was also my first lesson in immunity.

The church we normally attended actually was not in Donaldsonville but in the neighboring parish of Smoke Bend. The church in Smoke Bend was next to the Town & Country Nightclub where we went to drink and sin on Friday and Saturday nights. When the parking lot at the Town & Country got full, we naturally parked in the church yard. One night, the pastor, Father Lapere, became so incensed over us putting his holy land to such use that he retaliated by blasting out car windows with a shotgun. I, for one, never understood his fury, inasmuch as the Town & Country at least kept us in close proximity, especially at Christmas time when it was a regular custom the night before to stagger over for midnight mass. This custom, however, was not without some risk, as evidenced by the fact that on one Christmas Eve, I ended up drunk in the choir loft. At the most quiet and solemn moment in the service, I sang out an unsolicited and loud "Ahh men!" I was forcibly removed from the choir by some of the parishioners, and this became my first custodial experience. I also learned I could never break my mother's heart, permanently.

Donaldsonville is eccentric. Part of this may be attributable to the fact that it is always wrong. For example, Donaldsonville at one time thought it would become the State's capital. Indeed, the townspeople constructed a new building to house the government, only to have the capital removed to Baton Rouge after only three months in Donaldsonville. Another sign of this eccentricity is that people in Donaldsonville, unlike most people who build second homes in faraway places for a change in scenery, build second homes on the banks of the bayou across the street from their houses. I have often wondered what archeologists will make of this two thousand years from now when they find a matching cup and saucer in separate ruins one hundred yards apart.

I suspect it all goes back to the interdiction. When Father F. X. Cuppens, a Belgian native, began construction of the present church in Donaldsonville, a war broke out among the parishioners and he was chased out of town. The bishop retaliated by interdicting the town. Supposedly the interdiction was lifted around 1896, but no one can find proof of this because all of the church's records were destroyed in the great fire of 1911. According to Mr. Sidney Marchand, " . . . church news during said years is non-existent." My guess is the interdiction was never lifted.

Mr. Sidney was the town's historian. He was also a lawyer and a very distinguished-looking, white-haired gentleman. He wrote a number of books about Donaldsonville and his opening sentences, I wager, are among the most powerful in the English language. For example, in his book about the Donaldsonville Chief, the town's newspaper, he began,

> "On the Western Shore of LaSalle's great river, in Southern Louisiana, where a child of the Father of Waters—the Lafourche—begins its long journey to the open sea, and in the land where the plumed, jewel-

> bedecked and feathery Chief of the Chitimacha Indians held sway over two centuries ago, another more progressive Chief has established its present wigwam at 118 Railroad Avenue, in the city founded by William Donaldson."

Mr. Sidney's prose, however, dropped off considerably after his opening sentences, continuing, as he did, by reproducing newspaper articles, death notices and epithets, or by providing other valuable statistical information, such as, "Templet, H., Pvt. Co. V., Richardson's Battn. Rolls of Prisoner of War, C.S.A., paroled, Virginia, 1865."

After Mr. Sidney died, my father became the town's historian. He wasn't elected to the post, it just happened. All of a sudden, people just turned to him for historical information. When strangers came to town looking for something, the librarian or City Hall clerk sent them to "Mr. Bubba" at the B. Lemann & Bro. store founded by his great grandfather in the 1830s. Unlike Mr. Sidney, however, my father never wrote history; he talked history. My father also planted trees. Everywhere he went, he planted live oak trees.

My father didn't care very much for Aunt Delta. One reason for this was history. My father embraced history, while Aunt Delta fought history—recorded history, that is. She was always trying to alter its course. Take, for example, her forged birth certificate, which showed her to be at least ten years younger. And then there was the case of the missing bodies. For some reason, Aunt Delta moved some of her dead ancestors from the family cemetery at Linden in Natchez to some other cemetery, the whereabouts of which she now claims not to remember. History will never know what dark family secrets were covered up by that move.

Blackboard Jungle and *Rebel Without a Cause* were the movies that guided us through adolescence. Tugger and me. Tugger is Uncle's younger brother and my best friend. His father was the mayor of Donaldsonville, and Tugger and I would go around town demanding free drinks or free gasoline or free passage over the ferryboat, saying, "I'm Bubba Lemann's son and he's the mayor's son and we don't pay." This all ended badly for me. One day, Tugger and I stole a fifth of whiskey from his father's tavern and proceeded to drink it straight down, with me doing most of the drinking. Naturally, I became quite drunk. In a desperate attempt to sober me up, Tugger threw me in the Mississippi River. He walked along the bank holding my arm, dragging me up current then letting me float back down stream. The last thing I remembered was clinging to some bulrushes on the muddy banks of the river. Fortunately, a watchman at a nearby pumping station called the police and an ambulance to rescue me from the river. Before the police arrived, Tugger made me promise to say we had found the whiskey in back of the levee. Instead, when the police arrived, I said, "Tugger stole the whiskey from his Daddy's tavern, and he made me drink it!" That was my first lesson in turning state's evidence.

The next day, my father shipped me off to military school for my last two years of high school. Marion Military Institute is located in Marion, Alabama, not far from Selma. I was one of only a handful of Catholic students and, on Sundays, we were bussed to Selma for mass in a National Guard armory. It was at Marion, of all places, that my horizons were broadened. It was there, for example, that I learned in biology class that a man doesn't have fewer ribs than a woman. This would never have been revealed to me in Donaldsonville.

I learned another important lesson at Marion: I would never be a general. One weekend during my second year, having advanced to corporal, I was the ranking man on campus in my company. With the support of comrades-in-arms, I quickly imposed a reign of terror, making younger cadets kowtow, until my confederates revolted, tied me up, and threw me into a shower stall. Anarchy ensued. Needless to say, when the rank returned, I was busted and ended up graduating as a private.

College was no different. I flunked out of L.S.U. after the first semester. My father would say I was the only student who began college as a senior and graduated as a freshman. After flunking out, I decided to become self-educated. I told my father I wanted an unlimited supply of books and an apartment in which to study. At five-thirty the next morning, I found myself tarring hot tin rooftops on the plantation. Thus, another important lesson: there is a vast difference between identifying with the oppressed and actually being the oppressed. So, I left the hot tin rooftops after that summer and returned to college.

My youngest sister, Zabette, doesn't remember me without Roberta Ann. I began "going steady" with R.A. in high school, and we married while I was still in college. In fact, I only had two other girlfriends in Donaldsonville, Bobbie Gail Rodrigue and Ann Goette. I also went steady with Bobbie Gail and Ann, but they broke up with me. Bobbie Gail broke up with me when she discovered I was dating Ann, and Ann broke up with me after I married R.A. In between, it was the 3-M syndrome.

Our wedding was supposed to take place in the small church in Smoke Bend. After the invitations had been printed, Father Lapere refused to perform the ceremony on the grounds that I was a "Public Sinner!" While this would have been a pretty severe sanction for the choir incident alone, in defense of Father Lapere, I must say that it wasn't the only incident. I was found sleeping in the manger on a Christmas Eve and, on another occasion, I was caught hearing confessions. Fact is, I have performed, at one time or another, all of the sacraments . . . all without a license. Needless to say, Father Lapere's refusal to marry us caused quite a commotion with my mother and R.A.'s mother, Miss Roberta, both deeply religious women. They had to print an addendum to the wedding invitations announcing a change in location to the big church in Donaldsonville. To this day, I sometimes ascribe my name as Arthur A. Lemann III, B.A., LL.B., LL.M., and P.S., for "Public Sinner."

The big church in Donaldsonville was reigned over by Monsignor Edwin J. Gubler. Actually, the Monsignor reigned over all of Donaldsonville. He once told my father that since he was Monsignor, he should also be President of the Chamber of Commerce. As school children, we had a holiday for his birthday, except it was known as his "feast" day, the Monsignor having canonized himself even before death.

Industrialization didn't arrive in Donaldsonville until the 1950s. When this happened, the townspeople divided into the progressives, led by Monsignor Gubler, and the preservationists, led by my father. The progressives wanted huge petrochemical plants to locate along the Mississippi River. The progressives won, and many landowners (save the Lemanns) sold their sugar cane fields to the petrochemical plants. The progressives were so gleeful over the prospects of new jobs, they renamed the King of the local Mardi Gras ball, King Industrio.

The most picturesque building in Donaldsonville was the convent of the Sisters of Charity. Built in 1848, it was a lovely two story, brick structure with dormer windows and a cupola overlooking the river. A long alleyway of the whitest and purest Easter lilies one could ever hope to see enveloped the building, making it look like the home of Joan of Arc. During the Civil War when Admiral Farragut bombarded Donaldsonville, a cannonball flew through the convent's wall and, miraculously, landed harmlessly at the foot of a statue of the Blessed Virgin Mary, chipping away, as it fell, one of the Holy Mother's fingers. As school children, we would parade by and look in awe at the missing finger and cannonball lying at the feet of the Blessed Virgin.

After the progressives carried the day for the petrochemical plants, Monsignor Gubler decided to celebrate his triumph by constructing a new, windowless, concrete block building for the Sisters of Charity. But instead of building it in the backyard, he placed the concrete block building right on top of the Easter lilies, exactly one foot in front of the beautiful antebellum convent. Surviving Admiral Farragut was one thing, but surviving Monsignor Gubler was quite another.

When my father went to see the Monsignor about making financial arrangements for our wedding, he insisted that I attend private catechism classes. With one addendum already printed, I had no choice. When I arrived for my first class, the Monsignor began by saying, "Son, I understand you don't believe Jesus is the Son of God."

"Well, Father, I must admit I have my doubts," I said, squirming in the high backed chair he put me in.

"Son, let me ask you, when you were crossing on the ferry boat on your way here, if you had seen a man walking across the river, would you believe that to be a miracle?" Monsignor asked, taking a deep breath, and leaning back in his swivel chair.

"Well, Father, I guess so if I saw it with my own eyes," I stammered, caught completely off guard.

"And if I told you that was Jesus, would you then believe in Him?"

Monsignor asked omnipotently.

"Well, I guess so, Father," I meekly replied, trapped and cornered.

"Son, you don't have a problem at all," Monsignor said, smiling and reaching over to pat my arm.

Thus ended my catechism classes with the Monsignor, and two thousand years of skepticism. It was also my first lesson in good cross-examination.

R.A. and I were finally married in the big church, albeit sans flowers or music, a concession the Monsignor insisted we make in deference to Father Lapere and in light of my status as a Public Sinner. I then went to Loyola Law School where I was welcomed as a tuition-paying student under the Jesuitical rubric of no questions asked. For the first time, I excelled academically, finishing third in my class and serving as Editor-in-Chief of the Law Review. After law school, R.A. and I moved to Washington, D.C., where, following in Uncle's footsteps, I obtained an LL.M. from George Washington University.

I almost stayed in Washington and would have, had Dr. D. C. Foti had his way. Doc Foti, a dentist, lived next door to Miss Roberta on Bayou Lafourche. Now Doc truly was an eccentric, even by Donaldsonville's standards. Proof of this lies in the fact that Doc didn't build a second home across the street from his house. Instead, he built himself a church across the street from his house. When Monsignor Gubler refused to consecrate Doc's church, he started his own religion. The name plate on the door of his dental office read, "Rev. Doc. D. C. Foti."

The Rev. Doc became mayor of Donaldsonville, and when he went to Washington on town business, it was with the pomp accompanying a sub-Saharan potentate. The Rev. Doc was always accompanied by a large retinue of factotums, including a photographer who followed him around the hallways of the capitol taking pictures of whatever dignitary shook his hand. When the Rev. Doc found out I might be staying in Washington, he arranged an appointment for me with a Mr. Bienvenue, a third level bureaucrat at the Pentagon. A few days later, my mother called excitedly about my interviews with "Katzenbach and Ribicoff," two high-ranking Washington officials. She had heard of this from Miss Roberta. I'm not sure whether the misunderstanding resulted from the Rev. Doc's exaggerations, which he was known for, or whether it was due to my mother and Miss Roberta whispering in French when the topic involved her neighbor, an equally plausible explanation seeing that my mother and Miss Roberta, like many others in Donaldsonville, spoke French but didn't understand French.

R.A. and I returned to New Orleans. New Orleans is a patchwork collection of Donaldsonvilles stuck haphazardly together over time. Consequently, it too is a pretty strange place. Like Donaldsonville, it's a gumbo of cultures: Blacks, Jews, French, Italians, Arabs, Anglo-Saxons. One can cross a street in New Orleans and go from the south of France to North Little Rock. And it doesn't stop there. We have blacks with

French surnames dressing like Indian chiefs, Jews who go to mass on Sunday, Arabs who evict Anglo-Saxons, Irish pubs on Spanish streets, and a few Italians who, according to the United States Attorney, aren't in the Mafia. In fact, the last president of Deutsches-Haus, a German cultural club, was a Chinaman.

Like Donaldsonville, New Orleans can be wrong too. Consider the World's Fair and the casino fiascoes. In truth, about the only difference between the two places is that people in New Orleans don't build second homes across the street from their houses.

Returning to New Orleans was good for my well-being, inasmuch as I get dizzy whenever I go much farther north than Baton Rouge. I went to work for Polack, Rosenberg & Rittenberg, a small law firm founded by my cousin, Robert Polack. Bobby had been a partner at Monroe & Lemann, the big establishment law firm of my grandfather's brother, Montefiore Mordecai Lemann. According to my father, Uncle Monte was the greatest lawyer ever. I met him once when my father took me to his home to receive final approval for sending me to military school. At that time, all important decisions in the Lemann family were blessed by Uncle Monte. Why cousin Bobby left Monroe & Lemann to start his own law firm was a closely guarded family secret but, in any event, my father thought of him as the second best lawyer after Uncle Monte. Father was pleased. I became a real estate lawyer.

The Notarial Archives in New Orleans are located in the basement of the Civil District Court building. It is here that all important land records and other historical documents are kept. It is known as the catacombs. It is musty and damp, populated by mole-like notaries. Once in a while, I would catch a glimpse in the shadows of a small figure draped in black working feverishly in some large tome. Aunt Delta was busy . . . altering the course of history.

After two years of "running titles," I realized that, like the hot tin roofs at Palo Alto, the catacombs were not for me. And so I joined the faculty of Loyola Law School, where Uncle was waiting for me, having left Washington the year before to join the faculty. In Donaldsonville, we refer to blood strangers as uncle or nephew because our parents did and, I suppose, their parents before them. So you see, Uncle and I aren't really related, he is just the older brother of my best friend, Tugger.

Uncle is also a student of Donaldsonville, the difference between us being mostly one of technique. Uncle is more the fact gatherer. Take the case of Miss Francis. Miss Francis was Monsignor Gubler's housekeeper. She bought a home on the Mississippi Gulf Coast that the Monsignor used on weekends. She also bought him a brand new car to drive to and from the weekend home. When church money was discovered missing, the Monsignor blamed Miss Francis and she was branded an embezzler.

Now Uncle can tell you the dates when all of this happened, the make and model of the car, and the street address of the weekend home. In fact, Uncle can give you hundreds of facts about everything in

Donaldsonville. However, once a fact becomes chronicled, it becomes an absolute for Uncle. On the other hand, I limit my studies of Donaldsonville to only a few of its mysteries, such as the case of Miss Francis and the custom of building second homes across the street from houses.

Our Dean at the Law School was Marcel Garsaud. Mo was a very haggard man. Mo was haggard because Mo was a papist. If the Pope decided to retry Galileo, Mo would prosecute. It's not easy being a papist in the Twentieth Century, so he walked around in a perpetual state of gloom. He never whistled because it's hard, I imagine, to whistle a Gregorian chant.

Mo's wife, Fleta, was cute and vivacious. But she too had strange ways. Before Mo became Dean, when he didn't have to carry the weight of the papacy on haggard shoulders, Fleta looked like a nun. Oddly, once he became Dean, Fleta began to look like a starlet. She must have done it for the children because there's a lot to be said for having only one holy parent in a household at a time.

When Uncle and I joined the faculty in the early 1970s, a dramatic change was underway in legal education. For the first time, law schools began to place some emphasis on preparing law students for courtroom practice, as distinguished from the study of law under the Socratic method. Under the new "clinical education," senior law students, under faculty supervision, were allowed to appear in court to represent indigent clients. In my second year on the faculty, Uncle obtained a grant for the Law School to operate a Law Clinic, and I became its Director. Using criminal cases as teaching tools, and realizing that students learn more quickly when the stakes are high, the Law Clinic handled mostly felony cases. And, of course, since the highest stakes in criminal law are in murder cases, it was here that I began to fight prosecutors, judges, juries, the media, and public opinion—the dragons of the criminal justice system. It was in murder that I began to fight dragons.

ONE

The Honeymoon Knight

Janet Roby and Gregory Kress were married on St. Valentine's Day in Erie, Pennsylvania. Greg was a handsome young man who worked in his family's business as a promoter of a "personality development" system that had been invented by his father. The system was designed to motivate individuals, and Greg spent a lot of time marketing the program to social welfare agencies, once even spending eight weeks in an Alabama prison to teach the program to the inmates. He was, in the words of his father, "a traveling motivational therapist." His bride Janet was a pretty, petite blonde, whose father was an aide to the city's mayor. After the wedding, the young couple planned to fly to Hawaii, but a thick fog descended over Erie that night, causing a cancellation of all flights and, instead, Janet and Greg drove to New Orleans for their honeymoon.

Young, happy, carefree, and in love, the Big Easy was the place to be—the moonlit river, the quaint streetcars, the lovely mansions, the romantic French Quarter, the city that care forgot. But New Orleans can be unkind to strangers. The Big Easy on one street; the Big Killer around the corner. Janet and Gregory would take the wrong turn.

In New Orleans, the honeymooners stayed at the stately Fairmont, the old Roosevelt Hotel, which is located across Canal Street from the French Quarter. On Sunday, February 23, 1975, Greg and Janet slept late and then went to mass at a nearby Jesuit Church. After mass, they had dinner at Bailey's in the Fairmont, and then went to Bourbon Street. They ended up at the Silver Follies, a nightclub with a drag queen floor show. Once inside, they were befriended by another young couple; they drank together, laughed together, partied together, and had a good time together. At one point, the female ran her finger across Janet's face, telling her how pretty she was. But Valerie Manchester and Clifford McGraw weren't what they seemed to be. They weren't happy. They weren't carefree. They weren't in love. They were on the prowl. And they had found their prey.

Clifford McGraw was a bad man. As a teenager, he spent two years in the psychiatric ward of Charity Hospital. He then went to the State Reform School. As an adult, he was arrested at least nine times for serious offenses. Now in his early thirties, he had just been released from the Louisiana State Penitentiary at Angola after serving four years of a ten-year sentence for attempted murder. His girlfriend, Valerie, had dropped out of school in the tenth grade. She became pregnant and left the baby with her mother to raise. Valerie shifted from job to job, but mostly just lay around her parents' home and, as her mother once said, "You know how young'uns ain't too particular 'bout the way they do." In her early twenties, Valerie "took up" with Clifford McGraw in a dingy apartment at 516 Dufossat Street, a neighborhood which, in typical New Orleans fashion, was on the wrong end of an uptown street—one that begins with the rich and ends with the poor.

After the couples left the Silver Follies, they went to the honeymooners' room at the Fairmont where they had more drinks until Valerie and Clifford invited them to Dufossat Street for a midnight breakfast. The affluent Yankees, strangers in town, fell for the poor Southern trap. At the Dufossat Street apartment, more drinks, more laughs, a blaring radio. Then Greg went with McGraw into the bedroom to get some marijuana. Janet began to feel uneasy. Suddenly, she heard loud thuds and McGraw rushed out of the bedroom and began to strike her repeatedly with a heavy object, dragging her into the littered courtyard, where he continued to beat her savagely. Then cold steel, as her young and innocent face was ripped apart by the jagged edge of a rusty carpet knife. Darkness.

Her screams aroused the neighbors. Members of the New Orleans Police Department (NOPD) arrived shortly thereafter and found Janet, bleeding and unconscious in the trashy courtyard, the wedding rings missing from her fingers. They found Gregory dead in a pool of blood under a discarded mattress in the courtyard, brains splattered, six bullet holes through the head. His wallet and wedding ring were also missing. The police then saw Valerie, surly and indifferent, sweeping blood from her stoop nonchalantly. They arrested her and McGraw and charged them with first degree murder.

Janet was taken to Charity Hospital where she underwent six hours of major surgery. Her jaw and chin had been shattered, and she had a deep and gaping slash across her face. A number of her teeth had been knocked out. The police attempted to interview her but, delirious and semiconscious, she could only moan, "I can't find my husband." A few days later, the police visited her again and, this time, she remembered being struck in the face by Valerie as well as by McGraw.

Meanwhile, the two defendants had been taken to Magistrate Court for a first appearance. Magistrate Court, or "Magic Court" as it is sometimes called, is on the first floor of the Criminal District Court building, located on the corner of Tulane Avenue and Broad Street. For this reason, criminal court in New Orleans is simply referred to as "Tulane and Broad." At their first appearance, the Magistrate Judge (sometimes referred to as "Your Wizard") advised the defendants of their rights and, because they were indigent, appointed lawyers to represent them. Since the charge was first degree murder, no bond was set and they were remanded to Parish Prison to await trial.

The courthouse at Tulane and Broad is a massive concrete building that towers over the surrounding neighborhood of shacks, seedy motels, and cheap gin joints. Built in the early 1900s, its timeworn marble hallways lead into large, panel-walled courtrooms where the judges sit high on elevated benches that dominate the airy courtrooms like thrones. The prisoners, handcuffed and shackled, are kept out of sight in holding cells behind the courtrooms, like cattle in a loading chute, waiting their turn for justice, Tulane and Broad style.

Murder, rape, armed robbery, burglary, muggings, and serious drug offenses are standard fare. Tulane and Broad judges try more cases than anywhere else in the state, and they are understaffed, underpaid. Each day the courtrooms are filled with cops, victims, witnesses, prosecutors, defense lawyers, a few dragon slayers, and despairing prisoners waiting for justice. Justice is meted out like an assembly line in an abattoir—not as cleanly, swiftly, and decisively perhaps, but with the same deadly force. Because of the carnage, everyone at Tulane and Broad is callous. Every day, day after day, week after week, month after month, year after year, a mind-numbing exposure to the ugliest side of humanity takes its toll. Everyone at Tulane and Broad is callous.

After her initial appearance before the Wizard in Magic Court, Valerie was interrogated by Detective George Heath, allegedly after first being advised of her right to remain silent and the right to have a lawyer present. According to the detective, she confessed that the " . . . first time she set eyes on Janet and Gregory Kress she intended to rob them, they looked like a good mark . . . [and] that she cut Janet with [a] carpet knife."

In 1975, first degree murder automatically carried the death penalty in Louisiana. The elements of first degree murder were a specific intent to kill or to inflict great bodily harm, plus an aggravating circumstance, such as intending to kill more than one person, or committing a murder during the course of an armed robbery. This was the theory of the State's case against Valerie and McGraw. Under the law of principals, the fact that McGraw was the trigger-man was not a defense for Valerie, and as long as she had knowledge and intent to kill or to inflict great bodily harm, she too would be guilty of first degree murder.

The case was allotted to Judge Alvin Oser, a strong law-and-order type who had been an Assistant District Attorney (ADA) under Jim Garrison, the now famous District Attorney (DA) who was the subject of the Oliver Stone movie *JFK*. Judge Oser prided himself on being very studious, and unlike many other judges he did indeed spend much time reading advance sheets containing new decisions from the Supreme Court. Although many defense lawyers thought him too prosecution oriented, I thought he was a good judge, one who followed the law and permitted the lawyers to try their cases.

Judicial wisdom holds that those who commit crimes together should be tried together. Since there is always a potential for conflict between jointly charged defendants, Judge Oser appointed a member of the Orleans Parish Indigent Defender Program to represent McGraw and the Loyola Law Clinic to represent Valerie. Thus, the Law Clinic served a good purpose for everyone involved: Senior law students gained experience from working on a capital case, and the defendant received the benefit of the law school's resources.

Most murder cases don't involve eye-witness testimony because the eye-witnesses wind up dead. But, most murder cases, miraculously, involve confessions. To do Valerie any good, we had to bridge this moat by having her confession, in the parlance of Tulane and Broad, "throwed out."

At the suppression hearing, Detective Heath, a heavy-set, balding man, swore that Valerie freely and voluntarily confessed after he first advised her of her right not to confess. However, Heath made a fatal mistake. Instead of obtaining the confession on the night of her arrest, he waited until a lawyer had been appointed for her in Magic Court. And, of course, he failed to notify the lawyer before interrogating her. Judge Oser, being the studious judge that he was, "throwed out" the confession.

This was a major victory for us, and as was the custom at Tulane and Broad my students and I celebrated in a sleazy gin joint across the street from the courthouse. Win or lose, everyone went to the Miracle Mile after court at Tulane and Broad. As a result, half the people at the Miracle Mile were always celebrating and the other half were always commiserating. And of course, the commiserating drunks were always pissed off at the celebrating drunks. When you add the fact that the celebrating and commiserating drunks were alternately cops and criminal defense lawyers, the only thing predictable was that someone at the Miracle Mile would end the night with a bloody nose.

A murder trial renders the soul like no other human event. It is worse than a funeral because the dead don't rest. It is worse than war because God is not on both sides. It is worse than hell because the innocent are punished. A murder trial destroys the spirit. It is a place for dragons and dragon slayers.

The soul of Greg's father was the first to go. Jim Kress couldn't sleep; he couldn't eat; he couldn't work; he couldn't rest; he couldn't cry; he couldn't do what he most wanted to do—reach across the bar to the defense table and choke the life out of the lot of us. He stared with deadly eyes and taunted McGraw and Valerie by mouthing the word "nigger" over and over again. Jim Kress was so overcome with grief and hatred that he would not even talk to the Roby family, somehow blaming Janet for Greg's death. A murder trial renders the soul. . . .

The State presented its case against McGraw and Valerie following the typical pattern: the investigating officers laid out the evidence leading to the arrest; the coroner's evidence established the cause of death; the victim's family identified photographs of Gregory; and lastly, Janet gave her eye-witness account. No longer young, happy, carefree, and in love, she was now small and pathetic, with an ugly, jagged scar across her once pretty face. She recounted in painful detail a honeymoon night that ended in murder. She wept and fought for breath and composure, but she stuck by her story: Valerie had struck her in the face with a carpet knife while McGraw clubbed her with a heavy object.

I cross-examined her gently. Never attacking, I obtained what then appeared to be an insignificant piece of evidence—when Janet was struck in the face with the carpet knife, Valerie had on the same long black dress she had worn in the French Quarter earlier that evening.

This would become very significant evidence. According to the police, when they arrived on the scene, Valerie was wearing an old pair of blue jean shorts and a bloody blouse. The blood on her blouse was Type O. However, Janet and Gregory both had Type O blood and, without the more sophisticated testing used today, such as DNA analysis, the prosecutors were unable to demonstrate that the blood on the blouse came from Janet instead of Gregory. Moreover, no blood was found on the black evening dress, which opened the way for us to argue to the jury that the blood on the blouse came from cleaning up Gregory's blood, rather than from inflicting wounds upon Janet.

The decision of whether to put Valerie on the witness stand to tell her side of the story was, as in any criminal case, a difficult one. Although the jury would be admonished by the Judge that no inference of guilt should arise from a decision not to testify, conventional wisdom holds that juries don't always follow this instruction. On the other hand, if she testified, the jury might believe her to be a liar. And there was the additional problem of her confession. While the Judge had ruled that the State could not use the confession in its case-in-chief, the prosecutors could use it to impeach her if she testified inconsistently with the confession.

Valerie was not someone to meet in a dark alley. She was scarred, tattooed, belligerent, and emotionally flat. We spent hours, without much success, trying to soften her personality and make her more human. While it was risky, we sensed that the jury wanted to hear from Valerie in her own words. And so she took the witness stand. She testified that she never intended to rob or kill anyone, and that McGraw acted on his own when he murdered and robbed Gregory in the bedroom. She agreed with Janet that she had been wearing the black evening dress, but she denied ever striking her. Moreover, she said that it was only after McGraw had done his bloody work that she had changed into the blue jean shorts and blouse. At worst, she was only trying to help her boyfriend by cleaning up the bloody scene. Finally, she admitted making a statement to Detective Heath, but she denied the contents of the confession. Larry Centola, the prosecutor, charged in and cross-examined Valerie—devastatingly. "Why were you trying to clean up the blood?" he demanded.

"Because the house was in a mess," Valerie replied dryly.

"Why didn't you call for help?" Centola asked accusingly.

"I didn't call for help because I didn't have a telephone."

"Did you try to help her in any way?"

"No, I went back to my apartment."

"Why didn't you help her?"

"There was nothing I could do," Valerie said.

After we rested, having done all we could do, the State, as expected, called Detective Heath as a rebuttal witness. Over our objection, he slowly, effectively, and dramatically provided the jury with the full details of Valerie's confession: " . . . from the first time she set eyes on Janet and Gregory Kress she intended to rob them, they looked like a good mark . . . [and] that she cut Janet with [a] carpet knife."

A trial ends with closing arguments. The lawyers for both sides are given the opportunity to explain to the jury what they believe the evidence has proved—or has failed to prove. For dragon slayers, this is a most important part of the bout because often the theory of the kill doesn't fully develop until after the full head of the dragon presents itself.

As you might imagine, I'm a great believer in symbolism. It comes from my Catholic upbringing: the big sticks, the tall hats, the capes, the chain of beads, the holy water, the smoke, the bread, the wine. Because of this, I always use a white trial book, never a black one. And I always begin a trial dressed in a dark three-piece suit, underscoring its solemnity, and progressively wear a lighter one until the last day, when I appear all in white, representing the resurrection. There is also the matter of armor—the initialed cufflinks, the initialed shirt, the initialed belt buckle, the braces, the wristwatch, the pocket watch with gold chain through the vest, the Mont Blanc, the half-rimmed reading glasses, the expanding pointer, the chapeau—all accouterments necessary for a modern day dragon hunt. Arrayed in battle dress and blazoned with symbols, I beckon the jury to follow me to the land of truth and justice.

And so, on the last day of trial, I walked to the podium in a three-piece white linen suit and told the jury that, as with Tugger, the tragic events were all McGraw's fault, that Valerie just happened to be in the wrong place at the wrong time. After all, the only thing she had done wrong was to help out her boyfriend by sweeping up the bloody mess. I turned to face the jury directly and paused a moment before ending. Speaking very slowly and deliberately, I said:

> "McGraw condemned Gregory Kress to death—killed him

> brutally. McGraw condemned Janet Kress to a fate perhaps even worse because he condemned her to a living death. Don't let Clifford McGraw, at your hands, condemn Valerie Manchester to death. . . ."

The jury found McGraw guilty of first degree murder. For dragon slayers, sentencing is always the dreaded moment, the last rite, the ravishing of the vanquished. This is particularly true when a death sentence is imposed. Judge Oser, in fine form, pronounced:

> "It is the sentence of this court that you, Clifford McGraw, be remanded to the Parish Prison of the Parish of Orleans, there to remain in the custody of the Criminal Sheriff of the Parish of Orleans, and there to remain awaiting your removal to the Louisiana State Penitentiary at Angola until the day and hour fixed by the Governor of the State of Louisiana for your execution, at which time and place to be designated by the Governor of this State in his warrant, you, Clifford McGraw, shall then and there be put to death in the manner prescribed by law, that is, by causing to pass through your body a current of electricity of sufficient intensity to cause death and by the application and continuance of such current through your body until you are dead, dead, dead, and may God have mercy on your soul."

Years later, while he was on death row at Angola, a newspaper reporter asked McGraw why he didn't shoot Janet as well. "I ran out of bullets," he said.

Valerie fared better. She was acquitted of first degree murder, but she was found guilty of second degree murder. Believing her a part of the robbery scheme, but obviously accepting our argument that the blood on her blouse came from cleaning the crime scene, the jury concluded that she had not intended to kill anyone and had not been the one to slash Janet with the carpet knife.

The case was appealed to the Louisiana Supreme Court. Our principal argument was that the confession was erroneously admitted for impeachment purposes because the Judge had not required the proper foundation of surrounding circumstances that the jury needed to fairly weigh the statement.

I assigned a female student to argue the case before the Supreme Court. She was a very dedicated student, and she worked long hours preparing for the argument. She also had very big tits. Late on the eve of the argument, she called my home for some additional pointers. Over the years, I have come to learn that, as with certain medicines, my 3-M syndrome doesn't mix well with Jack Daniels. Caught in the mix, my last pointer to her was not to wear a bra for argument the next day. Unfortunately, R.A. overheard the lesson, and I was sentenced to misery for some considerable time thereafter.

The Supreme Court reversed the conviction and ordered a new trial. The Court found that the studious Judge Oser had committed error by admitting the confession without the proper foundation. In the meantime, however, Valerie had escaped from prison. She never learned that we had won her a new trial, sans brassiere.

TWO

The Doctor in Distress

Dr. Joseph Beasley was Dean of the Tulane University School of Public Health and Tropical Medicine. He was also the founder and Chairman of the New Orleans based Family Health Foundation (FHF). FHF had been started by him in the 1960s with a six hundred dollar contribution. By the mid-1970s, FHF had an annual budget of eighteen million dollars and was the leading organization of its kind in the world.

FHF was essentially a family planning clinic. What made it unique was Dr. Beasley's concept that, to be successful, a family planning clinic should provide overall health care. As he would often say, "You can't parachute condoms from a plane over India and expect the masses to use them properly." He thought the same was true for the poor and underprivileged in America. To successfully break the welfare cycle, women had to be educated about family planning, and the best way to do that was as a part of an overall health care program.

A simple concept, but a very controversial one. The medical establishment in New Orleans believed it was the beginning of socialized medicine. The public health establishment in New Orleans felt it was an invasion of its turf. And naturally, the politicians responded erratically. Some black politicians thought it was genocide. Some white politicians thought it was a good idea for precisely that reason. Altogether, it was exactly the kind of atmosphere that Gerald Gallinghouse, the United States Attorney in New Orleans, thrived upon.

Gerry Gallinghouse was a bully. He was known around New Orleans as Captain America. A Republican and Nixon appointee, he was politically conservative, yet not a typical establishment man. Grandiose, colorful, dramatic, aggressive, and tyrannical, he was a bull in a china cabinet in most cases and a bull in a medicine cabinet in this one.

Captain America launched a grand jury investigation into FHF that turned the Crescent City upside down. In typical Gallinghouse fashion, the investigation had no limits. The Board of Supervisors of Tulane University, a sacred cow of the New Orleans establishment, received subpoenas from the grand jury. The same was true for the Chancellor of the Tulane Medical School. And then the investigation became national in scope. The Rockefeller and Ford foundations, stalwarts of the American philanthropic establishment, were also implicated because of their heavy funding of FHF. Ultimately, Tulane University, the Ford Foundation, and the Rockefeller Foundation would be named as unindicted co-conspirators. This was heresy; some would say lunacy.

Dragons sometimes travel in herds. Captain America had the grand jury return three indictments against Dr. Beasley. The first one charged him, Eugene Wallace, and Oscar Kramer with conspiracy to defraud the federal government through the filing of false claims. Wallace and Kramer, both lawyers, had been key advisors to Dr. Beasley. The indictment alleged a fraudulent scheme to divert federal funds intended to reimburse FHF for costs associated with the construction of mobile clinics. According to the indictment, about fifty thousand dollars of falsely inflated costs had been used by the doctor to pay a bribe to Sherman Copelin, a young, upcoming black politician who was the Director of the New Orleans Model Cities Program. Allegedly, the bribe had been paid so that Copelin would not brand FHF a genocide program in the black community. The money had been paid to him through a New York consulting firm, the Scholarship, Education and Defense Fund for Racial Equality (SEDFRE). Under the alleged scheme, a contractor for the mobile clinics had sent the money to SEDFRE under the pretext of paying for a day-care study. According to the government's theory, Kramer and Don Hubbard, another FHF employee, then went to New York one weekend and completed the sham by preparing the day-care study on SEDFRE stationery.

Dr. Beasley wanted a "street fighter" to take on Captain America, so he hired Jim Garrison as his lawyer. Garrison at the time was in private practice following his defeat at the polls by Harry Connick, the father of the famous jazz musician. In many respects, Garrison was like Captain America. He too was physically towering and flamboyant—nothing like the character portrayed by Kevin Costner in *JFK*. He had a booming voice and a great courtroom presence. His fatal flaw as a trial lawyer, however, was his laziness. He simply didn't possess the self-discipline necessary to prepare properly for a complex trial.

The case was allotted to Judge Alvin Rubin, a tough judge, who ran a very tight ship. Tall and distinguished-looking, Judge Rubin knew all the tricks of the trade and was always in complete control. Thus, the stage was set for a battle of the Titans: Gallinghouse, Garrison, and Judge Rubin.

Right before trial, Wallace "flipped" by cutting a deal with Captain America. He agreed to plead guilty to a single count of the indictment in exchange for being placed in the government's witness protection program where he received a new identity, a home, and income. In addition to the deal with Wallace, Captain America also gave immunity to Copelin and Hubbard by promising not to prosecute them as a *quid pro quo* for the information they had provided to the government.

The trial of Dr. Beasley and Kramer began on January 10, 1975. Kramer was represented by John Volz, a former ADA under Garrison and the federal public defender. Prior to trial, Kramer had moved for a severance on the grounds that he was willing to testify for the doctor in a separate trial but not in a joint one. Judge Rubin deferred ruling, but after he testified, the Judge severed him from the trial. The jury, however, was unable to reach a verdict on Dr. Beasley and the case ended in a mistrial.

Judge Rubin set a new trial date for Kramer and a separate one for Dr. Beasley. Kramer went to trial first, and on March 11, 1975, the jury returned a verdict of guilty. Dr. Beasley's trial was scheduled to begin the next day. On the morning of trial, Garrison moved for a continuance, but the Judge denied it and forced the doctor to trial under the cloud of Kramer's conviction. Despite Garrison's oratory skills, the jury convicted the doctor. Curiously, Copelin and Hubbard were not called as government witnesses.

Dr. Beasley was devastated. FHF was in shambles and had been seized by the government. Jobless and nearly destitute, he opened a small private clinic in the French Quarter. To make matters worse, he still had two dragons to face. A doctor in distress and in need of a dragon slayer.

I was still running the Law Clinic. I loved what I was doing, but Tulane and Broad was still the minor leagues. The big show was at federal court. I must also confess to being somewhat of a snob, having become one, you will recall, as a result of the hot tin roofs at Palo Alto. The defense of street crime at Tulane and Broad is truly trench warfare, and frankly, I was tired of the stench. Most street crime defendants are uneducated, dull-witted, and sociopathic. I longed for the rich and educated sociopaths at federal court.

I met Joe Beasley at his home on Burgundy Street in the French Quarter. He was charismatic and handsome, with long, dark hair fringed with gray, and a solid, square jaw; pipe-smoking and debonair, he was a man with a mission, a driven soul, and we liked one another immediately. It seemed that destiny had brought us together, both Georgia born and both involved in University-backed programs to assist the poor. Unlike me, however, he was a high-roller. He wore custom-made shirts, thousand dollar suits, and Gucci loafers. He drove a Mercedes convertible. Quite a contrast to Clifford McGraw and Valerie Manchester. This indeed was a client I could "do lunch" with, and he introduced me to a lifestyle I have never left.

We agreed that I would represent him for a small monthly retainer, exactly five hundred dollars per month plus expenses. While this seems a mere pittance today, it wasn't a bad supplement to a law professor's salary in 1975. I told him, however, that because it was such a high profile case, and because of the institutional jealousies between Tulane and Loyola, I wanted approval from my Dean.

I went to Mo's home that evening. Although faculty members weren't permitted an outside practice, I told him that as a clinician, I needed to broaden my experience as a federal litigator. He seemed particularly haggard that evening. As I gulped my Jack Daniels, he moaned and groaned profusely while sipping cautiously from his glass of sherry. Fleta, on the other hand, looked especially sexy as she sashayed about in a new starlet outfit. Not finding any scripture proscribing my request, however, Mo blessed my representation of Dr. Beasley. The big show.

My star student at the time was Sean O'Grady, a veteran who had lost a leg in Vietnam and walked on a prosthesis with a cane. He was from an old, politically active, New Orleans family; his grandfather and uncle had both been judges at Tulane and Broad. With all the makings of a great trial lawyer—a quick mind with the ability to think on his feet or, in this case, foot—he was a good-looking, wounded and decorated war hero, who would one day be capable of charming a jury into doing anything. He and his wife, Maddie, also Irish and as pretty as Sean was handsome, became close friends of mine, and he volunteered to help "after hours" in representing the doctor.

The second indictment also charged Dr. Beasley with a conspiracy to defraud the federal government through the submission of false claims. In a nutshell, the government's theory was that the doctor, through FHF, had caused others to donate "federal" dollars to Tulane University, which in turn had donated the "federal" dollars to the State as matching funds for more "federal" dollars to support the family planning program. Allegedly, the doctor had accomplished this scheme by persuading FHF vendors to make contributions to Tulane in order to begin the process. One such vendor, Software, Inc., an Oklahoma company, had sold a computer program to FHF, and in turn had donated two hundred thousand dollars to Tulane. The indictment charged that the software product was worthless, and that the whole transaction was a sham designed to use "federal" dollars to match more "federal" dollars.

In preparing for trial, O'Grady and I realized that Garrison had made two crucial mistakes in defending the first indictment. First, he hadn't called Dr. Beasley as a witness. As a general rule, one cannot ask a jury to acquit a defendant—especially a professional one—without having him take the witness stand to explain his innocence. The fact that Garrison believed the doctor would make a bad witness, however, didn't come as a surprise. Feeling persecuted, the doctor had adopted the stance of a martyr. During his trials on the first indictment, he had sat through the proceedings with detachment and indifference, aloofly reading the newspaper. Undoubtedly, this had come across as arrogance to the jury. A monumental mistake. A defendant cannot hold himself above a trial without holding himself above the jury. Rather, a defendant must begin a case on the same level as the jury and end it with the jury on a mountaintop gazing down upon the lowly prosecutor and, if necessary, the judge also. In other words, Dr. Beasley had to descend before I could resurrect him.

The second mistake Garrison had made was in attempting to win the case on cross-examination alone. Sometimes a criminal defense lawyer has no other choice, but this was not that kind of case. Whenever the government is the alleged victim in a case, prosecutors invariably rely upon bureaucrats for their witnesses—people who, like them, take a very narrow view of things. Prosecutors do this because they realize there is too much flexibility on the higher rung of government, and prosecutors don't like flexibility. It is much the same in war. When a general falls in battle, it's from a shot fired by an enemy foot soldier, not an enemy general. Garrison had contented himself with cross-examining enemy foot soldiers. Our strategy, in contrast, was to call enemy generals to the witness box, if need be, as our own witnesses in order to force the trial onto the higher fields of justice.

We also added an unorthodox member to the defense team. Joe Walker, a well-known political pollster, was retained to help select the jury. While his expertise was selling politicians to voters, selling a defense to jurors is much the same process. This, of course, was not the kind of tactic taught in law school, but one never learns how to fight dragons in law school.

Our major problem in preparing for trial was Beasley himself. He truly viewed himself as a missionary and as a prophet, and so the world itself became the stakes in his battle with Captain America. Joe was so intense, and the times so stressful, that furniture literally vibrated around him. As a release, he went on drinking binges for weeks at a time. When O'Grady and I drank with him, we stuck to the usual Jack Daniels, while he rotated from bourbon to Scotch to gin to vodka to brandy and back again to bourbon. And when he drank, he would get mean as hell, calling me the "Uptown Jew" and O'Grady the "Gimp."

He was just as volatile with women. When we first met, Joe was still married to his second wife, a beautiful woman from Norway whose best friend Kari, also from Norway, was married to George Guild, a New Orleans physician. Not surprisingly, Joe and Kari fell in love; the two doctors began to hate one another intensely, bitter divorce actions ensued, and we became embroiled in representing them in these domestic wars.

After the divorces, Joe and Kari married. I was best man. In the beginning, bliss. Kari, an armful of woman, had a wonderful Norwegian accent and a very sensuous voice. My nickname, Buddy, became "Boudee." Joe was simply "Bees-Lee." But then Joe and Kari began to fight, exchanging tirades that sounded as though they had been written by Tennessee Williams. In fact, one night at Sardi's, the great playwright came over to our table to see Kari, an aspiring actress, and as he left I thought, "If only you knew the raw material you're leaving behind." In

New York, we always stayed at the Plaza. Through the hotel walls, I could hear them arguing through the night, and all the while, I had to remain focused on trying to keep Joe out of jail.

Trying a case in federal court is much different than trying one at Tulane and Broad. Federal judges are appointed for life and have the time and staff to work comfortably without worrying about being reelected. As a rule, they are remote and arrogant. While Tulane and Broad judges shoot from the hip, federal judges take careful aim. And the quality of federal crimes is choicer—not much blood and guts, more fraud. Federal crimes are crimes of the mind. State crimes are crimes of the heart. Defendants in federal court wear coats and ties, while defendants at Tulane and Broad are shackled in flaming orange coveralls stamped "Orleans Parish Prison." The atmosphere is also different. In federal court, it is antiseptic, much like a pharmacy. Tulane and Broad, on the other hand, reminds me of the big church in Donaldsonville—lofty and full of sinners.

Every criminal trial pits king against commoner so, in that sense, every criminal trial is a political one. But when the indicted subject is also a pretender, with a competing cause, loyal serfs, and a flag of his own, you have the trappings for a real political trial. Such was the Beasley case. Captain America led the forces of the establishment. I was Dr. Beasley's knight.

The trial began in March 1976 before a visiting judge from the Southern District of New York. Judge Edmund L. Palmieri had been appointed to the bench by President Eisenhower, and he had the reputation for being a very conservative judge. The principal Assistant United States Attorney (AUSA) was Don Richard, a law school classmate of mine and a dangerous prosecutor—for he appeared to be such a nice guy.

But this time, we were ready. No longer presenting himself as a high and mighty big shot, Joe had become a house-calling doctor. Also, a loving father. His daughter Beth, a Tulane student who looked twelve, came to court every afternoon at three-thirty dressed in a pleated uniform with a canvas book bag on her back, like an eighth grader from Sacred Heart Academy.

Again, Wallace was the government's principal witness, testifying he and the doctor knew all along that they were violating federal criminal laws by structuring transactions to channel money for matching funds. Although given immunity, I nonetheless forced him on cross-examination into taking the Fifth Amendment since his tax returns had failed to report income for work performed outside his normal duties as an FHF employee. A defense lawyer's dream. The government's case began to unravel.

As planned, we called enemy generals with a much broader view of the world than the foot soldiers relied upon by the government. We also called top state officials, including Charles Roemer, the Commissioner of Administration, and Governor Edwin Edwards. I asked Governor

Edwards whether he had ever received anything of value from the doctor. With his typical flair, he responded, "No," and then pausing, with impeccable timing, he added, "Except for a packet of birth control pills, which I assure you I didn't take!" Everyone laughed, including Judge and jury, always a good sign in a criminal case.

I had two unexpected visitors in the courtroom that day. One dressed in black and hooded; the other in seersucker suit and polkadot bow tie. Looking as though they had just arrived from Tara, my father and Aunt Delta actually had just come from the next closest place in spirit, Galatoire's. Old New Orleans. People go to Galatoire's not just to eat, but to watch other people eat. To enhance the ritual, the walls of Galatoire's are lined with mirrors—musty, old mirrors that allow people to watch other people sitting behind them eat. Old kings and young queens from most of the carnival krewes go to Galatoire's for lunch and to watch one another eat. I watch the young queens, but once in a while, after a few drinks, I catch glimpses of my long dead great grandfather and his brother sitting at a corner table discussing commerce and sugar cane.

It was strange seeing my father and Aunt Delta together. Aunt Delta, like my mother, is a very handsome woman. But unlike my mother, Aunt Delta hides her beauty behind her veils and hoods, I suspect, in order to hide her wickedness. Aunt Delta is a man-eater. After putting her husband to rest some fifty years ago, she went through a long succession of lovers, her weapon of choice being poison—slow poison, but not the swallowing kind, the kind that penetrates by telepathy. Because of this, her male companions are mostly gay, while real men like my father, sensing the danger, keep a safe distance away.

When my father and Aunt Delta visited court that day after lunch at Galatoire's, they left my mother in the lobby of the Monteleone Hotel. While it was *comme il faut* for my father to leave my mother sitting alone in the lobby of the Monteleone in the middle of the French Quarter, he would never have even dreamed of escorting her into the hotel's bar, the Carousel, which is located just a few feet away. There were good reasons for this. In the first place, the bar in the Carousel rotates, and my father didn't care much for modern day gadgetry. But more importantly, working girls occasionally frequented the Carousel. New Orleans is truly a town of close quarters and fine lines—lines that are not always visible to outsiders.

My mother stayed in the Monteleone lobby that day because she was too nervous to attend my trials. In that regard, she was a lot like R.A. In fact, R.A. got so nervous over just hearing about my courtroom adventures that she would have to take to her bed. Actually, I liked it that way.

This would be the only time my father visited me in court. The fact that the Beasley case did not involve dead bodies but something approaching a business transaction (although in his book, a shady one) made it more palatable for him. Aunt Delta, on the contrary, became a regular courtroom visitor. Dead bodies suited her just fine.

Throughout the trial, the government maintained the silly notion that so-called "federal" dollars remained "federal" dollars and couldn't be used for matching funds even though the money had been earned. Arguing that this was as absurd as saying that money paid to White House gardeners remained "federal" dollars, I told the jury, "As long as they spray the roses, that's their money."

I also attacked the government's claim that the computer program, which had been purchased from Software, Inc., was worthless simply because it hadn't been used:

> "Now, it's true that the products were never fully implemented. That's true. But look—if you have a contract with the State of Louisiana to build a road, and they agree to pay you what it costs to build that road, and you have to go and buy a road grader to build that road, and you buy a road grader. Now, a road grader is no different from this (pointing to the software program). If you don't use the road grader, it ain't worth nothin.' You've got to use it. So you bought the road grader, and here's the road grader (indicating the software program). Now, after you buy the road grader, if the weather is bad and you can't use it, that's not a crime. Well, the weather for Family Health got bad in August of '73."

Most importantly, I argued that Dr. Beasley's actions were inconsistent with criminal intent. He had obtained supporting legal opinions and had openly entered into the transactions with unlikely co-conspirators: Tulane University, the Ford Foundation, and the Rockefeller Foundation. Again in my three-piece white linen suit, I cajoled:

> "Now, I'm going to end with this thought:
>
> Many of you, either personally or as a family, have gone through surgery, and you know when you go in that room, and when they put the gas on you, and the lights go out, your life is then in the hands of the surgeon.
>
> When you take this case from the Judge and you go to your deliberation room, the lights for Dr. Beasley are going to go out. He's going to be waiting for you to come back and tell him your verdict.
>
> Now, unlike the surgeon, there is not just one hand on the knife; there are twelve hands, and one slip and a nerve can be severed. So all twelve of you must guide that knife.

> I'm going to suggest that you will come back, and you will say, 'Dr. Beasley, we have done exploratory surgery; we've examined you for six days; we've looked at you from head to toe, and we find, Dr. Beasley, that you may have a little fever, you may have a little virus, doing things too fast, you may have a little rash of negligence about you, you may have had one bad boil, meaning Eugene Wallace, but, Dr. Beasley, we don't find cancer; we don't find the malignancy of guilt.'"

After the jury retired to deliberate, the long wait began. This is the worst time for a dragon fighter. Indeed, it is exactly like waiting in a hospital during life or death surgery on a loved one. This time, however, I had an unlikely companion waiting with me. Morey Sear, a U.S. Magistrate, was seeking an appointment as the next federal judge, and his competition was none other than Captain America.

The jury returned a verdict of not guilty. The federal courthouse at the time was in the French Quarter in a majestic old building that used to be the home of the Louisiana Supreme Court. Across the street was one of my favorite drinking places, the Napoleon House. Like the Miracle Mile, the Napoleon House served as an oasis for weary federal litigators. Unlike the Miracle Mile, however, the Napoleon House crowd never became too rowdy or confrontational because it was mostly a one-sided crowd. The long-haired writers, poets, and artists who regularly hung out there, along with the operatic music in the background, kept the cops away. After the Beasley trial, it was raining as we walked there for an all-night party. Dr. Beasley, ecstatic, told the clamoring reporters, "It's raining, but not on my parade tonight."

But there were still dragons on the loose. Unexpectedly, however, Captain America retreated and ran for cover by voluntarily dismissing the third federal indictment. Our celebration was cut short because the Orleans Parish DA, Harry Connick, indicted Dr. Beasley along with Copelin and Hubbard for the same alleged bribe which had been the subject of the first federal indictment. While jeopardy doesn't exist between federal and state sovereigns, such double prosecutions are rare because of their fundamental unfairness. Something rotten in Denmark was smelling at Tulane and Broad.

The state case was allotted to Judge Matthew Braniff, who was widely considered around Tulane and Broad as a mean old bastard. Courthouse lore has it that the Judge once sentenced a young man to ninety-nine years in the state penitentiary at Angola.

"I don't think I can make it, Your Honor," the young man complained.

"Do the best you can, son," the Judge growled.

Actually, Judge Braniff had appointed me to my first criminal case while I was still a real estate lawyer at Polack, Rosenberg & Rittenberg. I went to see him about the case and, surprisingly, he was very courteous to me. As we spoke, older lawyers milled about in his chambers and one of them interrupted to say that his client had agreed to plead guilty. The Judge then excused himself to take the bench, saying, "Wait just a minute while I go out and give this motherfucker some justice." As an innocent young lawyer, I was horrified by his callousness.

Judge Braniff had a rough and tough past. He joined the Royal Canadian Air Force at age seventeen as a combat pilot to fight the Nazis before we entered the war. After the war, he became a prosecutor, then a defense lawyer, and finally, Judge. He personified Tulane and Broad: he wasn't bright, but didn't care to be. A lawyer practicing in Section B soon learned the futility of citing a precedent from the Louisiana Supreme Court. To cite a United States Supreme Court case was grounds for the death penalty. As the Judge often said, "I'm only interested in Section B jurisprudence!" Sometimes, however, he did have a softer side. When the Law Clinic began operations in Section B, he seemed to enjoy working with the law students. He would also give a break to first offenders, but for the typical repeat offender, going before him was an early visit to hell.

One day the Law Clinic had a case scheduled for trial before Judge Braniff and I was supposed to personally assist the student practitioner. In this particular case, O'Grady was the student and, having great confidence in him, I told him to try the case alone. When the Judge demanded to know where I was, O'Grady said I was out of town on business. That evening, the Judge saw me on TV at the federal courthouse with Dr. Beasley. The next day he confronted us and I responded, "Judge, O'Grady lies a lot," thereby endearing us both to him.

Copelin and Hubbard hired Richard Sobol, a Washington, D.C. lawyer, to handle their case. Dick Sobol was a bright lawyer whose practice was primarily civil rights. The fact that he was bright, however, was the third strike against him for Judge Braniff. The first two: he was a civil rights attorney, and he came from Washington, D.C.

Dick filed a motion to quash the indictment on the grounds that a federal prosecutor may not grant immunity and then, in bad faith, provide the immunized evidence on a "silver platter" to a state prosecutor. We subpoenaed the United States Attorney's files and found to our delight that much of what Copelin and Hubbard had told the federal prosecutors was inconsistent with the government's theory of the case. At a hearing, we were able to demonstrate that Captain America had in fact turned over to Connick immunized evidence that was used to obtain the state indictment. My problem, however, was that Dr. Beasley had not been given federal immunity, so we didn't have the same argument for dismissal as Copelin and Hubbard. All I could do was argue double jeopardy under the Louisiana Constitution, a meritless argument, but I made it anyway because, after all, we were dealing with Section B jurisprudence. Judge Braniff quashed the indictment against Copelin and Hubbard and, surprisingly, against Dr. Beasley as well. It was probably the only time a defendant benefited from Section B jurisprudence.

With the state indictment behind us, the only remaining dragon was the federal appeal. I wrote the brief. These were the days of manual typewriters, and it was a long and arduous process. I needed another secretary, and my next door neighbor suggested a friend. The next day, I interviewed Elizabeth DeWeese Neilson. I say "interviewed" advisedly, because no one interviews Beth. No one interviews Beth because no one can get a word in edgewise. She speaks faster than the speed of sound, and she types faster than she talks—actually, she does both at the same time. She was petite, attractive, and stylishly dressed. I hired her. She was a godsend; she became my "Della Street," and she has been with me ever since. In relaxed moments, of which there are few, I call her "Slim."

Our principal argument to the Court of Appeals was prosecutorial misconduct. We argued that Copelin and Hubbard had given exculpatory information to the prosecutors that should have been disclosed to the defense. We also argued that Captain America had misused the grand jury. Once a grand jury returns an indictment, the government and the defendant should be on an equal footing, but that had not been the case here. Ronnie Moore, the Executive Director of SEDFRE, had twice given testimony to the grand jury that the SEDFRE transaction was legitimate. Some nine months later, and only a few months before trial, Captain America threatened him with perjury and brought him before the grand jury for a third time, where he supposedly "recanted" his prior testimony. In truth, this was "ass-saving," not recantation, and it should have been disclosed to the jury for what it was.

Nonetheless, the Court of Appeals would not reverse Judge Rubin. Almost apologetically, the Court wrote:

> "It should be noted that this Court entertains no doubt as to the many good things accomplished by the Family Health Foundation and the appellants. Their work for the individual, the scientific and professional communities, and society as a whole is admirable and commendable. Nonetheless, their greed provoked criminal actions which cannot be ignored or excused."

This opinion represents the worst side of our judicial system, and to have suggested that Dr. Beasley was motivated by greed was wrong. There was no evidence that he did what he did for monetary gain. Undoubtedly, had he been engaged in the same type of machinations in the military to obtain more weapons for his troops, he would have been awarded the Medal of Honor. The truth is that Dr. Beasley was prosecuted because he was involved in an innovative social welfare program that threatened the status quo.

Our last step was the United States Supreme Court. I had never argued a case before the Supreme Court, and Joe and I agreed we should have someone in the lead with a national reputation. He settled upon Leonard Boudin, a New York lawyer well known for representing left-wing clients such as Cuba and the Communist party. Joe liked the idea of someone from the eastern liberal establishment representing him because it fit in with his perception of being a political scapegoat.

I came to know and admire Leonard as a great lawyer. To my surprise, however, I received an unexpected lesson from him. When the legal pleadings were ready for filing, he was still due ten thousand dollars on his fee. At Joe's request, I called him to explain that the doctor was having cash flow problems. Curtly, he replied, "Better he than me!" I was shocked to hear such a capitalist remark from the great socialist lawyer; to this day, however, Slim scolds me for not always following the wisdom of Leonard Boudin.

But even with his help, the Supreme Court would not review the case. Armageddon had arrived. I had slain three dragons for Dr. Beasley, but I could never slay the one that had run over Garrison. Dragon-smitten, wounded and singed, Joe Beasley had to go to jail. But like everything else he did, he did it in grandiose style. Almost immediately he established himself as a kind of Captain Hawkeye Pierce. He ran an underground clinic, where he either correctly diagnosed real illnesses or provided the symptomatology for feigned illnesses, both invaluable commodities in prison. When I visited him, inmate "orderlies" served us martinis. The system might constrain the man, but never the spirit.

The night Kari returned from taking him to prison, she invited me over for a drink. They had a lovely, but strange home in Faubourg Marigny, an old Creole neighborhood across Elysian Fields from the French Quarter. The house was three stories, with the kitchen oddly situated on the third floor. We sat on a magnificent patio in the moonlight like Lancelot and Guinevere. She was a beautiful woman with long blonde hair and, as we drank, she gave me a long Scandinavian look and began to undo her hair, letting it fall and cap her Nordic breasts. I put down the drink and walked out of the strange house. It was too soon, even for one stricken with the 3-M syndrome.

When he got out of prison, Dr. Beasley established a successful medical career in New York. Judge Rubin was promoted to a higher court. Jim Garrison was elected to a state court. Sherman Copelin became a very powerful member of the Louisiana Legislature. Morey Sear, not Captain America, became the new federal judge. And for me, the Beasley case was my first real taste of dragon blood. The taste has never left me.

THREE

THE ROOK

Jean Pierre LaVergne came from a lovely family in Canada. The family, however, was cursed with a physical malady known as hyperthyroidism. People with this condition typically become overly active, and frequently cannot function as ordinary people. Jean Pierre, his mother, and a sister suffered from this condition. At the time, a common treatment was a thyroidectomy, whereby a portion of the thyroid is removed to produce less hormone. Jean Pierre, his mother, and sister underwent thyroidectomies. But in the case of Jean Pierre, the surgeon removed too much thyroid, causing him to develop hypothyroidism. People with this condition become overweight, sluggish, lethargic, and, if untreated, they can become comatose and die. The disease is gradual, becoming progressively worse, and it must be treated medically with thyroid supplements. It also requires frequent monitoring to assure that the patient is receiving the proper amount of medication.

Unlike his sister, who went to graduate school, Jean Pierre was a poor student. He eventually dropped out of school, became a drifter, and hitch-hiked around the country doing odd jobs. For the most part, he didn't take proper care of himself. In the summer of 1977, he was living in New Orleans with two roommates, Mary Ellen Proper and Theodore "Teddy" Stire. One night, while Teddy was asleep, Jean Pierre crushed his skull with a hammer. He then picked up Mary Ellen from her job and took her on an all night, non-stop trip to Lubbock, Texas, where he was arrested for murder.

Jean Pierre's family retained me to represent him. The case was allotted to the studious Judge Oser. I moved immediately for the appointment of a sanity commission, which determines a defendant's present ability to stand trial and his sanity at the time of the offense. Dr. Kenneth Ritter and Dr. Ignacio Medina were appointed to the sanity commission.

Judge Oser always appointed Dr. Ritter and Dr. Medina to sanity commissions. As a matter of fact, all of the Tulane and Broad judges appointed them to sanity commissions. One reason for this, I suppose, is that the two doctors never disagreed with one another, meaning the judges didn't have to decide whose opinion was right or wrong.

Dr. Ritter looked like a psychiatrist. He wore horn-rimmed glasses and sported an Edwardian beard. He also talked like a psychiatrist and, although born and raised in Louisiana, he spoke with a slight Austrian accent. A workaholic, he examined hundreds of defendants to determine present capacity and past sanity; he was perpetually either examining them or testifying about them in court. His examinations usually lasted forty-five minutes and, from that brief encounter, he was able to determine whether a defendant understood the nature of the proceedings and whether he was sane at the time of the offense. I always marveled at these findings since many of my Law Clinic students never understood the nature of the proceedings against their clients.

Dr. Medina, on the other hand, didn't look like a psychiatrist. That wasn't surprising, inasmuch as he wasn't a psychiatrist. Indeed, he didn't even look like a doctor and he certainly didn't speak like one. Actually, no one at Tulane and Broad even knew if he had a tongue. You see, Dr. Medina never testified in court. Since his opinions were always the same as Dr. Ritter's, the ritual was for the lawyers to stipulate that, if called to testify, his testimony would be the same as Dr. Ritter's. No one at Tulane and Broad deviated from this protocol.

Although some might think Dr. Ritter a hack, I knew better. We had worked together on many occasions when he was either a state witness or a defense witness. He was usually right. And he was right about Jean Pierre. He diagnosed him as having myxedema psychosis, a rare mental disorder brought on by hypothyroidism. Because of this, he concluded that Jean Pierre was insane at the time of the offense but, as long as he was on the proper medication, he was capable of standing trial and assisting his counsel. Dr. Medina silently concurred.

In speaking to Dr. Ritter, I learned that the Chairman of the Psychiatry Department at the LSU Medical School, Dr. William Easson, was a leading authority on myxedema psychosis. I retained him as an additional expert witness and, after examining Jean Pierre, he confirmed the diagnosis of Drs. Ritter (and Medina).

At that time in Louisiana, the law presumed everyone sane and, therefore, a defendant had the burden of establishing the defense of insanity by a preponderance of the evidence. If sufficient evidence of insanity was produced, the burden of proof shifted to the State to prove sanity beyond a reasonable doubt.

All dragon slayers know that insanity is not a popular defense. This is especially true with so-called temporary insanity where, as in this case, a defendant becomes sane simply by taking pills, and insane simply by not taking them.

The case was prosecuted by Joe Meyer, the best prosecutor in the DA's office. The victim had been Orleans Parish Sheriff Milton Stire's nephew and that, no doubt, had something to do with his being assigned to the case. Joe Meyer, who was my age and a long-time friend, had begun his professional career as a legal aid lawyer, perhaps an unlikely beginning for a prosecutor, but precisely what made him a dangerous prosecutor. For example, an ex-cop who becomes a prosecutor will continue to think like a cop, going for the overkill—the Achilles heel of most prosecutors—while Joe, in contrast, would be more subtle, more crafty, more attuned to a defense lawyer's way of thinking. A formidable foe.

Because of the medical aspects in the case, my cousin, Walter, a medical student at Tulane, assisted me, the Judge allowing him to join us at the defense table. Walter was the same age as Jean Pierre, mid-twenties, and fat, balding, lethargic, and eccentric. In fact, Walter looked more like the one suffering from myxedema psychosis.

The trial went quickly and uneventfully. After all, we weren't contesting the fact that Jean Pierre killed Teddy. During our case, Jean Pierre's mother and sister established the family's history of hyperthyroidism and the botched surgery on Jean Pierre which caused his hypothyroidism. Drs. Ritter and Easson (but not Medina) gave their expert opinion that Jean Pierre was insane when he crushed Teddy's skull with the hammer. Overconfident because of his natural talents as an advocate and relying upon the typical jury's aversion to the defense of temporary insanity, Joe did not bother to present contradictory medical evidence. In hindsight, this was a huge mistake. And so I hammered away in closing argument at his failure to rebut:

> "The only evidence from the witness stand that you can consider—because that was the only evidence that you heard—was that Jean Pierre LaVergne, on August 15, 1977, was legally insane. That's the only testimony that you have heard. There was not one person, there was not one doctor, there was not one psychologist, there was not one fortuneteller, who got on that stand and told you that on August 15, 1977, my client was legally sane. No one disputed the testimony of Dr. Easson, Dr. Ritter. No one. There has not been one iota of evidence to dispute what the doctors have told you.
>
> What Mr. Meyer wants you to do—and if you analyze his remarks to you, both the remarks that he gave a few minutes ago and the remarks that he will give following the conclusion of my remarks—is simply this: That you twelve fine folks should not believe the testimony of Dr. Ritter and Dr. Easson. When you boil it down to the rock bottom of his case, it is simply that he wants you to come to the conclusion that Dr. Easson and Dr. Ritter were wrong.

Now, he doesn't want you to do that on the basis of another doctor taking the stand and disputing what Dr. Easson and Dr. Ritter have to say. He wants you to do that based upon what he tells you are symptoms or what he tells you is mental illness or what he tells you is legal or non-legal psychosis. The bottom line is simply that. That is what Mr. Meyer wants you to do."

Anticipating Joe's argument that Jean Pierre was sane because he fled the scene and acted rationally by driving to Texas in an attempt to escape punishment, I told the jury:

"He will go to great lengths about whether or not on August 15, 1977, my client had too much energy or not enough energy, and he will attempt to use those symptoms—symptoms that deal with what the doctors told you. And you have to be very careful because it's very, very confusing. Those symptoms that he is going to talk to you so much about have to do with the symptoms of hypothyroidism, a physical condition—the symptoms about being sleepy, the symptoms about hair falling out, the symptoms about the dry skin. Whatever those symptoms are, they all deal with the medical, physical condition of hypothyroidism."

As I recounted these symptoms, I pointed to the defense table behind me, where cousin Walter sat oafishly. I then focused upon the difference between the mental illness and the physical condition, at the same time emphasizing that myxedema psychosis, unlike schizophrenia, had an organic etiology:

"What the doctors attempted to explain is that as an offshoot of this physical illness called hypothyroidism, a person may, because of this organic change in his body, may develop an entirely separate illness, psychosis. He may become crazy. As a result of the physical changes, the chemical change taking place in his body, he becomes demented. He begins to hallucinate. He becomes paranoid. He becomes suspicious. He becomes crazy. All as a result of what is going on chemically within his body.

He is trying to confuse the two. He is trying to say that because on August 15 Jean Pierre LaVergne was not comatose, because he wasn't laying out like a Zombie, because he wasn't purely myxedematous or hypothyroid, that he was not crazy. But they are two different things.

> The doctors attempted to explain that the psychosis, the mental illness, may come at any time. There is no set pattern. . . .
>
> What Mr. Meyer is going to try to do today is to bring you back to an image of mental illness that goes back centuries ago when medicine was very, very poor, and we just locked everybody up; and we have all these images that we have seen in old movies and books, and he wants to portray to you that a person in order to be mentally ill must be a person who is in a comatose state or a person who is hysterical or mad, who can't eat, can't feed himself, can't control his bodily functions, can't do anything—but that's not what the doctors told you. A person can be insane, but yet he can eat, he can breathe, he can go to the bathroom, he can drive an automobile, he can make decisions. He is not stupid. Those are two different things. We are not talking about intelligence versus stupidity. We are talking about legal insanity versus sanity."

Another plus in the case from our standpoint was that Joe never offered a viable motive for the killing. I took advantage:

> "Now, His Honor will instruct you—and I think it's an important instruction—that while motivation, a motive—we hear a lot about motives when we read detective books—while a motive is not required, the State is not required to prove a motive as an essential element of the crime. The Judge will tell you that the law does assume that people do things with a motive, and that if there is evidence of motive, then you can infer from that evidence of motive that the defendant had specific intent. But he will also tell you that if there has been no evidence of any motive, that you can infer from the failure of the State to prove motive, you can draw an inference that the person did not have any specific intent.
>
> The point of the matter is that it was a senseless crime. There was no motive. There was no reason. There was no logical reason. There was no sane reason. There was no good reason. There was no jealousy. There was no animosity. There was no hostility. The poor young man was sleeping. Sleeping. No threat. No threat to a sane person. No threat to a sane person."

Ultimately, I knew that Joe's biggest weapon would be the understandable reluctance of a jury to acquit someone on the grounds of temporary insanity. "Mr. Meyer will tell you, ' . . . do you want to put Jean Pierre LaVergne back on the streets with a pill bottle and tell him to take his pills?'" I had to explain to the jury that under Louisiana law, when a person is found not guilty by reason of insanity, he is institutionalized in, " . . . the East Louisiana Jackson Hospital that Dr. Ritter told you was a prison hospital. Bars. Guards. Security. But at least a hospital where this person, a medical patient in the Twentieth Century, deserves to be." It was also crucial to let the jury know that once committed, Jean Pierre wouldn't be released until Judge Oser determined not that he was sane, but that he was no longer a "threat to himself or to others." I had every reason to believe it would be a calm day at Tulane and Broad before the Judge allowed that to happen. So I ended on our strongest point:

> "Keep in mind one thought when Mr. Meyer is talking to you, one thought, and that is this: You have had a lesson in medicine today. You have been taught by Dr. Ritter, and you have been taught by Dr. Easson. They have given you a medical class in psychiatry, in medicine, in myxedema psychosis. They have told you that, based upon everything that they know about this case, it is their opinion that on August 15 Jean Pierre LaVergne was legally insane. Mr. Meyer wants you and will ask you to do one simple thing. He wants you to come back and announce that your teachers, Dr. Easson and Dr. Ritter, are wrong. Flatly wrong. Because he says they are wrong.
>
> If you have a member of your family who becomes ill, if you take that loved one to Dr. Easson and Dr. Ritter, and they examine that child, and they tell you that child has to go into the hospital, would you take that child to Joe Meyer and ask him, 'What is your medical advice?' Or would you take him to someone on the jury sitting next to you right now? 'What do you think? Should he go in the hospital or not?' And perhaps Dr. Meyer here would say, 'No. No. Don't put him in the hospital. He is alright.' Now, who would you believe? You would have to go, wouldn't you, with Dr. Easson and Dr. Ritter. You might not want to do it. You might prefer to believe Mr. Meyer. You might prefer to believe somebody else who is not a doctor. You might prefer to do that. You might not want to believe what Dr. Ritter and Dr. Easson have told you. You might not like it at all. But what would you do? What would be your duty? Your duty would be to do what the professional

> doctors tell you. Now, when I selected you ladies and gentlemen, I asked each of you would you consider this defense. Would you require me only to prove it by a preponderance of evidence and would you do your duty? That's what I asked you. I relied upon your word that you would."

The jury returned a verdict of not guilty by reason of insanity. As the jurors filed out of the jury box, many of them went up to Walter and congratulated him. Although some skeptics believe differently, it was only then that I realized the jury might have acquitted the wrong man. But then again, one never knows with dragon slayers.

FOUR

The Candy Knight

Dr. Mark Sheppard lived a double life. In St. Petersburg, Florida, he was a prominent, wealthy anesthesiologist . . . and straight. On weekends in New Orleans, he was gay. But not a typical gay. Rather, Dr. Sheppard got his thrills from sex with black street hustlers. It was the danger of these encounters that aroused him.

On a rainy Monday morning, January 23, 1978, Dr. Sheppard failed to show up for surgery in St. Petersburg. A Missing Person's Report was filed with the NOPD. Dr. Sheppard had arrived in New Orleans on Thursday, January 19, and had been staying at the Ursulines Guest House in the French Quarter. Detective George Heath, the same detective who obtained Valerie Manchester's confession in the Honeymoon Murder Case, went to the Guest House. The manager Jim Owens showed him Dr. Sheppard's room, where he found among other things a receipt from John T's Restaurant dated January 19. He also found a bust of Andrew Jackson, supposedly worth fifty thousand dollars, which Dr. Sheppard had brought to New Orleans to donate to a local museum.

Owens told Detective Heath that Dr. Sheppard, a regular customer, had spent that Thursday night with a black male prostitute. The last time Owens had seen the doctor was when he and the prostitute left the next morning. While Owens was unable to identify the prostitute, Detective Heath learned that Dr. Sheppard liked to play pool at a place in the French Quarter called Cigar's.

Detective Heath interviewed Billy Barr, the owner of Cigar's, who said that he knew the doctor well and that he was a regular customer who spread a lot of money around the place. Barr remembered the doctor being in his place recently and that he had been playing pool with Ponce Woods, a hustler. Indeed, Barr said the doctor had given Ponce an expensive, handmade pool stick in an alligator case. Barr also said the doctor spent a lot of time with a black guy named Candy—that, in fact, Candy had been there while the doctor and Ponce played pool. Later that night, according to Barr, he had to evict Candy for causing some kind of disturbance.

Influential friends of the doctor started a ruckus with the NOPD over his whereabouts. A private investigator from Florida had been retained and was snooping around in New Orleans. The press had gotten wind of the story, and the tourist-conscious city fathers didn't want another embarrassing headline. The phlegmatic Detective Heath was replaced by a hot shot homicide detective, John Dillmann, a dashing, Hollywood detective stereotype, who ironically looked a lot like the now infamous Mark Fuhrman.

Detective Dillmann went to John T's Restaurant. The owner knew Dr. Sheppard and recalled him dining there recently with a black gentleman named Larry Cephas. Detective Dillmann located Cephas, who readily admitted having spent that night with the doctor at the Ursulines Guest House. Consistent with what Jim Owens had said, Cephas claimed he and the doctor had left together the next morning and that the last time he had seen the doctor was at the corner of Royal and Ursulines streets, when Dr. Sheppard said he was going to the French Market for coffee and doughnuts. Cephas agreed to take a polygraph test. He passed.

Almost a month later, Dr. Sheppard's body was found in the city dump on Almonaster Avenue. He had been strangled with an electrical cord, and a black sock had been stuffed down his throat. The electrical cord and a gold necklace were still draped around his neck. An empty wallet was found nearby.

Detective Dillmann took his investigation to Florida. While going through the doctor's house, he discovered some diaries which revealed that the doctor had made other visits to New Orleans in January. The entry for January 2, 1978, according to Dillmann, read:

> "Check into the Ursulines at $22 @ day instead of the $75 demanded by the Noble Arms because of the Sugar Bowl. I put away my luggage and walked over to Esplanade and Marais and went to John Smith's apartment. He had been in bed with a sore throat—enjoyed seeing him. Then walked down to Cigar's to find that he had decided to close for the day because of the Sugar Bowl."

The entry for that day also indicated that Dr. Sheppard had gone "to see the Kari and Joseph Beasley house. . . ." I would not learn of this coincidence until many years later.

There were other references to a John Smith in Dr. Sheppard's diaries. Thinking he was on to something, Detective Dillmann called New Orleans to have a rap sheet run on a John Smith who lived in the neighborhood of Esplanade and Marais streets. When the rap sheet came back showing a young black male with an alias of "Candy," the name mentioned at Cigar's by Billy Barr, Detective Dillmann thought he had his man.

He returned to New Orleans to hunt for Candy. Discovering that Candy's girlfriend Daisy Scott lived at 1423 Marais Street, Detective Dillmann and his partners arrived at the Marais Street apartment with guns drawn; but instead of finding them, they found a white couple, Curtis and Karen McKnight, who said that they had been living in the apartment since early February and that they didn't know Candy or Daisy. Allegedly, the McKnights consented to a search and, seeing bloodstains throughout the apartment, especially in the bathroom, Detective Dillmann was convinced he had located the crime scene. As he would later write:

> "At apartment D on 1423 Marais Street we hit the mother lode, an evidentiary gold mine.
>
> The blood droplets near the front door were just a hint, a teaser, of what would follow. The shabby apartment had many terrible secrets to reveal, and so clear were they to a trained eye that, had the dwelling been human, I believe it would just have been waiting for our overdue arrival to blurt out the savage scene it had witnessed.
>
> Several times, as my gaze traveled from living room to kitchen to bathroom to bedroom and out to the dingy enclosed hallway, I wanted to punch my fist into the air and shout 'Eureka!'
>
> A detective can devote a lifetime to the job and never encounter a case such as Sheppard's and ten lifetimes before finding <u>this</u> murder scene. It was so much sweeter, this dream moment for a cop, because a good, professional investigation led us to the find."

Tracking down Daisy's new apartment, Detective Dillmann finally caught his suspect hiding in a closet. Candy was arrested and taken to the police station and, after a lengthy interrogation, Detective Dillmann and Sergeant Steve London obtained a confession. In many respects, the two detectives were alike: soft-spoken, articulate, smooth. Very experienced, and realizing that any confession would surely be attacked in court, they taped Candy's confession. London advised him of his rights, including the right to remain silent and to have an attorney present, and Candy waived those rights.

> London: "Has anybody threatened or beaten you into giving this taped statement?"
>
> Smith: "They haven't."

London: "Have you been promised anything in return for this statement?"

Smith: "No, I have not."

London: "Are you handcuffed at this time?"

Smith: "No, I am not."

London: "How many police officers are present in the room at the time of this statement?"

Smith: "One."

London: "No, there are . . . ."

Smith: "Two."

London: "Do you know their names?"

Smith: "No, I don't."

London: "Let this tape reflect that Detective John Dillmann and Sergeant Steve London are present. John, let me direct your attention to Friday, January 20, 1978, at approximately 9:00 A.M. Can you tell me what occurred at this time?"

Smith: "On Friday?"

London: "On Friday."

Smith: "On Friday morning at nine there were two dudes waiting to rip off the doc. I didn't even want them to rip the doc off, but they insisted, they needed the money, so I gave them the permission to go ahead, they could rip him off. But I never knew that anything like this was going to take place until it happened, and after it had happened, it was too late for me to really do something. Well, maybe I should have did something, I could have did something, but I was just silent and just let it go ahead. I hadn't did no crime, well, I didn't think I had committed no crime, I hadn't murdered nobody. I mean, I was a witness, I was there, I seen. . . ."

London: "John, how long have you known Doctor Sheppard?"

Smith: "Since 1976, 1977."

London: "Could you describe your relationship with Doctor Sheppard?"

Smith: "Well, yeah, the doc took a great interest in me. He said I had a nice body, and he just took a like to me."

London: "Have you seen him often?"

Smith: "Yes, I see him every time he come into town. He would have a way for me to know his telephone number so I could call him and let me know where he was at, and leave me a key."

London: "This address, 1423 Marais, apartment D, is that where you used to reside?"

Smith: "Yes."

London: "Would you please explain to us how Doctor Sheppard came to be at 1423 Marais Street, apartment D, on Friday, January 20, 1978?"

Smith: "All right. On Thursday afternoon, all of us were in the pool hall shooting pool and I sat with the doc for a while and he said he had some kind of dinner. He had to go to dinner with someone, so he said he would see me that morning, that Friday morning 'cause we already had decided that from Thursday afternoon, that he was going to come to see me that Friday morning. So, that's how he eventually came there 'cause he had already decided that he was going to come over there."

London: "Would you please relate everything from the moment he entered your apartment, everything that transpired and occurred that Friday morning?"

Smith: "Doc came in. I was in the bedroom. As you know, this is a three-room apartment, bedroom, living room, and kitchen, and I was in the bedroom. The doc came in, he said, 'Good morning.' He took off his clothes and went to the bathroom. Okay, that's the only thing that occurred. He go to the bathroom and they put a gun to his head and told him to lay to the floor, which he did, and. . . ."

London: "Who did this?"

Smith: "Patin. So, they searched him for money. He didn't have no money on him but I think forty dollars. That's about all that took place. They decided that the doc could identify them if they were to just took the forty dollars and left, so they wanted to know what to do, what to do, what to do. So, they came up with the idea to kill him, you know, so they did."

London: "All right, how did they? Describe to me exactly what occurred inside the bathroom."

Smith: "He took a cord off a radio that I have and put it around his neck and took a sock and stuck it in his mouth to keep him from screaming."

London: "Did the doctor struggle at any time while this happened?"

Smith: "No, he wanted to say something but the dude wouldn't let him speak, you know. I don't know what it was but he tried to say something, but he wouldn't let him say nothing. So he didn't put up no struggle."

London: "What was your participation in this?"

Smith: "Well at first I was frightened, you know, I was very scared. I had never seen nothing like this take place and I wanted to run, but if I had run, you know, it still would took place in my, you know, all this took place where I live. And if I had ran, either way, it would still be on me, you know. So after it happened, I just told them like it was. I said, well, you all going to have to dispose of him from here because this is where I live, and I did stay there until at least about two or three weeks after."

London: "John, how did they remove the body of Doctor Sheppard from your apartment?"

Smith: "By carrying him downstairs."

London: "All right, did they wrap him in anything?"

Smith: "They had a sheet off my bed."

London: "Would you describe that sheet?"

Smith: "Yellow sheet. And a bag, a garbage bag, a trash bag, they pulled that over him and they took him out to the car."

London: "Did they take him out to the car in the daytime, or was it in the night?"

Smith: "It was in the night."

Dillmann: "During the course of your involvement with Doctor Sheppard, did you become involved in any sexual relations?"

Smith: "Yes."

Dillmann: "Was this one time, twice, numerous occasions?"

Smith: "I had sex with him more than a dozen times."

Dillmann: "Would he give you money, presents, or anything?"

Smith: "He would give me money and buy me whatever I wanted."

In response to questions from Dillmann, Candy stated that he was born in New Orleans but raised in Pensacola, Florida, and that Dr. Sheppard had once paid for him to come to St. Petersburg, where Candy stayed with him in his home "for about a week."

Dillmann: "Who did you reside with at the Marais Street address? Who lived there with you, John?"

Smith "Oh, I lived with a partner of mine. His name is Red. That's the only name I know him by is Red. That's all we ever called him."

Dillmann: "Did he move in with you when you first rented the place?"

Smith: "No, he didn't. I had been staying there and he told me one day that his mom was going to put him out and he needed a place to stay, but he had a job so, quite naturally, I let him stay."

Dillmann: "Do you know anything else about Red. Do you know his mother, his father, his sisters, brothers?"

Smith: "Never met none of his relatives."

Dillmann: "Do you know where he worked?"

Smith: "He used to work off of Decatur. He don't work there no more. He quit that job."

Dillmann: "To your knowledge, he's just a hustler from the Quarter? Is that correct?"

Smith: "That's right."

Dillmann: "Can you give me a description of Red?"

Candy described Red as a black male seventeen or eighteen years old, standing six-one or six-two and weighing one hundred twenty-five or one hundred thirty pounds, clean-shaven, with a "little bush" of hair. He said he knew nothing else about Red, including his last name.

Dillmann: "Do you know any of his friends?"

Smith: "Harold Patin, that's the only one."

Dillmann: "Who actually strangled the doctor?"

Smith: "Patin and Red."

Dillmann: "Both?"

Smith: "Yes."

Dillmann: "You also mention that a sock was placed in Doctor Sheppard's mouth. Is that correct?"

Smith: "Yes. They were looking for something to put in his mouth and they seen the sock and they just decided to put it in his mouth. That's what they did."

Dillmann: "How many times would you say that Doctor Sheppard had been to your apartment?"

Smith: "This was the second time."

Dillmann: "It was only the second time? When was the first?"

Smith: "Just before this visit. He had made one visit, only about two or three weeks beforehand."

Dillmann: "Getting back to Thursday, January 19, 1978, you mentioned that you were shooting pool in Cigar's. Was that when you made arrangements with Doctor Sheppard to come to your apartment the next day?"

Smith: "Something like that. He was going to take someone out to dinner, and he wanted to know if it was all right that we could get together that morning. So I said, 'yeah.' Well, he asked me do I still live there. I said, 'yeah.' He said, 'why don't I drop by in the morning.'"

Dillmann: "Was Harold Patin or Red in the pool hall at that time?"

Smith: "Harold was in there with me."

Dillmann: "Am I correct that Doctor Sheppard was coming

to your apartment on the morning of January 20, 1978, to engage in sexual relations with you? Is that correct?"

Smith: "Right."

Dillmann: "Now, after he left the pool hall, who approached you, or were you approached? How did your conversation originate about ripping off the doctor? Would you relate that to me in detail?"

Smith: "I passed back by the pool hall about ten and there was nobody in there, so I left. Then I ran into the other little dude, Red, and we talked, and he was telling me about how bad hustling was, and people weren't buying nothing, and he needed some money, and this and that. And they decided that if I knew the doc and he just came in town that he would be a good person for them to rip off."

Dillmann: "John, now when you say rip off, do you mean they were going to rob the doctor?"

Smith: "Right."

Dillmann: "They were going to rob him of his money?"

Smith: "That's all they said."

Dillmann: "And you knew that the next morning they were going to rob him of his money?"

Smith: "Right, I did."

Dillmann: "And they were going to use your apartment as the place to rob him of his money? Is that correct?"

Smith "Right."

Dillmann: "The express purpose of their being at your apartment was to perpetrate an armed robbery on Doctor Mark Sheppard, is that correct?"

Smith: "Yes."

Dillmann: "And you had knowledge of this?"

Smith: "Yes. I did. Well, I didn't have no knowledge of this armed robbery. All I know was that they were going to take the money. I didn't know, you know, that there was going to be no armed robbery."

Dillmann: "But you knew they were going to rob him?"

Smith: "Right."

Dillmann: "All right, were you going to get any of the money from the robbery?"

Smith: "All I was doing was letting them be in my apartment. At that time I had money so I didn't need no money. I was just letting them make them some money."

Dillmann: "You weren't going to get any of the money?"

Smith: "No. If I wanted any money, I was going to get it anyway, you know, 'cause all I had to do was ask for it."

Dillmann: "You were just furnishing them a place to rob Doctor Sheppard, that's what it amounted to?"

Smith: "Yes, that's what it amounted to."

Dillmann: "How did Red and Harold find out that the doctor was going to be at your apartment Friday morning?"

Smith: "I told them."

Dillmann: "Why did you tell them?"

Smith: "I just told them so that they could make some money."

London: "Didn't you think that if they robbed Doctor Sheppard in your apartment with you there, and then left and didn't do anything to Doctor Sheppard, that Doctor Sheppard would naturally know who you are and could go to the police and say you assisted in this robbery? Didn't you think about that?"

Smith: "Well, I had figured that the doc was going to recognize them. Well, I thought that he would."

London: "All right, you thought he would, so you previously stated in this tape that the reason Doctor Sheppard was killed is because he could make an identification. Is that correct?"

Smith: "Uh-huh."

London: "Well, then you must have known that he was going to be killed ahead of time."

Smith: "I didn't know that they was going to kill him, no. All I thought, they were just going to take his money. As far as the killing part, I didn't know this."

London: "Did you think that Doctor Sheppard would turn you in to the police after this robbery?"

Smith: "I didn't."

London: "Why didn't you?"

Smith: "Because Doc knew me for two years and I knew that the doc, even knowing him, you know, the doc, you know, being with him, I was qualified to make money on my own 'cause he ain't never had seen me really just down and out broke. Sure he did me a favor, but he know that I was making money and I could make money. I shoot pool, I shoot dice, you know, and like I say, I was letting them make them some money. You know, I could make money myself, you know."

London: "All right. After Doctor Sheppard was killed, the body stayed in your apartment until after midnight. Is that correct?"

Smith: "Uh-huh."

Dillmann: "I'd like to take this a little bit slower. John, you mentioned earlier in this statement that the doctor arrived at your home about nine o'clock that morning."

Smith: "Uh-huh."

Dillmann: "So when he arrived that morning, who was at your apartment with you?"

Smith: "Harold and Red."

Dillmann: "Red was your roommate, and the second subject's name is Harold Patin?"

Smith: "Uh-huh."

Dillmann: "Would you give me a description of Harold Patin?"

Candy described Patin as five-nine, one hundred sixty or one hundred sixty-five pounds, twenty-five or twenty-six years old, medium build, with a "little mustache" and "just regular combed" hair. He said that Patin lived in the Lafitte Project with "some chick" and that he had seen him "once or twice" since Sheppard was killed.

Dillmann: "Have you seen Red since the doc was killed?"

Smith: "I done seen Red about twice, once in the pool hall. He said that he had got a job."

Dillmann: "Did he mention where he was working?"

Smith: "He didn't."

Dillmann: "Okay, John, let's get back to the morning of January 20 when Doctor Sheppard arrived at your apartment. He knocked on your door, is that correct?"

Smith: "Uh-huh."

Dillmann: "Who answered the door?"

Smith: "The door was open. I said, 'come in.'"

Dillmann: "Where were you when you said come in?"

Smith: "I was in the bedroom."

Dillmann: "That's the rear bedroom, is that correct?"

Smith: "Uh-huh."

Dillmann: "What happened when Doctor Sheppard walked into your apartment?"

Smith: "He came on straight to the bedroom. Spoke and started getting undressed."

Dillmann: "Where were Harold Patin and Red at that time?"

Smith: "In the bathroom."

Dillmann: "You mentioned earlier that they had a pistol, is that correct?"

Smith: "Uh-huh."

Dillmann: "Can you give me a description of this pistol?"

Smith: "Well, the pistol was phony, it wasn't no real pistol. It wasn't no blank pistol but it sounded like a blank pistol. It had a plug in the end, you know, like a little red plug in the end of a toy pistol. The pistol wasn't real, it was a little play gun."

Dillmann: "Now, as soon as the doctor got into your apartment, he took off his clothes?"

Smith: "Uh-huh."

Dillmann: "What was Doctor Sheppard wearing that day, do you remember?"

Smith: "A pair of, I think, gray pants . . . gray pants, and a shirt. He just pulled off his pants and he said, 'I got to go to the bathroom.'"

Dillmann: "All right, now, this is very important, John: Do you remember, when he took his pants off, did he have underwear on?"

Smith: "Well, I didn't pay no attention, but I think he did. I'll say he did."

Dillmann: "What clothes did Doctor Sheppard have on when he walked into the bathroom."

Smith: "A shirt, a T-shirt, and socks."

Dillmann: "Once he got to the bathroom, what happened?"

Smith: "I heard the noise. I know that they was in there, you know, doing what they had planned to do. But I wanted to say before he went in there, because at the last minute, I still wanted to cop out from doing that and from even letting them rip him off. You know, I wanted to cop out. I said, when he was going in the bathroom, you know, I wanted to say, 'well, hey doc, don't go in there, let's go somewhere else,' you know, like that. But I didn't say nothing after I heard the tumbling."

Dillmann: "You heard the tumbling, you said?"

Smith: "Right. I walked from the bedroom. I looked in there and he was laying on the floor."

Dillmann: "Did you go into the bathroom?"

Smith: "I went to the kitchen. When I got to the kitchen, I automatically see what was happening, you know."

Dillmann: "Where exactly was the doctor lying at that point?"

Smith: "Across the floor. Half of his body was in the bathroom, and half was in the kitchen."

Dillmann: "Was he on his stomach?"

Smith: "His stomach."

Dillmann: "And what were Red and Harold doing at that time?"

Smith: "Well Red was getting something to cover him with . . . to put on his body."

Dillmann: "He was still alive at that point, wasn't he?"

Smith: "Yeah, he was. So they asked, you know, how much was it? There wasn't but forty dollars."

Dillmann: "How did you know about the money?"

Smith: "How I know how much money the doc had?"

Dillmann: "Yes."

Smith: "Well they had left it, ah, you know, the doc had pulled off his pants in the room."

Dillmann: "Am I correct in assuming that while they grabbed the doctor in the bathroom and held him with the fake pistol, you went into the doctor's pants and removed the money?"

Smith: "Well I did."

Dillmann: "What did Harold and Red say?"

Smith: "Nothing, but that it wasn't worth, you know, the while for them to, you know, to have robbed because there wasn't no money. You know, they had did something that they didn't get no money or nothing out of it and had taken a chance at getting some time."

Dillmann: "Now you stated they mentioned that it wasn't worthwhile robbing him for forty dollars and that they could get some heavy time for that, is that correct?"

Smith: "Uh-huh."

Dillmann: "Is it at that point that they mentioned killing the doc?"

Smith: "Well not at that particular time. They stood there for a while and everybody was wondering what they were going to do. Well I was getting ready to leave myself, you know, like I was scared from the jump, you know."

Dillmann: "Did you give either Harold or Red the money at that point?"

Smith: "I left it in the wallet. I just laid it back on the dresser. I didn't put it back in his pants. And I was standing in the other room, right there, so I could see in the kitchen door. So I was standing right there and I was talking to them and they were saying, well, they had to dispose of him, and I was wondering what. . . ."

Dillmann: "They said they had to dispose of him?"

Smith: "Right. And so they didn't have nothing to kill him with. Like I said, his gun was, you know, that wasn't no real gun or nothing. And that's when they decided they had to strangle him. They didn't have nothing to strangle him with, so my radio was sitting there."

Dillmann: "Where, exactly, was the radio?"

Smith: "It was on the table, the table just as you walk in the front door, you know, the table that sit there. I had it there with the cord plugged in the bottom. Red went and got the radio and he just put one foot on it and snapped the cord out. And then just wrapped it around the neck and he started pulling."

Dillmann: "John, was just Red choking the doctor with the cord?"

Smith: "Well Red, he put the cord around the neck first to choke him, but apparently he didn't have enough strength to choke, and Harold grabbed the other end."

In a series of questions, Dillmann in effect asked Candy to affirm that Red and Patin wanted to kill Sheppard so he couldn't identify them, that both men took part in strangling the doctor, and that Candy had a clear view of the act. Candy affirmed these things in brief responses—"Right," "Uh-huh," etc.

Dillmann: "About how long did it take to strangle him?"

Smith: "Five or six minutes."

Dillmann: "What was the doctor doing while this was going on? Did he struggle at all, John?"

Smith: "Yeah. After they started choking him then, you know, quite naturally, he started, you know, pulling. Then that's when Red, you know, sat on his leg and fought to put the cord on his foot."

Dillmann: "Was the doctor able to say anything? Did he scream for any help?"

Smith: "He didn't scream."

Dillmann: "He didn't say a word at all?"

Smith: "He didn't say anything."

Dillmann: "Did he appear scared to you?"

Smith: "Well really, he wasn't scared, I think, because, like I said, me and the doc had been knowing one another a long time and he didn't feel that nothing was going to happen 'cause he know that, I guess, you know, that I wouldn't do anything to him like that, to harm him. He really figured that they were just going to rob him, you know, probably then go head home."

Dillmann: "I see."

Smith: "And so after he did struggle, after they put the cord around his neck, you know, he started struggling then."

Dillmann: "After they strangled the doctor, you mentioned

they went and got a sheet?"

Smith: "Uh-huh."

Dillmann: "What was the reason for getting the sheet?"

Smith: "To cover him up."

Dillmann: "Can you describe the sheet to me in more detail than just being yellow? Anything else about it that you can remember?"

Smith: "I think it's the one that covers the mattress. It got elastic on the thing."

Dillmann: "You're saying it was a fitted sheet?"

Smith: "That's what it is."

Dillmann: "Who went and got that sheet?"

Smith: "Red."

Dillmann: "And he wrapped the doctor in the sheet?"

Smith: "Well he put it up around from his shoulder to his head."

Dillmann: "Okay, now, the cord is already around the doctor's neck, then the sheet was around his head. Is that correct?"

Smith: "Uh-huh."

Dillmann: "And the stocking?"

Smith: "That was the first . . . the stocking was to keep him from screaming."

Dillmann: "Before they strangled the doctor with the radio cord, they retrieved a pair of panty hose or stockings, and they put a sock in the doctor's mouth to keep him from screaming, is that correct?"

Smith: "That's correct."

Dillmann: "Who got the panty hose?"

Smith: "Well the panty hose was already in the bathroom."

Dillmann: "Who did the panty hose belong to?"

Smith: "My old lady."

Dillmann: "What is her name?"

Smith: "Daisy Scott."

Dillmann: "Is that the woman whose home you were at when I picked you up?"

Smith: "Right."

Dillmann: "So the sheet is around his head, the stocking is used as a gag, and the cord is around his neck, right? Did they use any other sheets?"

Smith: "Nothing but a green trash bag."

Dillmann: "What did they do with that trash bag?"

Smith: "Put it on his head, you know, just put it over him."

Dillmann: "Did they use any other sheets?"

Smith: "Not to my remembering."

Dillmann: "So what happened next? The doctor is dead, they have him wrapped up in a sheet; they have the plastic bag over his head. Then what did you do?"

Smith: "Well I told them I was going home."

Dillmann: "John, you were home."

Smith: "Yeah, but what I was saying, I was getting away from there, I was leaving there. I was going to spend some time somewhere else. So I went on to my old lady and I laid there in bed."

* * * * *

Dillmann: "John, when you left the apartment, you left Harold and Red there?"

Smith: "Well Red was getting ready to come outside with me, but Harold, he was running around up in there. I think he was looking for a little more money. He figured there was more than forty dollars."

Dillmann: "Who took the money, John?"

Smith: "Ah, they split it up. It wasn't but forty dollars, they had twenty dollars apiece. They went and got speed, and Harold, I think he finally wound up in the project. I don't know where Red went."

Dillmann: "When did you next come back to the apartment?"

Smith: "Well I didn't come to the apartment. I went to the project where Harold live and I was telling him about, you know, this lady that I dig and that, you know, I was welcome to, you know, come home and stay, 'cause that is home, you know. Come home and sleep. So he said, I told him that, well, buddy, you know, you got to get this, this man's body out of there. And it's up to you all to get him out of here."

According to Candy, Patin said he would move the body but needed a car. "So I said, bro, you have to get one now, you know." Candy said that "later that night," Patin borrowed a car from "a partner" at about one or two o'clock in the morning on Saturday (January 21).

Dillmann: "Do you know who Harold Patin borrowed the car from? Do you know the gentleman's name?"

Smith: "Ah, wait now, he was another one that we call Red."

Dillmann: "He was another Red."

Smith: "Yeah, but he got a lot of hair. I don't think he had knew why he was lending his car, you know, 'cause I had asked, I said, 'bro,' I said, 'the car,' I said, 'the dude know what you gonna do with the car?' He said no, but he said 'I just got it,' he said 'I got to return it back in an hour or so,' he said, 'but he don't know nothing.'"

Dillmann: "Can you give me a description of this car?"

Smith: "Chevrolet, white, sixty-three or sixty-four, something like that."

Dillmann: "Then you and Harold went back to the apartment?"

Smith: "Uh-huh."

Dillmann: "Red wasn't with you?"

Smith: "No."

Dillmann: "When you went back upstairs, the doctor's body was in the same position?"

Smith: "Uh-huh."

Dillmann: "John, this is important. Was there any blood at that time in the bathroom?"

Smith: "There was blood, you know, wasted over the bathroom but I don't know where it had come from, but it was there."

Dillmann: "Do you think possibly it might have come from the doctor?"

Smith: "It had to. There wasn't nobody else it could have come from."

Dillmann: "The blood was on the floor? In the bathroom?"

Smith: "Uh-huh."

Dillmann: "So you and Harold took the doctor's body out, is that correct?"

Smith: "Right."

Dillmann: "You took it down the steps?"

Smith: "Uh-huh."

Dillmann: "Who carried the doctor's head?"

Smith: "Patin."

Dillmann: "And what did you carry?"

Smith: "The feet."

Dillmann: "All right, now this is very important, John. Listen to me. At any time during the course of going down the steps into the alleyway, did you bump up against that wall?"

Smith: "We stopped on the step, the first step, you know, just coming around it, we stopped right there. That was the only stop."

Dillmann: "To your knowledge, was there any blood dripping from the doctor?"

Smith: "No."

Dillmann: "Do you think you might have brushed up against the wall coming down the steps with the doctor's body. Is that possible?"

Smith: "It's possible, yeah."

Dillmann: "Now, the doctor's upper torso was covered with the sheet and the plastic bag. Is that correct?"

Smith: "Right."

Dillmann: "What about his legs? Was the rest of his body covered with anything?"

Smith: "Yeah, it was."

Dillmann: "What was it covered with, John?"

Smith: "Sheet."

Dillmann: "What color sheet?"

Smith: "Well it got to be white. There wasn't another yellow one. It had to be white."

Dillmann: "What about the rest of the doctor's clothes?"

Smith: "I think they all was in the bag."

Dillmann: "So you're saying the doctor's clothing was put in the plastic bag that was put over the doctor's head, and then the rest of his body was wrapped in a white sheet, and you and Harold Patin carried the body down the stairwell to the alleyway and then out to the Chevrolet?"

Smith: "Right."

* * * * *

Dillmann: "Who drove the car?"

Smith: "Patin."

Dillmann: "And you rode on the passenger side, correct? How did you determine what to do with the body?"

Smith: "Well I didn't determine. He determined to take it to the dump. I didn't know where the dump was. He just picked a spot and that was it."

Dillmann: "Where did you dump the body?"

Smith: "On the side, I don't know the name of the street. It's on the side of the road, somewhere, you know, off from the dump."

Dillmann: "On the side of the road out by the dump? Is that what you're saying?"

Smith: "Yeah. It's not the dump but, you know, it's the road going to the dump."

* * * * *

Dillmann: "Now, why did you decide to stop there?"

Smith: "We just picked a location."

Dillmann: "And then you and Harold—I don't want to put words in your mouth—but then you and Harold took the body out of the car?"

Smith: "Right."

Dillmann: "And dumped it? Is that correct?"

Smith: "Right."

Dillmann: "What did you do next?"

Smith: "Got in the car and drove on. I came back home. I laid down and went to sleep and he came over that morning and helped clean up."

Dillmann: "Who came over that morning?"

Smith: "Harold."

Dillmann: "Did you see Red?"

Smith: "Not right then. I seen Red about a week afterward."

Dillmann: "What did you do in the apartment to clean up?"

Smith: "Nothing but mop the blood up."

Dillmann: "You mopped the blood up?"

Smith: "Well it wasn't really mopping. We did it with some towels."

Dillmann: "And what did you do with the bloody towels?"

Smith: "Just put them in a trash bag and sent them to the dump."

Dillmann: "John, since Doctor Sheppard has been killed, have you and Red and Harold discussed the murder at all?"

Smith: "No."

Dillmann: "It's just been completely forgotten about?"

Smith: "Uh-huh."

London: "John, can you read and write?"

Smith: "No."

London: "Do you have any problem understanding what we're saying?"

Smith: "I don't."

London: "Are you on any medication right now that would prevent you from fully understanding what we're doing?"

Smith: "No."

London: "You are aware, aren't you, that the entire conversation is being taped?"

Smith: "I am."

London: "And this information was given freely and voluntarily?"

Smith: "It was."

Dillmann: "John, why havc you made this statement? For what reason?"

Smith: "I guess my conscience."

Dillmann: "Has it bothered you, John?"

Smith: "It has. My old lady could tell something was bothering me, but she ain't never know what it was."

London: "And nobody promised you anything in exchange for your statement?"

Smith: "No. Nobody promised me nothing."

Anticipating an accusation of police brutality, the detectives then took Candy to the Coroner's Office to have him photographed, head to toe. The photographs were clean. The case made, Detective Dillmann would later write:

> "I thought we had John Smith wrapped into a neat little package. There would still be plenty of work to do tying Patin and perhaps the two Reds into the murder and its aftermath, but Candy, I genuinely believed, had condemned himself."

The arrest received extensive news coverage, and shortly afterwards, Detective Dillmann was contacted by Alton "Red" Tumblin, who volunteered that he knew Candy and Patin and that he had loaned them his car in January, maintaining, however, that he didn't know why they had wanted his car. The car was impounded and searched for evidence. Red (pronounced "Raid") said he knew the other "Red" (also pronounced "Raid"), who had been Candy's roommate. Red led Detective Dillmann to Red.

When Detective Dillmann captured the second Red, whose real name was Wendell Blanks, he admitted having been Candy's roommate, but denied any knowledge of Dr. Sheppard's murder. Nonetheless, based on Candy's confession, Red was arrested for first degree murder; however, because the State had no witnesses against him, he was released when the grand jury refused to indict him.

Wrapping up his investigation, Detective Dillmann also seized a radio from Daisy's apartment which allegedly had a new electrical cord attached to it. The only loose end was Patin but, try though he did, the detective could never find Patin.

Candy's case was allotted to the mean old bastard. There is an old saying at Tulane and Broad that a case didn't need a prosecutor if it was allotted to Section B—Judge Braniff would handle that detail. But in this high profile case, Connick's office would take no chances and, again, the best prosecutor, Joe Meyer, was assigned to the case.

The Judge appointed the Law Clinic to represent Candy. Since we used certain cases to try to reform the legal system by expanding the rights of indigent defendants, and believing in a complex case such as this one that a free lawyer wasn't enough and that a free investigator was needed as well, we demanded one from the Judge. The mean old bastard must have liked us. He granted the motion.

Gary Eldredge was more of a Columbo than a Sam Spade. Actually a lawyer who didn't like lawyering, Gary was a terribly disheveled mumbler who gave the appearance of being in a perpetual state of confusion. He was, however, a damn good investigator—and the very best when it came to the kind of French Quarter characters we had to deal with in this case.

All dragons fight dirty, and this one was no different. Although the bloodstains in the Marais Street apartment had been classified as Type B, the State claimed it didn't know Dr. Sheppard's blood type. Here was a medical doctor who had served in the military and who had worked at several hospitals and the prosecution didn't know his blood type! The truth had to be that the doctor's blood type was something other than Type B.

Gary scoured the country for the doctor's blood type but he, too, came up empty-handed. At least the prosecution would not be able to match the blood at the alleged crime scene with that of the victim, no small advantage for the defense in a murder case. Also, the police claimed they couldn't identify the blood in Red's car, supposedly because the specks were too small. More reasonable doubt.

Lady Luck always plays a role in dragon fighting. Shortly before trial, Red Tumblin was murdered, and the evidence about lending his car to Candy and Patin went to the grave with him. Further, the McKnights, the couple occupying Candy's old apartment when the bloodstains were found, mysteriously disappeared.

We prepared Candy for trial by buying him a suit and a pair of dress shoes from the Salvation Army. He was a quick study during rehearsals. Candy had very little formal education, but he was streetwise. He was, after all, a hustler and con man who earned a living by deceiving people into believing him. A star in the making.

Trial began on February 6, 1979. In a first degree murder case, the jury is death qualified, meaning prospective jurors with conscientious scruples against the death penalty are excluded. Consequently, one ends up with death-seeking jurors—"Archie Bunkers," as I call them. In this case, however, I wasn't overly concerned with Archie Bunkers because I figured they would feel the doctor got his just desserts, being homosexual and messing with black street hustlers. At least six Archie Bunkers were selected and seated in the jury box.

The State called Detective Heath to outline the early stages of the investigation. On cross-examination I established from him what seemed to be two minor points: first, he had recovered Dr. Sheppard's wallet from his room at the Ursulines Guest House; and second, he had recovered some telephone message slips from the Guest House manager. Joe Meyer didn't know where the defense was going.

Next, the State called the crime scene technicians who had recovered the doctor's body and his personal effects from the city dump. On cross-examination, I focused on two items the State had introduced into evidence: first, a photograph of a wallet; and second, the gold chain taken from Dr. Sheppard's neck. Joe began to fidget in his chair.

The prosecution ended with Detective Dillmann playing Candy's confession to the jury. I cross-examined. Cross-examination is perhaps the most valuable weapon in a dragon slayer's arsenal, but it's also the one most likely to backfire. Knowing that this dashing, Hollywood type detective was a very controlled witness and that he wouldn't deliberately give me anything, I didn't confront him head on. It was his demeanor that I wanted the jury to ingest, a demeanor former Louisiana governor, Earl Long—known as Uncle Earl—would have described as "smooth as a peeled onion." I ended my cross-examination seemingly without laying a glove on him.

As our first witness, we called Jim Owens, the Guest House manager, who testified that, after last seeing the doctor on that Friday morning, he had received over the weekend a number of telephone messages for him. Significantly, some of those messages, which he had turned over to Detective Heath, had been from Candy Smith! Why would Candy be calling Dr. Sheppard on Saturday if he had murdered him on Friday? Joe began to squirm in his chair.

We also showed Owens the necklace the police claimed to have removed from the doctor's body. Holding the necklace high for the jury to see, Owens dramatically proclaimed that Dr. Sheppard's chain and medallion had been real gold, not the dime store trinket he was holding in his hand. Obviously, someone in the police chain-of-custody had substituted the trinket for the real stuff. During the next recess Joe, sensing that his case was falling apart, exploded by flinging the fake necklace at the nearest police officer.

Gary had located the landlord of the Marais Street apartment. The landlord testified that there were no bloodstains in the apartment after it had been vacated by Candy and before it was occupied by the McKnights. This testimony was corroborated by Daisy, who also swore that Candy had been with her on the morning of the murder. We also introduced the opinion of an expert witness that the electrical cord used to strangle the doctor had not come from the radio seized from Daisy's apartment.

Gary had also uncovered some other interesting facts which we presented to the jury. For example, Dr. Sheppard had changed his will two days before his final trip to New Orleans and, mysteriously, one of the beneficiaries had been in New Orleans during the weekend of the murder.

We ended with Candy. As expected, he was a good witness. Acknowledging their sexual relationship, he admitted having seen the doctor at Cigar's on that Thursday and that they were supposed to meet the next day. From that point on, however, his testimony differed from his confession. He insisted the doctor had failed to appear the next day, and that he had left messages over the weekend for him at the Guest House. He swore that his confession was false and that Detective Dillmann had told him what to say before it was taped. He also swore the detective had forced him into giving the false account by pulling hair from his face and by beating his testicles and feet with a blackjack. It wasn't possible for him to be the murderer, he said, because not knowing how to drive, he couldn't have transported the body to the dump. His *coup de grace* was that he had invented the facts about Red and Patin in the hope that they could prove their own innocence, and thereby exonerate him. In other words, Candy, the inveterate hustler, had made the ultimate gamble: his confession would prove his innocence.

In closing argument, I referred to Candy's "confession" as merely his "statement," naturally:

> "Now, there is something about this case that I'm going to tell you now that may shock you because it is something that has never been said, but it's the truth. And that is this: when you carefully analyze the State's case, when you carefully analyze and think about everything that Mr. Meyer has told you and everything that Mr. Meyer will tell you when he comes back with his rebuttal, this will be revealed to you. And I agree with him. He does not want you to believe this statement. Mr. Meyer does not want you to believe this statement, and the reason he doesn't want you to believe this statement is he knows, just as I've suggested to you, that out of this statement—a lawyer reading this statement could find neither first, second, nor manslaughter. . . . You carefully analyze all of his arguments and that will be the bottom line because a trained legal mind looking at this can only find the situation of a person saying, 'I've witnessed something that I didn't intend to happen.'
>
> * * * * *
>
> Now, how can he ask you to convict on something that he himself doesn't believe in—doesn't believe in. You see, what he wants you to do is to look at this statement and pick and choose, and he wants you to believe that this statement is a lie. Just like I want you, and suggest to you that this statement is a lie. But then, he wants you to make a big leap—a big jump. He wants you to say, well, because it's a lie, because it couldn't have happened that way, it must have happened this way. But which way. Maybe Patin did it. Maybe Patin didn't do it. Maybe Wendell Blanks did it. Maybe Wendell Blanks didn't do it. Maybe John Smith did it this way. Maybe he did it that way. Maybe Patin wasn't there. Maybe Wendell Blanks wasn't there. Maybe John Smith did it all himself.

Everything is a maybe—speculation. You see, he wants to go from this, a lie, to a conviction. You can't do that."

I then explained my theory of what actually happened:

> "Now I'll tell you the way the case went down. The way the case went down was just the way I suggested it to you in the opening statement. First of all, a prominent doctor ends up missing in the City of New Orleans. At that time, Detective Heath who is now in Juvenile, but then was in Homicide—since brought back to Juvenile—Detective Heath was in charge of the case, and he goes to the Guest House, and what does he get from the Guest House? The doctor's wallet, the doctor's credit card, a glove, telephone messages. All right. But then, Heath has that. Heath has it. Okay. Dillmann is not in the case at that time as Officer Heath told you. Then, in February, a month later, the doctor's body was found. Now all of a sudden there is a serious situation in the hands of the New Orleans Police because now, not only are we dealing with—we're not just dealing with a missing person, some eccentric wealthy doctor from Florida—now all of a sudden, New Orleans has a homicide on its hands, a very tragic homicide that's got to be solved. Dillmann then takes over the case, but Dillmann doesn't know what Heath found out in the Guest House. So Dillmann goes to the scene where the body was found and he finds a wallet. . . . So Dillmann figures, an empty wallet . . . robbery."

Completing the circle by converting Candy's confession into his defense, I told the jury:

> "When you examine this statement, this statement is consistent with the way Dillmann felt the crime had occurred. Dillmann felt that the crime occurred in the Marais Street apartment. So that's what it says. Dillmann felt that there was a lot of blood involved—on the walls—splattered. Now, you tell me, assuming you believe this statement, how a person can be strangled with something in his mouth, lying face down, can have blood splattered all over. But, it was consistent with what Dillmann thought was his case. He had to get blood in the Marais Street apartment.
>
> The real telltale is the wallet. Dillmann had to get the wallet because robbery was the motive. There was a wallet

> found with the doctor's body. He didn't know that Dr. Sheppard's wallet was in the Ursulines Guest House. So, there's a wallet involved. 'I went through the wallet, and we threw the wallet with the rest of the doctor's clothes in the bag, dumped it out there'—the wallet—the wallet—the wallet. Well, you see, the killer, or the witness would have known that the wallet wasn't there, that there was no wallet involved. Heath even knew that. But Heath wasn't making this case. But Dillmann thought that he had to explain the wallet. But the real killer, and the real witness or witnesses, or real killers, or whoever they were, would know that the wallet wasn't involved."

The jury deliberated for approximately three hours before sending a message to the Judge. All of us, O'Grady, Slim, Gary, and the students, had been smoking cigarettes and pacing the floor in the hallway. We rushed into the courtroom as the Judge ascended the bench and as the jurors took their places in the jury box. The foreman announced that the jury was hopelessly deadlocked. A mistrial was declared.

Everyone, as usual, went to the Miracle Mile. Unlike cases with a verdict, where one drunk side is pissed off at the other drunk side, with a hung jury, both drunk sides are pissed off at one another. Perhaps it's no coincidence that the Coroner's Office is located across the street from the Miracle Mile.

From time to time, discharged jurors also went to the Miracle Mile. Slim claims that my 3-M syndrome requires that I keep a pretty woman on the jury and that it's usually the pretty juror who hangs us. But that was not the case this time. To my great delight, the pretty juror in Candy's case joined us, and while she had voted for acquittal, we also learned that I had made a near fatal mistake: the six jurors who had voted guilty were the Archie Bunkers. And so, I had been only half right: the Archie Bunkers hadn't liked the doctor, that much was true; but they had disliked Candy even more—their attitude, according to the pretty juror, was, "Let's kill the nigger too while we can."

Joe and I both made adjustments for the second trial, and in jury selection I obviously stayed away from the Archie Bunkers as much as possible. Also, by this time, Patin had been found and arrested. Gary interviewed him, and miraculously, he had an airtight alibi. Candy's gamble was paying off, and we called Patin and his alibi witnesses during the second trial.

Joe made more drastic changes. He didn't call Detective Dillmann as a witness, and he also tried to shift the motive from robbery to jealousy. In closing argument, I rubbed salt into his wounds:

> "Now, Ladies and gentlemen of the jury, as I told you when I selected you, I think that the evidence shows that

this statement is consistent with the way Dillmann thought the case went down, but you all are deprived of what Dillmann thought. It's Dillmann's case. He's the Dick Tracy. He was the honcho. He was the crime solver. But now you just have to take my word for it that this is what Dillmann thought. You don't have Dillmann's testimony. That's incredible to me, absolutely incredible. And I want to remind you that there is a law—I'll read it to you because I think it's—this law says—it's Title 15, Section 432: 'That evidence'—now, of course, testimony is evidence—'that evidence under the control of a party, and not produced by him, was not produced because it would not have aided him.'"

As for jealousy, I argued:

"And the most important question is why, if jealousy was the motive, why would he kill the doctor and not Ponce Woods. When have you ever heard of a jealous whore killing her customer instead of the other whore that the customer has turned to. The doctor was the goose that laid the golden egg for Candy. If another person was getting some of the golden eggs, what would you do? You don't kill the goose that lays the golden eggs. You kill the other person who is running off with the golden eggs. So, that doesn't fit. . . ."

Joe's strongest points throughout the case had been that if Candy were truly innocent, why did he confess, and if Detective Dillmann were truly a bad cop, why didn't he coerce a more condemning confession. Good points. Sometimes, a dragon fighter can only deflect the streams of fire:

" . . . as I told you in the opening statement, what has bothered me a great deal, what I'm very afraid of, what is the sensitive thing in my case, is why—why John Smith, why do you in the first place make any statement? Why did you do that? Why? Now, he is going to argue and he is going to argue very effectively—Mr. Meyer—that none of you would have done that. None of you, if you can even envision a possibility that you might one day be confronted by a police officer and questioned about a crime—none of you would do that. Well of course you wouldn't. I wouldn't have done it. He (Meyer) wouldn't do it. And you see, in this country we're supposed to have a trial by peers. Well John Smith doesn't have a trial by peers. If he had a trial by peers, I'd have an easy job. If he had street people on there, hustlers, people who have been harassed, people who've been afraid of police, people who've been kicked around, people who would survive in a jungle, I wouldn't have any trouble at all. But I don't. He doesn't have a trial by his peers. He has a trial by his superiors—people who live differently. None of you would have done that. Of course not. And he's going to say, well, convict him because he acted differently than you would have acted. And he's going to argue that point eloquently and logically perhaps, and with some force and persuasion because he knows the audience he's talking to. And he knows that you all would have the most difficult time understanding, trying to understand, why someone like John Smith would make any statement to the police unless he was guilty."

And the jury did have a difficult time. They deadlocked again—this time eight for acquittal and four for guilty.

Trying cases is hard work; retrying them is murder. In many respects, good trial lawyers are like stage actors, with one important difference: trial lawyers need spontaneity and, unlike actors, they don't improve over a long run. Joe and I were exhausted and, realizing that the State would prosecute Candy at least for a third time, I half-jokingly suggested that we should turn the case over to others. He agreed and I put O'Grady on the point for the third trial.

When the third trial began, however, I showed up without O'Grady. The State, on the other hand, having fallen into my trap, sent in a rookie to replace Joe. Detective Dillmann would later say that I "double-crossed" them. Maybe so. But remember, I am a dragon slayer not a dragon savior.

When the rookie prosecutor appeared in court with his pretty, young fiancé for moral support, I walked up to him and taunted, "I'm going to beat your ass in this case and fuck your girlfriend, too." Anything to unnerve a rookie.

The State made another big mistake the third time around by reducing the charge from first degree to second degree murder. A death-qualified jury was no longer required. Goodbye, Archie. Also, on a charge of second degree murder, only ten of the twelve jurors had to agree on a verdict.

The State brought back Detective Dillmann as a witness for the third trial but, by now, I had fine-tuned my characterization of him:

> "And let me tell you about Dillmann. Dillmann is smooth, very smooth. Dillmann is like those yard lizards, they sit out in the sun, they're all pretty and green, and they, you know, they put out their throat and all of that, and as

> much as you want them to change colors, you can't get them to change colors. But when they want to change color, they've got a dark side to them. And they can change. Now you've got to believe that Dillmann, when he testified, and on that tape which he knew the jury was going to hear, he had his pretty green side up, his pretty green side up. But there's a dark side, and that dark side was when they were in that interrogation room, just the two of them—just the two of them for forty-five minutes before the tape started. And that's when this story was concocted. That is when this story was concocted."

The jury returned a verdict of not guilty. The vote was ten to two. As I was walking Candy down the steps of Tulane and Broad, he asked, "What you want me to do with this suit, Bro?"

"Keep it," I said, handing him twenty bucks. "Candy, you better get your ass out of this city. These cops are madder than hell. They're gonna' be after your black ass for sure."

"Yeah, you right, Bro. Where should I go?"

"Candy, it don't make no fuckin' difference. Just get out. Go to some nowhere place. Maybe Yazoo City."

"Alright, Bro. Thanks for everything," he said as he walked off into the darkness.

I never saw him again but I know he didn't follow my advice. Years later, I received a call from Daisy. She wanted to know if I would represent Candy because he was back in jail.

"What's he in jail for, Daisy?"

"Auto theft."

"Auto theft?" I repeated in shock.

"Yes, sir. That's the charge they got on him."

"Daisy, that's impossible. Candy can't drive. Don't you remember, that was part of our defense. He couldn't have brought the doctor's body to the dump because he couldn't drive," I said emphatically.

"Oh, no," Daisy said, "Candy drives."

FIVE

The White Knight

On June 12, 1963, civil rights leader Medgar Evers was assassinated outside his home in Jackson, Mississippi. Shortly afterwards, a fertilizer salesman, Byron de la Beckwith, was arrested and charged with murder. "Delay," as he was called by his friends, admitted the murder weapon was his but claimed it had been stolen from his house. He was tried twice in 1964 for murder but both trials ended with hung juries. The jury, all white, did not convict him; they didn't acquit him either.

Ten years later, Delay was arrested by the NOPD as he entered New Orleans on I-10. The police had been informed by the FBI of a tip from a confidential informant that he would be coming to New Orleans to bomb the residence of A. I. Botnick, a civic leader and member of the Anti-Defamation League. The tip included detailed information that Delay would be arriving in the Slidell area sometime after dark on September 26, 1973; that he would be driving a white over blue Oldsmobile with two radio antennae on the rear; that his car would bear a substituted license plate numbered 61D2390; and that he would be carrying a fully loaded forty-five caliber automatic pistol in his waistband. Sure enough, at midnight on the night in question, the police spotted his car entering Orleans Parish. They stopped him and ordered him to place his hands on the police car. The police frisked him and found the fully loaded forty-five pistol. Searching the car, the police found a box containing several sticks of dynamite, a time clock, and numerous wires. Also, a map of New Orleans with red tracings to Botnick's home.

Delay was first tried in federal court for interstate transportation of explosives. A federal jury of eleven whites refused to convict him. The State then charged him with transporting explosives without a license. The case was allotted to my neighbor, Judge Charles Ward, and the trial was at Tulane and Broad. This time, a jury that included five blacks found him guilty. The Judge imposed the maximum sentence of five years at Angola and, since Delay claimed to be an indigent, he also appointed the Law Clinic to handle the appeal.

Delay was imprisoned during the appeal process so we communicated by mail, but I say this with reservation, since the communicating was mostly a one-way street. He bombarded me with hate mail about "niggers," "Jews," and "Catholics." Strangely, the fact that I was a Catholic lawyer with a Jewish name, a free-thinking spirit, and worked for the Jesuits, didn't seem to phase him in the least. To my surprise, years later he would say," . . . those Catholic boys sure saved my ass down in Looziana."

Delay was a psychopath who stood for everything I despised. He was a racist, a bigot, a hatemonger, and probably a murderer. While a student at LSU in the early 1960s—a time of freedom riders, young liberals from the North coming South to show us the way, and of reverse freedom riders, bigots from the South riding North in Greyhound buses to defend the old ways—I had written to the school newspaper:

> "We Americans walk proudly to and fro in our land of freedom and liberty and look down superciliously with scorn and contempt at our bestial brethren across the straits who are engulfed by the terrifying atheistic and fraternal miasma of Communism.
>
> We graciously place ourselves in the limelight of world diplomacy as a grand example of true Christian and democratic brotherhood; yet, ironically, we chase what obviously we consider the 'lesser breed' around the countryside with the voracious, slobbering, and canine mouth of a greyhound."

I concluded the letter, written as you can see, in the florid style of Mr. Sidney Marchand, by calling upon the student body, the future "carpenters, mechanics, electricians, and Babbitts to lay down their tools momentarily and, Oh! bibliophiles, lead them!" Shortly afterwards, the door to my dormitory room was set on fire. My father considered sending me back to the hot tin rooftops at Palo Alto.

According to Aunt Delta, Mississippi is divided into two places: Natchez and the Delta. I'm not sure why this is. She certainly doesn't draw cultural differences, inasmuch as to her, blacks are "darkies" no matter where. All I know is that if she is going to a wedding or a funeral, say in Gulfport, she is off "to the Delta." People like de la Beckwith, the kind of white knight one might find on a Mississippi backroad with a sheet over his head, don't exist in her world. She predates them. Aunt Delta may not love—but she doesn't hate.

To be a dragon slayer, one must separate personal feelings from professional duty. We are amoral, hired gun-slingers. We don't make moral judgments about our damsels in distress any more than surgeons do with patients. At Loyola, Mo and I had an ongoing dialogue about this. The Jesuits (and Mo) postulated that the Law School should have "Christian goals." My retort was that there is no such thing as a Catholic lawyer, or a Jewish lawyer, only lawyers who happen to be Catholic or Jewish.

This isn't an easy concept for many people. My children and R.A. often confront me about some of my unsavory clients. I explain that, like prosecutors, dragon slayers are also law enforcers—but against the king. The legal rights are paramount, not necessarily the people who exercise them. This dogma also serves as a good sleeping dram.

And so the Law Clinic prepared a brilliant brief in Delay's behalf. We argued that the statute under which he was convicted was unconstitutional; that the Judge erred in not changing the venue from New Orleans; that his arrest and the subsequent seizure of the evidence from his car was unconstitutional; and that the prosecution engaged in unfair tactics to inflame the jury. All to no avail. On February 28, 1977, the Supreme Court, with one justice dissenting, affirmed the conviction.

Delay served out his sentence at Angola. He was released from prison in 1980 and undoubtedly returned to hatemongering. Then in December of 1990, he was indicted in Mississippi for a third time for the murder of Medgar Evers. Because the first two trials had ended in mistrials, it did not violate double jeopardy to try him for a third time. On February 5, 1994, twenty years after the first trials, de la Beckwith was convicted of murdering Medgar Evers. This time the jury consisted of eight blacks and four whites. The wheels of justice turn slowly.

SIX

Dragon Fields

Law professors are strange. Most of them teach law because they can't practice law. This phenomenon is unique to law schools. For example, medical school professors also practice medicine. But it goes much deeper than this. English professors teach writing, although many don't write novels. Yet English teachers know how to write. Music teachers teach music, although many don't compose music. Yet music teachers know how to play music. In contrast, law professors don't know how to practice law. For that reason, law schools historically have had absolutely no relevancy to the practice of law. For instance, I learned none of my dragon slaying skills from law school. As you know, I learned cross-examination from Monsignor Gubler, fee-splitting from Boo-Boo and Sonny, legal research from Aunt Delta, self-discipline from my father, commerce from Jacob Lemann, and chivalry from my mother. And so young lawyers were expected to learn how to practice law after graduation on unsuspecting clients. It was much like a Spanish teacher who didn't speak Spanish sending students off to Spain to do the best they could.

Deep down, law professors know they are irrelevant—and I suspect that's why they're so weird. Show me an upbeat law professor, and I'll show you a manic depressive without Lithium. This mania becomes most apparent at faculty meetings. At faculty meetings, law professors know they're being watched only by other law professors, and so it is there that non-practicing professors practice law. The slightest point of discussion has to be fully briefed and argued as though being presented to the United States Supreme Court. Also, older, unpublished professors at faculty meetings condemn younger professors for not publishing. I'm sure it's the same at all law schools but it's worse at Catholic law schools where one must cope with the added irrelevance of religion.

Clinical education changed some of this. To the students, it was the best thing since confession. Not unexpectedly, the non-practicing faculty frowned upon clinical education, supposedly because it was below the dignity of the ivory tower but actually because it reminded them of their own irrelevance. In many law schools, the lawyers who operated the clinical programs were often treated as second class citizens in the academic community. I was fortunate in having been on the regular faculty before becoming a "clinician," but even then, I had to guard against the hot tin roofs.

The Law Clinic was so popular we had a waiting list. There are only so many students a lawyer can supervise, so after O'Grady graduated we hired him as Assistant Director. But even so, we still had more applicants than we could supervise. Some of the rejected students nonetheless volunteered to serve as paralegals for the student practitioners. One such paralegal came by every morning, opened the office, and made coffee for the rest of us.

The Law School was located in a new building which resembled a set from a science fiction movie. The Jesuits, following in the holy trail of Monsignor Gubler, built the new building in the name of progress and demolished three St. Charles Avenue mansions in the process, one of which had been my great grandfather's townhouse. Gone are the Easter lilies.

Classrooms were located on the second floor of the Law School building, and the non-practicing faculty had their small offices on the third floor. The Law Clinic was on the first floor, directly behind the Moot Courtroom, in a suite of offices that had been designed originally as chambers for visiting judges. In other words, a showplace. Thus, by sheer accident, I ended up with the largest office in the building. We even had our own kitchen. On Friday afternoons, O'Grady and I cooked gumbo, jambalaya, or sauce piquant for our student practitioners. The strong smell of onions and garlic sauteeing in the Clinic's kitchen permeated the third floor, undoubtedly contributing to the tension between us lowly clinicians and the non-practicing faculty.

We ran a pretty loose ship, more like a MASH unit than a traditional law office. Sink or swim was the teaching philosophy. Because the clients would do the sinking, the students realized all the more the importance of their mission. Some discovered they couldn't take the heat. One student, standing next to a convicted murderer at sentencing, passed out cold when the judge said," . . . by causing to pass through your body a current of electricity of sufficient intensity to cause death and by the application and continuance of such current through your body until you are dead, dead, dead, and may God have mercy on your soul." Others flourished. Another student, putting aside the fact that she was a nun, loved divorce cases; she was known as the divorcing nun. O'Grady once tried to get her in full habit to appear before a jury on behalf of a rapist, but she only did divorces.

Mo and I constantly bickered over the budget. However, I had a powerful advantage. Whenever we ran short of money, I would have Slim hang a sign on the door proclaiming, "CLINIC CLOSED DUE TO LACK OF

FUNDS." When this happened, our motley clientele would mingle around the Law School and accost Mo, demanding to know, "Where's my lawyer at?" Naturally, this sent shudders through his already haggard nervous system and somehow he always found the money we needed.

From time to time, I would also threaten Mo with going straight to the Jesuits for money. The prospect of my meeting face-to-face with Jesuits made him particularly nervous. At one Christmas party, after being introduced to the University's new president who had recently become embroiled in an investigation involving fund-raising activities at his former post, I offered him the services of the Law Clinic, saying I knew he had "taken the vow of poverty." Mo shrank two inches. It turned out that the new president really didn't need a lawyer after all, seeing that he mysteriously disappeared overnight on reassignment to some unknown place. Stalin, I reckon, learned a lot from the Jesuits.

After the Beasley case, my private practice grew and R.A. and I moved to a larger home on Constance Street near Audubon Park, where we still live today. With four children, Rachel, Arthur IV, Amy, and Jonathan, I found it increasingly difficult to live on a law professor's salary. Drawing upon my sense of commerce, I began to look for greener pastures.

Already a Public Sinner, I decided I might as well become the United States Attorney. I was offered the appointment to replace Captain America by Senator J. Bennett Johnston. However, I needed the concurrence of Senator Russell Long. I met with him in Washington and, while we had a very cordial meeting, he reminded me of our families' past animosity. Uncle Monte and Huey Long had been bitter foes.

Another more serious obstacle I had to overcome was Judge Rubin. He and Senator Long had been law school classmates and remained close friends. The scuttlebutt was that the Senator would defer to the Judge on the appointment of the new United States Attorney. On the surface, Judge Rubin and I were very civil to one another, but our relationship had been strained by the Beasley case. In denying the motion to continue, the Judge had said that Dr. Beasley had "gambled and lost" that his trial would follow on the heels of a Kramer acquittal. In our appeal brief, I had written that a federal judge should be more than "a croupier of constitutional rights." I don't believe the Judge ever forgave me for that comment. I also don't believe he thought me enough of a company man to be United States Attorney. As I said, Judge Rubin was a very wise man. I never received the appointment. Instead, John Volz replaced Captain America, and thus ended my career as a heretic.

My best friend in law school was Frank A. Marullo, actually Francesco Americano Marullo. The son of a policeman, Frank was fairly representative of the Loyola Law School student body. Our students were lower to middle-class, the product of public or parochial educations. The typical Loyola graduate wasn't hired by the big establishment law firms as were the Tulane graduates but, rather, became solo practitioners who represented clients in personal injury, domestic, or criminal cases. And politics.

Most of the judges, legislators, and elected officials in New Orleans were Loyola Law School graduates.

Following in this tradition, Frank ran for the New Orleans City Council two years after graduation. I was his campaign manager. While we lost the election, we made a very credible showing and earned a place in the political ranks of New Orleans. Shortly afterwards, he ran for the Louisiana House of Representatives. His opponent, the incumbent, was backed by the powerful local assessor. We worked night and day, knocking on every door in the district, but our attack was not always frontal. At one point, we closed our political headquarters and sent an emissary to the Assessor to negotiate a surrender. Secretly, we opened a new headquarters and planned a last minute blitz, all the while negotiating terms of surrender. This was the same tactic that Detective Dillmann later would accuse me of using in the Candy Smith case. The gambit worked, and Frank pulled off an upset victory. He served in the legislature until Governor Edwards appointed him to a judgeship at Tulane and Broad.

I, too, ran for public office, the same city council seat that Frank had sought unsuccessfully. We ran a very serious campaign, with O'Grady acting as my campaign manager and Maddie serving as campaign coordinator. Then, two weeks before the election, an epidemic broke out. Until then, I hadn't realized that my 3-M syndrome was contagious but, sure enough, O'Grady caught it from me. To make matters worse, the 3-M syndrome is fatal with the Irish.

O'Grady had been sleeping with the prettiest law student at Loyola. Maddie must have suspected because one day while he was supposed to be in court, she saw his green convertible parked in front of the pretty student's apartment. As was his custom, O'Grady had hung his prosthesis on the bedpost, but in their haste to mate, they had neglected to lock the front door. Maddie threw open the door screaming. O'Grady quickly disengaged from the pretty law student, but he couldn't get his leg on in time.

O'Grady ran off to Mexico with the pretty law student and Maddie went home to cry on her parents' shoulders, leaving the campaign in shambles. R.A. stepped in and tried to keep the momentum going in our favor, but it was too late. I lost the election by thirty-six votes. Thus ended my career as an elected official.

I did, however, become the Wizard in Magic Court at Tulane and Broad. The Supreme Court appointed me to fill a temporary vacancy. I enjoyed being the Wizard. I think it helped me become a better dragon slayer. It's good to know how a wizard thinks.

During the Candy Smith case, one of the students working with me, George Blair, leaned over in the middle of the trial and whispered to me, "The Dean say I gotta' drop the Clinic."

"What the fuck you talkin' 'bout, George?" I thought that perhaps the stress of the trial had gotten to him, or that the stress of being a papist had finally snapped Mo. "The Dean say 'cause I'm flunking contracts, I gotta' drop the Clinic."

I was so pissed off I wanted to move for a mistrial. Why should a student doing "A" work in the Clinic, like George, be required to drop my course because he was doing poorly in some other professor's course.

This nonsense all began because Mo had decided to allow a Jesuit lawyer to serve on the faculty as Chaplain. Then, bowing to pressure, he had appointed the Chaplain and some non-practicing professors to a committee to study whether we were practicing Catholic law in the Clinic. In my absence and in the middle of the Candy Smith trial, the faculty had adopted this ridiculous resolution punishing my students for doing poorly in some other professor's class. Mo had forsaken me. Uncle claims that his had been the only dissenting vote.

It was time to move on. And since dragon fighting lay ahead, I might as well get paid handsomely for it. After nine years in the ivory tower, Slim and I sallied forth on our errantry into downtown New Orleans ready for the hunt.

SEVEN

The Brotherhood

As a child, when we came to visit city cousins, we came on Airline Highway—the major thoroughfare connecting the west with downtown New Orleans. During the 1940s and 1950s, Airline Highway was the hottest strip in town. In fact, it was known as the "Miracle Mile." All of the new motels, restaurants, drive-in movies, and night clubs were located there, and the classiest joint of them all, the Town & Country Motel, was owned by Carlos Marcello, the reputed Mafia kingpin of the Gulf South region. As we drove by, my mother would refer to him as the "Damn Dago!" Airline Highway ran into Tulane Avenue, and as we passed the intersection at Broad, I stared with fascination at the massive building on the corner, not knowing what it was.

By the 1980s, Airline Highway had become a ghost strip. Progress had taken a different turn. Gone were the bright lights and heavy traffic. Even the vacancy signs on the motels no longer blinked. It was now a low-life area filled with junkies, cheap prostitutes, and sex shops. But Carlos never left. Until he died, he kept his office at the dilapidated Town & Country on the dilapidated Airline Highway.

Carlos came from a large family, six brothers and two sisters. He was the eldest and the only one not born in the United States. Pascal was the middle child. While Carlos and his other brothers were involved in real estate, restaurants, motels, and the amusement business, Pas didn't do much of anything. During the late 70s, he hung around the Town & Country doing odd jobs and running errands for Carlos. He also watched over the seedy lounge in the Town & Country.

One evening a woman came into the lounge looking for "Mr. Pas." Jenny Mae was in her mid-thirties, with a good figure, but by no means a beauty. She told Pas she was down on her luck and needed extra money. She said that she worked a few card games as a dealer, but that things were slow and she wondered if she could work a few nights as a barmaid. Pas hired her.

After working a couple of nights, Jenny Mae quit the barmaid job, but she continued to come into the lounge and talk about needing extra money. Finally, Pas said that he had a friend, Van, an electrician, who might be interested in meeting her for some "extra money." Pas arranged a meeting with Van, but at the appointed time, Jenny Mae failed to show up. Returning a few nights later and offering to make amends, she said that Van's first night would be free and that Pas "could have some too." She agreed to meet Van the next day in Room 211 of the motel. But when he arrived for the tryst, so did the Jefferson Parish Police. Pas was then arrested for pandering. Jenny Mae, an undercover deputy sheriff, had been secretly taping her conversations with him.

Pas was tried, convicted, and sentenced to jail. Looking for someone to handle his appeal, he was introduced to me by Provino "Vinny" Mosca, a former student of mine at the Law Clinic. Vinny's father, Nick, was a chef and co-owned the Elmwood Plantation Restaurant with Joe Marcello, Carlos's brother. Legend has it that Nick's father had been Al Capone's chef before he was brought to New Orleans in the 1930s to cook for Carlos. After Elmwood burned, Joe and Nick moved to the French Quarter and reopened La Louisiane, the famous restaurant once operated by "Diamond" Jim Moran. La Louisiane was a very elegant place. The tables were discreetly set apart and rested upon a thick, mauve carpet that seemed to cushion all light and sound—the dim lights from the garish chandeliers and the sweet sounds from the Tony Bennett or Al Martino albums playing softly in the background. Control was the main course at La Louisiane, and words were measured as carefully as the rich, Italian sauces. Everyone whispered at La Louisiane.

Vinny had not been a typical law student. He had spent years in a seminary studying to become a priest and, because of this experience, he was rather naive in many ways. While he was in law school, I had introduced him to Uncle's friend, Lynn, a young widow with three small children. They fell in love, and soon afterwards he invited me to lunch at La Louisiane where he introduced Lynn and her three children to Mr. and Mrs. Mosca, telling his parents in the same breath that they planned to get married. Vinny's mother dropped her fork mid-way through the announcement. People looked over and wondered why she had lost control.

Pas was nothing like I expected. Far from being a wiseguy, he was a fat, jolly, kind-hearted man, a "teddy bear," as Slim would say. Every time he came to the office, he brought us a couple of dozen doughnuts, which he would then eat himself while waiting in the reception room.

Pas had not testified during his trial, and his lawyer had told the jury that he hadn't testified because he was "uneducated." In rebuttal, the DA had said that the real reason Pas hadn't testified was because he didn't want to face cross-examination. Because a prosecutor can never refer to a defendant's decision not to testify, this became the strong point of our appeal. The Supreme Court agreed with us and granted Pas a new trial.

Vinny and I tried the second case together. Pas took the stand this time and told the jury his side of the story. Furthermore, Jenny Mae admitted on cross-examination that there had not been prostitution going on while she had worked as a barmaid in the lounge. Again, luck played its role. Incredibly, the police had destroyed some of the tapes. And Jenny Mae's husband, Deputy Favolora, had been the supervising officer with the power to turn the recording switch on or off at will from his listening post outside of the lounge.

Juries typically are told that they are the judges of the facts and that "Hiz Honor" is the judge of the law. A jury's function is to "take the law from the judge" and apply it to the facts of the case. At the end of a case, the judge "instructs" the jury on the law by reading statutes that are often so confusing that lawyers earn a livelihood by fighting over their meaning. Therefore, in closing argument, the dragon slayer must explain to the jury what the law truly means. And so I told the jury:

> "Prostitution is the 'practice of a female of indiscriminate sexual intercourse.' . . . Now the key word is . . . 'indiscriminate' . . . the difference between indiscriminate and discriminate is the difference between a crime and . . . something that is not a crime. . . . A female can have sexual intercourse with a male for compensation as long as it's discriminate. . . . For example, if I have a mistress and if I pay her room, if I pay her rent, if I pay her car note, if I buy her clothes, if I give her money—that's not a crime. It's not a crime. It's not prostitution. In the South, we say I'd be a sugar daddy. But that's not prostitution—and she's not a prostitute. She's a mistress."

All trials re-create history, and I suspect that's why Aunt Delta is so fond of them. Prosecutors re-create the crime with actual characters and, more often than not, this leads to a conviction. One way to counter this is for the dragon slayer to reenact the scene through different characters hoping that the jury will see the matter differently:

> "Let me tell—you know I can walk on a street—forget an undercover operation—I can walk on a street and see a police lady standing on a corner in uniform on the beat. And I could go up to her and I'd say, 'How do you do, officer?' And she says, 'How do you do?' And I say, 'What is your name, officer?' 'Oh, I'm Officer Jane. What is your name?' 'My name's Buddy Lemann, officer. How do you like your job?' 'Oh, I like my job okay. You know we work really hard. We don't get paid very much but other than that, the job is all right. But you know, I work a little card game when I'm off duty. I work a little illegal card game

and I make extra money that way. But I really wish I could make more because times are tough.' And I'm standing right on the street corner with a female officer in full uniform and I say, 'Oh, is that true, Officer Jane?' She says, 'Yes, I've got my little card game going on.' So I'm thinking—well, the lady is obviously—she's not above the law. I mean, she's a policewoman but nobody's perfect and if she wants to participate in a little illegal activity at night with a little card game to make a little extra money as a waitress, it's all right with me. So I'm thinking, okay. And she says, 'I need some extra money.' And she says, 'You know, I love clothes. I love clothes, and my lifelong dream has been if I could meet somebody who would just take me out and pop out all of these clothes for me.' 'Well, Officer Jane, I have a friend—I have a friend who might be—who might want to meet you—might want to take care of you.' 'Oh, you do? Well, that sounds interesting. Do you think I'd like him?' 'Yeah, I think you'd like him.' 'Now, you're not suggesting to me—you're not suggesting to me, are you, that I just go out with any Tom, Dick, and Harry?' 'No, no, no. This is a friend of mine. He's a classy guy. He's a neat guy. He's got an Eldorado—takes little trips. Might want to take you on a little trip.' She says, 'Oh, that sounds very appealing to me and I really appreciate your wanting to help me out. Well, let me think about it a little bit. Well, you know, I think I may want to do that.'

Now, has a crime been committed? Has a crime been committed? I'm on the street corner and I'm telling this female officer, you know, I think that's what you ought to do. You ought to get yourself a sugar daddy. You ought to get somebody to take care of you. You want clothes? He'll buy you clothes. You want to take trips? He'll take you. Am I committing a crime? No, I'm not committing a crime! I can even go further than that. I can say why don't you go out and turn tricks? I can preach on a street corner the virtues of prostitution and I'm not committing any offense, because all I'm doing is talking and talking is protected—but he didn't even go that far! She said, 'You mean you want me to sleep with just anybody?' 'Oh, I don't want you to be a hooker, officer— Officer Jane. I'm not talking about you being a hooker. I've got a good friend of mine. He might be willing to meet you. Are you interested?' 'Yes, I'm interested.' 'Okay, Officer Jane, I'm going to call.' So I call Vinny, my friend, Vinny. 'Say,

Vinny, I just met this policewoman. She tells me she needs a little extra help—needs a little extra money—and she's a good worker. She's a good police officer but she tells me—she tells me she's playing a little—has got a little illegal card game going at night. That's what she tells me. Now, whether she's lying to me or not, I don't know. But Vinny, she tells me she's got a little card game. She must be all right. I mean, you know, she's a cop but she's a human being and she wants a little extra money and she wants to meet somebody who might want to help her out a little bit. Would you be interested?' 'Well sure I'd be interested.' 'Now do you have a place?' 'I don't have a place to go though.' 'Oh, that's all right. I keep an apartment—me, I have an apartment that my mistress stays in. I maintain it and she's not there today.' So I tell Vinny, 'Go and use my apartment. Go use my pad. Take her there. See if you like her—if you like one another. See what happens.' So he does that and then the next day he calls me—he says, 'Buddy, guess what? Your police lady didn't show up.' So I run into Officer Jane and I say, 'Officer Jane, I had you all set up with my friend. You didn't show up.' 'I'm sorry. I really blew it. I'm sorry. Tell you what I'm going to do. Tell your friend I want to meet him tomorrow. Tell your friend I'm going to give him a break. Tell your friend that it's all going to be for free. What did you want out of this? You're being so nice to me, Buddy. What do you want out of this?' 'I don't want a thing, Officer Jane.' 'You don't want any of the money or any of the jewelry or anything that I get out of it?' 'Not a thing. I'm putting two friends together. Look, if you don't like it, don't do it.' 'Oh, you're not going to have—your feelings won't be hurt at me if I don't do this?' 'Oh, Officer Jane, no, no, no, no, no.' 'You mean you'd still talk to me?' 'Sure, Officer Jane.' 'I tell you what, Buddy. I feel so bad about it, tell your friend Vinny I'll meet him tomorrow and we'll get together and we're just going to get together and he doesn't have to worry about helping me at all. And I'll tell you what. You've been so nice to me, I'm going to give you some of it too.'

Now what would I do? I guess I'd do like Mr. Pas did. I'd go for the pass."

I then focused the jury's attention on the fact that this was not a typical undercover operation stumbling upon crimes in progress; rather, this was a sting operation targeting Carlos Marcello's brother with the purpose of creating crimes:

> "Ladies and gentlemen, this is not what this country should be about! In this country, no matter who your brother is, no matter whether you are Catholic or a Jew, or Irish or English, or Black or Indian, or German—it doesn't make any difference. Everybody in this country is entitled to a fair trial. And I want to remind you again as I told you earlier, you do your duty as a citizen! You see, he mentioned something about the State not being on trial. Well, of course the State is on trial! Every lawsuit involves two litigants and both litigants are on trial. And of course the State is on trial. They have a lawyer here, don't they? Protecting their rights, don't they? Of course they're on trial. And the defendant is on trial. And if you feel that this evidence—controlled, orchestrated, molded by that liar Favolora—if you think that this is sufficient, then it would be your duty to convict my client.
>
> On the other hand, if you feel that the State, as I submit, has failed—and failed miserably to prove any crime, then it becomes your duty as a citizen to find him not guilty. You enforce the law against the State as well as against an individual. That is what makes this country different from Nazi Germany—that in your twelve hands, you have the power to say, 'State of Louisiana, you didn't make a case and we're going to enforce the law against you because, when you bring a person into a court of law and accuse him of committing a crime, if you fail to prove it, you must lose the case. We enforce the law against you.' And you do this country great service when you do that because you send a message. . . ."

The jury returned a verdict of not guilty. Pas was a free man. Vinny, the ex-seminarian, was still blushing over being thrust into the role of Lothario. At the victory party, I met Carlos for the first time. He said, "Lemann, ain't nobody in my family ever made money sellin' pussy." Carlos and I would soon be spending a lot more time together.

EIGHT

THE PAGANS

Joseph Hauser was a twice-convicted insurance swindler, a career con man. He was first convicted in federal court in California and received a sentence of thirty months. While that conviction was on appeal, he was indicted on federal racketeering charges in Phoenix, Arizona. He pleaded guilty to three counts of the Phoenix indictment and faced a maximum sentence of fifty years. Hauser was also an admitted perjurer. In short, he possessed all of the qualifications to become an agent provocateur for the federal government.

Hauser was a friend of Irving Davidson, a veteran Washington lobbyist, a consummate deal maker and a very colorful and interesting character who counted Richard Nixon, J. Edgar Hoover, and Jimmy Hoffa among his friends. In 1975, Davidson introduced Hauser to Richard Kleindienst, the former Attorney General of the United States, and Kleindienst supposedly was instrumental in helping Hauser get a multimillion dollar insurance contract from the Teamsters Welfare Fund. According to Hauser, he paid Kleindienst two hundred fifty thousand dollars as a finder's fee for helping him get the Teamsters contract.

In June of 1976, Hauser purchased the National American Life Insurance Company from Jules and Roger LeBlanc of Baton Rouge. He purchased NALICO with premiums received from the twenty-four million dollar contract with the Teamsters. It was during the negotiations with the LeBlanc brothers that Davidson introduced Hauser to Carlos Marcello.

When Hauser agreed to become a government agent in the Spring of 1979, the government instigated the so-called "Brilab" (after bribery and labor) sting operation. The government created a sham company for Hauser, Fidelity Financial Consultants. Next, the government created an aura of legitimacy by falsely representing to the public that Fidelity had a close and unique association with Prudential Insurance Company of America. The government also created for Hauser two business associates (a nephew and friend) by the names of Michael Sachs and Larry

Golden (actually Special Agents Michael Wacks and Larry Montague). The government also provided a secretary, a swank Beverly Hills office, and extravagant travel and entertainment expense accounts. Lastly, the government created the mission: approaching citizens to help obtain insurance contracts for Prudential with the incentive that Fidelity would share huge commissions with anyone who helped.

Hauser was instructed to approach Davidson and to renew his acquaintance with Carlos. He secretly taped his telephone conversations with Davidson. The first recorded conversation occurred on February 8, 1979, and Hauser's recent plea in the Phoenix case was discussed. From the beginning, he pressured and played upon Davidson's sympathy for his financial plight. He told him: "I don't have five fucking cents." He explained the conviction in Phoenix by saying, "I ran out of money, I couldn't go on with a lawyer any longer. . . ." He pleaded:

> "Oh, God, the problem is—is a very simple one—is that my financial position is beyond belief. It is so beyond belief that, uh, I just can't describe it to you. Ah, there are crises and there are crises, but this is the super, super crisis."

Finally, Davidson agreed to see if Carlos would help Hauser get some insurance business. They came to New Orleans and met with Carlos at the Maison Dupuy Hotel in the French Quarter. Hauser had a tape recorder hidden in his briefcase:

> Carlos: "What kind of business?"
>
> Hauser: "Insurance business, prepaid legal, health, any, any kind of business."
>
> Carlos: "I don't think so; I don't know Joe, what kind of business you talking to me, what kind of insurance are you talking?"
>
> Hauser: "Any kind."

* * * * *

> Carlos: "What's it, an old company, or are you starting a new company?"
>
> Hauser: "No, it's an agency that has a contract with one of the biggest companies in existence. . . ."

* * * * *

Hauser: "Ah, can you help me get some business? I'm coming to you like my father for help."

Carlos: "No, but I mean I'm telling ya, you see, I'm—that's not my line of business and I'm in the dark, you gotta' tell me look, you, what kind of business you want, charity business, Blue Cross or—or—city business or? . . ."

Carlos, an avid reader of the *Times-Picayune*, loved politics and closely followed governmental affairs. He also loved being a power broker and, after asking whether Hauser had read a recent news article reporting that the City of New Orleans was changing its insurance contract, the following exchange took place:

Hauser: "Could we bid on it?"

Carlos: "Sure you can bid on it if it come out on a bid date, the council put, filing a suit so they gotta' come before the council."

Hauser: "You have anything, you have any 'juice' there?"

Carlos: "Yeah, I got all, I got'em all where I want 'em. I got to tell 'em, look, put it in this company here, let him bid on it, let it come out for bid!"

Hauser: "Oh, I love you, Carlos."

Carlos: "Can they bid now?"

Hauser: "Yeah, yes, we can bid tomorrow morning."

Carlos: "You can?"

Hauser: "Yes."

Carlos: "All right, well then, you've given me something to go to work on right now."

Hauser: "I can bid tomorrow morning."

Carlos: "All right. What kind of deal can I make if you know what it is?"

Hauser: "I have to know what benefits they want. Here's what I have to know—what dollars they have to spend, what benefits they want."

Carlos: "All right, the City of New Orleans, like I say."

Hauser: "I have to be able to talk to somebody."

Carlos: "All right. The cit—all right, I get you all the information, tell you what they paying now, what they benefit is and everything."

Carlos spoke in soft, raspy tones, with poor grammar. His speech had a very poetic cadence to it, almost musical—like hearing Verdi. He loved to brag and exaggerate but possessed the wisdom acquired over hundreds of conversations with deal makers. To him, a telltale for legitimacy was a connection to a big, established company and not, as he would say, with some "shoobie shoo fuckin' insurance company." Satisfied with Prudential, he continued with the meeting:

Carlos: "I'll, I'll give you all the information I can get; that's why I wanna' get one of these fellas tonight, first thing in the morning and find out what they gonna' really do, how long it's gonna' take, you know, they going to court."

Hauser: "And whatever we have to take care of we'll take care of."

Carlos: "That's all."

The meeting ended with Carlos promising he could get " . . . Jefferson Parish, too . . . that's the main one. . . ." When Hauser asked, "You got juice out there too?" Carlos replied:

> "I got connections, yeah. I know everybody from fucking Grand Isle all the way to Raceland, man . . . all the way to Houma, you know. . . . It take me two days if I stop at each one of 'em house to say hello, right. Yeah, it's really somethin' to see. . . . I got two Italian boys. They state representatives, Guarisco and Siracusa. . . . I know all these people. . . . Go there and gotta' get the right people. Say, 'Here $5,000, $10,000. . . .' It takes time to get where I am at. To know all dese people—governors, business, the attorney general. They know me."

Hauser then completed his mission by saying, "You're the boss," and Davidson added, "You have the respect, Carlos."

After this New Orleans meeting, Hauser kept the pressure on Davidson to get him "new clean business to start off on a fresh footing." At one point, Davidson reported that Carlos would help because "it has merit, it's clean." Hauser told Davidson that his company was ready to write "a perfectly legitimate case," but that, "One Heeb to another," he was desperate:

> "I, I don't know how to express myself to you, Irving. I am right now [in] as bad shape as I've been in the last three years. I am in the worst shape that I've ever been in my entire life.
>
> * * * * *
>
> I, I desperately need either one or two things—either some money, or I need some relief. I'm—here's what—here's the position I'm in. Barbara is hitting her head against the wall.
>
> * * * * *
>
> We're three months behind in our rent. I owe on my tuition for my kids.
>
> * * * * *
>
> Steven had a serious problem to graduate.
>
> * * * * *
>
> My phone—I have until Monday to be shut off. I have, ah, electric bills. . . ."

Through the summer of 1979, Hauser kept the pressure on Davidson: "I'm desperate, Irving. . . . I'm running out of time. . . . I'm pleading with you, I have nowhere left to turn; Prudential gave me a shot and they gave me a shot to underwrite cases; is there any way in the world you can help me out?" But nothing happened. It appeared that the sting was going to be a flop and that Hauser would be without the brownie points he desperately wanted in order to minimize his jail time.

This time, however, it was the dragon who got lucky. In the fall of 1979, the Louisiana governor's race was gaining full steam. It was a wide open election since Governor Edwards had already served consecutive terms and could not run for re-election. As Carlos lamented, "Edmund

[sic]. . . . He is the strongest sonofabitchin' governor we ever had. He fuck with women and play dice, but won't drink. How do you like 'dat?"

Naturally, every candidate wanted campaign contributions, and in Carlos's words, "They all want money. . . . Just like all you wants money. . . . Everybody wants money. . . . Anytime a politician goes in there, he wants money. . . ." This was also exactly the type of mold in which to fester a sting operation. Accordingly, the government instructed Hauser to tell Davidson and Carlos that Prudential was willing to make substantial campaign contributions to candidates willing to help obtain business from the State. This fit right in with Carlos's perception of himself as a power broker.

Charles Roemer, the Commissioner of Administration and the number two man in state government, was also serving as the campaign manager for Edgar "Sonny" Mouton, a state senator from Lafayette and a candidate for Governor. Believing that Mouton had a good chance of winning, Carlos made arrangements to meet with Roemer through a mutual friend, Aubrey Young, a minor official in the Edwards administration.

Carlos introduced Hauser and undercover agent Wacks to Roemer on September 10, 1979, at the St. Ann Hotel in the French Quarter. Meeting privately with Wacks, Roemer agreed to help obtain state insurance business for Prudential. According to Wacks, Roemer also agreed to an equal split of the anticipated one hundred thousand dollar per month commission. However, when Wacks offered a ten thousand dollar contribution to the Mouton campaign, Roemer responded by saying that he usually didn't talk to people who contributed less than twenty-five thousand dollars.

Unexpectedly, the dragon then ran into a serious problem. The government was naturally anxious to make campaign contributions, knowing that it would later label them as bribes. Carlos, however, was against paying anything to a politician before results were produced. As Carlos said:

> "Man, I know better than you, man, 'bout them politicians. . . . They take your fucking money, man, they tell you good-bye, man. . . . I put $2,000 in McKeithen's pocket. . . . I hate the motherfucker, take my money and don't do nuttin' for me. . . . I went with him before, when he wasn't nuttin'. . . . I had McKeithen for eight years. That sonofabitch got $168,000 my money, and then that sonofabitch too scared to talk to me. How do you like that shit?"

Nonetheless, the government ultimately had its way, and on September 25, at the Hilton Hotel in Baton Rouge, Hauser gave Roemer a fifteen thousand dollar campaign contribution for Mouton. In accepting the contribution, Roemer said, "I've already laid some of the ground work for the insurance business," and that he wanted " . . . it to look, you know, clean as a wind driven snow."

Meanwhile, Lieutenant Governor James Fitzmorris, a well-known New Orleans politician, was also running for Governor. Wisely, Carlos decided to cover the fifteen thousand dollar bet on Mouton by keeping the other ten thousand dollars Prudential was willing to pay as a "saver" for Fitzmorris. That way, Carlos said, "We got two shots."

Vincent Marinello, a lawyer and Fitzmorris supporter, was introduced by Carlos to Hauser and the undercover agents. Vincent was told that Hauser and the agents were insurance people who were interested in making campaign contributions in order to help them get business in Louisiana. Eager to raise money for his candidate, Vincent took Wacks to meet with Fitzmorris on September 27 in the State Office Building in New Orleans. Fitzmorris said that he would be happy to assist them in obtaining business, but he observed that:

> "The Edwards administration has played their cards so close to their chest, I don't know what the hell is going on . . . but once we get in there we'll see what they have."

After the meeting, Vincent told Fitzmorris they had "some change for you . . . a couple of bucks."

Reluctantly, Carlos agreed to make the contribution even though, in his words, Fitzmorris was:

> " . . . honest. You see, he's an honest, honest man. The bastard don't care for money. . . . You wouldn't believe that, but that's the truth. He's a fifty-eight-year-old motherfucker been—how you say, you know, no money. He never did have no big money. That's all. If he had $20, $25,000, he had plenty money. Maybe—I don't think he ever had that kind a money in his life."

Carlos arranged a luncheon meeting at Impastato's, telling Hauser to "bring the papers." After lunch, Hauser gave Vincent the ten thousand dollars for Fitzmorris. Several hours later, Vincent reported, "I delivered the newspaper today and everything was taken care of."

Always anxious to pass the honey pot around, Hauser met again with Roemer and gave him another ten thousand dollars for Mouton's campaign. With a degree of chutzpah that was disarming even to Hauser, Roemer said, "It really would be a help to me if you could give me twice that much, I'm talking about fifty . . . anytime between now and election day." Roemer explained: "I know I'm asking, you know, I'm asking for, for a lot but . . . the delivery mechanism doesn't depend on Mouton. The delivery mechanism depends on my relationship with the current Governor."

Ironically, neither Mouton nor Fitzmorris, the two federally-backed candidates, made it through the first primary. Instead, Dave Treen and Louis Lambert would face-off against one another in the general election. For sure, Carlos didn't like Treen: "Treen is our enemy, man. . . . This motherfucker he ain't goin' to do nothin' for nobody. . . . He and his people they is aristocrats. He not goin' for our kind of people. But them sumbitches is wheelin' an' dealin,' man."

Treen wasn't the only one "wheelin' an' dealin'." Unbeknownst to Carlos, the government, through another source, had also given Lambert ten thousand dollars for his campaign. Altogether, the government contributed forty-six thousand dollars in taxpayers' money to candidates in the Louisiana elections. The only federally-backed candidate to win was Bobby Freeman, who replaced Fitzmorris as Lieutenant Governor.

During the second primary, Hauser and the undercover agents came to New Orleans, and while in Carlos's office at the Town & Country they wrote a proposal for Prudential to underwrite Louisiana state employees' life insurance program at a savings of one million dollars per year. The agents had Carlos's secretary mail the proposal to Roemer. This mailing would eventually cause Carlos's downfall.

Ultimately, Treen won the governor's election, and he was scheduled to take office in March. Carlos then began jockeying for input into the new administration, and at one point he thought Fitzmorris would be the new commissioner of administration. When Vincent told him Fitzmorris would not be the new commissioner, the following exchange took place:

Carlos: "Fitz is chicken, more chicken than anybody I ever seen in my life!"

Vincent: "He don't have enough balls . . . that lyin' sonofabitch. I went to the wrong man, damn it."

Carlos: "How old are you?"

Vincent: "Forty-three."

Carlos: "Well you done learned somethin' now. When you as old as me, you'll know more than the fuckin' President of the United States."

Carlos began to concentrate on getting the job done before the change in administrations. By the end of January, it appeared the State's insurance contract would soon be put to bid. Carlos gave the undercover agents a tentative outline he had received from Roemer. When they began to discuss the commissions, the undercover agents suggested Carlos should receive the lion's share because he had "masterminded the deal." With his typical graciousness, Carlos responded, "No, it ain't the money, forget the money. I'd be just as proud as you to make the deal. I just wanna' be proud 'dat I can do somethin' like 'dat."

The subpoenas hit on February 8, 1980. Davidson received one in Washington and Governor Edwards received one in Baton Rouge. The Governor told Roemer about the subpoena and he, in turn, sent Aubrey Young to see Carlos:

Aubrey: "All right. Now the papers that Roemer gave you. He said if you got them, please destroy them."

Carlos: "What papers?"

Aubrey: "Explaining that insurance, whatever it was. He said he gave you some papers last week. To show you how they bid. How it works."

Carlos: "Oh man, I done disappear with them mother-fuckers. I don't need nothin' like that."

Aubrey: "He's afraid. 'Cause you know that could get a subpoena or somethin', and he said, you know, if they ask about you, he was going to say: 'Hell yeah I know you.' He said, 'I'm talking to him about oil and waste,' and, you know, I said, 'Well, shit, they ain't got nothin' on him.'"

Carlos: "They ain't got nothin' on him. Because, fuck, there ain't nothin'."

Aubrey: "But he wanted me to come tell you. You know, they after him again. You see, they popped him."

Carlos: "They ain't gave . . . tell, tell Roemer we ain't gave him no money. Nobody give him nothin'. Just tell him ain't no money passed. Nothin'. No money. Okay?"

Aubrey: "Ya'll talkin' business. Oil and waste."

Carlos: "Yeah. We talkin' about our garbage deal."

Aubrey: "Oil."

Carlos: "If he wants to tell 'em that, tell 'em, as far as me, I ain't gonna tell 'em nothin'. They can, they can come here forty times, but I ain't—you know, I'm gonna take—tell him, look, look, tell him look, Carlos don't care if he gets subpoenaed forty times. . . . I got subpoenaed with the, with the President, the Vice, the, the, the United States. . . ."

Aubrey: "Told him."

Carlos: " . . . district attorney, I mean, ah, the attorney general and all. Tell him I just take the Fifth Amendment and that's it. They ain't gonna get a fuckin' thing from me."

Aubrey then explained that Roemer was afraid it was a federal sting, but Carlos was equally confident that it wasn't:

Carlos: "Tell him the insurance man, I'd put my head on the chopping block."

Aubrey: "All right."

Carlos: "Look, the man's in jail. Forget about him, man. He ain't gonna' say nothin.' And his two nephews . . . don't worry about it. Look, he ain't give no campaign money. He ain't never. All they talk about is insurance. And they given 'em the letter to show what they can save 'em, a million dollars."

Aubrey: "Well, that clears him."

Carlos: "Yeah, that's it. Gonna' make him look good."

Aubrey: "That's right."

Carlos: "That's all. Ain't no more. Ain't no use to talk about it. Look, don't worry about it at all. Okay? And if I hear anything, I'll call you right away and say, 'Look, they got subpoenaed too, and I know what. . . .' Look, don't worry about it."

Aubrey: "I ain't worried about it."

Carlos: "'Cause he ain't done nothing."

Aubrey: "I don't know."

Carlos: "I don't believe. He ain't scared, huh?"

Aubrey: "No, it don't bother him."

Carlos: "He don't, he ain't scared."

Aubrey: "He, he's got some balls."

Carlos: "You wanta' eat?"

Carlos was dead wrong. The grand jury returned the indictment on June 17, 1980, charging Carlos, Roemer, Davidson, and Marinello with racketeering in a scheme to obtain insurance contracts through bribery. Aubrey Young was later added to the indictment as a defendant.

Vinny Mosca and I were having lunch when the news of the indictment broke. Corporate lawyers in New Orleans have lunch at the Boston Club; criminal defense lawyers have lunch at La Louisiane. Whenever O'Grady and I went there, we watched in gleeful anticipation as conspiracies were hatched at various tables and counts were confected between courses.

Vinny wanted to know if I would be willing to represent Vincent Marinello. I knew Vincent a little from La Louisiane. He was best friends with Carlos's youngest brother, Sammy, who managed the restaurant. Vincent had lunch there daily, arriving at eleven-thirty in the morning and not leaving until four o'clock in the afternoon. I couldn't imagine when he practiced law (and concluded that he probably didn't). If given a choice between an honest buck and a fast buck, he invariably went for the fast buck. Not necessarily illegal, mind you, but fast. I told Vinny I would be happy to represent Vincent.

Carlos would be represented by Russell Schonekas. He had represented Carlos intermittently for many years. An authentic New Orleans character and a smart lawyer with the ability to relate to juries, his weakness, like Jim Garrison's, was an inability to pay attention to detail in a complex case. He was a "legal pad" lawyer—one who began a trial with a blank legal pad and went from there.

Russell would not be the only lawyer representing Carlos. Henry Gonzales from Tampa, Florida, the standby lawyer for Santos Trafficante, another alleged Mafia chieftain, was in New Orleans to represent Carlos. Henry was a bon vivant and could eat more than any man I knew—until I met his young son one night at dinner in a Tampa restaurant. I tried to keep up with them and ended up sick for two days. Henry, who knew his way around a courtroom, was a good lawyer but he didn't appear to get along well with Russell. In fact, both were very much alike—good on their feet, but neither having much taste for preparation.

Much of the preparation work would be thrust upon Vinny, even though he was fresh out of law school.

Roemer would be represented by Mike Fawer. I was one of the few lawyers who got along easily with Mike. A former federal prosecutor from New York, he was extremely high-strung and at times abrasive. But he was bright and an excellent tactician. Davidson would be represented by Tom Dyson of Washington, D.C., with help from New Orleans lawyer Frank DeSalvo. Aubrey Young would be represented by Risley "Pappy" Triche of Napoleonville, the next town down Bayou Lafourche from Donaldsonville. In all, a good defense team.

The prosecution was led by John Volz, my old rival to replace Captain America. Also on the government's team was Eads Hogue, the head of the Strike Force, Al Winters, the First Assistant, Richard Simmons, and John Voohries. We would be in for a tough fight.

The case was assigned to the former United States Magistrate, Judge Morey Sear, with whom I shared the agonizing wait for the jury to return its verdict in the Beasley case. This would be his biggest case since "ascending" to the bench. He had a flair for administrative detail, and he spent considerable time insuring that the trial proceeded without a major glitch.

The amount of preparation was Herculean. We listened to some thirty-five thousand taped conversations. Roemer, a computer whiz, was of great assistance in computerizing the evidence for us. But no amount of computers could shorten what my client had said on the tapes. Vincent loved to talk.

During the long hours of preparation, Vincent and I became close friends. However, his wife Delores presented a different problem. Lust. In her mid-twenties and a former Miss Arkansas, Delores could have been a *Playboy* centerfold. They lived across Lake Pontchartrain in Mandeville in a home with a swimming pool in the backyard and, while we worked over the weekends, she sunbathed in a bikini. This was most difficult for me. There is no known antidote for the 3-M syndrome. A Mandeville mirage can be a powerful one and before long, I was gazing at Dulcinea sunning under a Castilian sun. I had to repress the thought of throwing the case in order to console Delores while Vincent went away to prison.

Trial began in March 1981. Jury selection alonc took weeks, which is unusual in federal court where the lawyers normally are not permitted to ask questions during *voir dire*. Instead, "Hiz Honor" will usually ask a few "closed-ended" questions, such as "You will give the defendant a fair trial, correct?" thereby effectively assigning a defendant's fate to a faceless jury. Because of Carlos's notoriety, however, we were permitted to ask some questions, and by the time the Judge took over the questioning, we had taught him how to conduct a meaningful *voir dire*.

The government excused every prospective juror of Italian descent, including married women with Italian-sounding maiden names. At one point, believing that a prospective juror's mother was Italian, Carlos whispered loudly that the man was a "Lebanee," hoping that the prosecutors would overhear him and keep the man as a juror. Parenthetically, according to Carlos, besides Italians, blacks, French, Jews, and Chinese, everyone else in the world was Lebanese. In any event, the ruse didn't work, and the government excused the "Lebanee."

Just as dragons need dragonflies, dragon slayers need butterflies. A dragon slayer without butterflies should retire. No matter how many times one has approached a jury, the fear must never go away. Fear is the catalyst that flames the intensity, the emotion, the edge needed to dramatize a client's plight. Ho Chi Minh once said a day of freedom is worth more than a thousand in jail. The dragon slayer alone stands between freedom and the fires of prison.

And so with butterflies, I told the jury in the opening statement: "Mr. Marinello comes here today not as he has on other occasions pleading the cause of someone else; he comes here today as a citizen accused. I have the honor and pleasure to represent him in pleading his case to you, his fellow citizens." I then humanized him by telling the jury about his background:

> "Vincent is forty-four years old. He was born and raised in the City of New Orleans. His mother and father separated when he was nineteen years old, and he and his mother operated a sandwich shop on Tchoupitoulas Street. . . . He worked his way through college at Loyola and then on to law school. He graduated from Loyola Law School in 1961 and then he went into the Armed Services. He served his country for two years as a military policeman. In 1963, upon completion of his service, he started a law practice. Since then, as always, he has operated a one-man law firm. . . ."

Next, I explained the relationship between the characters in this drama:

> "Marinello knew Mr. Fitzmorris from back in 1965 when my client first got out of law school, finished the service, and started practicing law. He was introduced to Mr. Fitzmorris when he ran for Mayor of the City of New Orleans. He was defeated then by Mayor Schiro. But in 1965, my client, as a young lawyer, did what many young lawyers do who were practicing on their own. Politics is a good way to meet people, to make contacts, to build one's business. And as a young man, he supported and helped Mr. Fitzmorris. He drove an automobile for him; he was a chauffeur. He attended political rallies with him. And he did that in '65, he did that again in 1969 when Mr.

Fitzmorris ran the second time. That time he was defeated by Mayor Landrieu. Now in 1979, Lieutenant Governor Fitzmorris was running for Governor. And he comes to Marinello and he requests that Marinello attempt to raise money for him. And substantial amounts of money are required to run for Governor of the State. As a matter of fact, Marinello was requested to sign a twenty-five thousand dollar note for Mr. Fitzmorris. Of course Marinello did not have that kind of wherewithal to be able to sign a twenty-five thousand dollar note. But he was asked by Fitzmorris, and he did go out and attempt to raise contributions. He went to a number of people, and one person that he went to was Mr. Marcello. This was in August of 1979. He had known Mr. Marcello; he had met him on three or four occasions. He was not very close to him. He was, however, very close to two of Mr. Marcello's brothers. . . .

In August of '79, he goes to Mr. Marcello and tells Mr. Marcello that his friend, Lieutenant Governor Fitzmorris, is running for Governor; he thinks he's got a good shot at winning, needs an awful lot of money. 'He wants me to sign a twenty-five thousand dollar note. I can't really afford to undertake that kind of an obligation. Can you help me locate people or will you yourself be willing to contribute to Fitzmorris' campaign?' This was back in August of '79. Time goes by, Mr. Marcello decides to support Sonny Mouton. However, it's in September that Mr. Marcello tells Marinello, 'I have people from Prudential, the largest insurance company in the United States, these individuals are coming here'—and this is, by the way, you have to understand, the evidence will make this clear, this is not a situation where you have two people or three people who say, 'I'm going to open up a little insurance company and we're going to write insurance for Prudential.' This is not what the script written by the prosecutors and the federal police, that's not the way it read. It was much different. It was big time. The scam and the scheme and the script that the government agents were telling was that, 'This is a unique situation we have'—meaning Hauser, Wacks, and Montegue masquerading as insurance brokers; 'we have a unique contact with the president of Prudential in Newark, New Jersey. We deal above and beyond little insurance agents. We have direct contact with the top corporate echelon, and Prudential has authorized us to spend unlimited amounts of money to help Prudential secure large insurance contracts.' And in the words that you will hear from Hauser on the tape when he begins to explain this to Marinello, he tells them, 'It's mind boggling. You're a young man. You have no idea the amounts and the kinds of money that we're talking about. I have a blank check. I can buy unlimited. I can contribute unlimited amounts.'"

Dragon slayers use opening statements to plant the lances they hope to thrust at trial's end. In this case it was very important to distinguish between the payment to Fitzmorris, which involved Vincent directly, and the payments to Roemer, which only involved him indirectly:

> "Now it is true that Marinello is told, and he's told by Mr. Marcello, 'These people are interested in writing the insurance for the State of Louisiana, but you have—but you, Mr. Marinello, have nothing to do with that. We're handling that through Mr. Roemer. You have no involvement with that. You are not part of this transaction. However, why don't you go up to Lieutenant Governor Fitzmorris and, if you can get him to agree to meet with these Prudential agents, they may be willing to contribute substantial sums to Fitzmorris' candidacy.' And indeed, on the next day, September 27, Marinello brings one of the agents to Mr. Fitzmorris. And that conversation between the agent and Mr. Fitzmorris is taped. And you will hear that. And you will see that that is a classic conversation between a candidate who's running for Governor—who's running for public office—and a person who is brought to him as being someone who is just coming into the state representing a company that wants to make contacts and wants to make political contributions. There is absolutely nothing criminal about that conversation, but there is a lot of talk about favors by Fitzmorris. 'Yes, I'll be happy to help you fellows. I'll be happy to try to introduce you to people. I'll be happy to open doors for you. And I certainly will appreciate it if you see fit to contribute to my campaign.'
>
> That is the price we pay in this country for free elections, for a free democracy. That is the way that the system operates. The evidence will show—because I intend to show you—that in campaigns, large sums of money are raised because the donor of those sums clearly expects to receive a benefit. It may be simply to be invited to the Inaugural Ball, it may mean having certain matters

> favorably considered by the Governor. It definitely is based upon the contributor expecting benefits—expecting something in return. Nothing illegal, nothing to the detriment of the State of Louisiana. And it is very clear that the way this whole thing was sold, the starting premise was that, 'This is Prudential. We are the biggest insurance company in the United States, and we will save the State of Louisiana a million dollars.' . . . And you will see from the conversation that Fitzmorris desperately would have liked to have received contributions from these people and, in fact, he ultimately did. It's also clear, however, that at the time this ten thousand dollar payment was made to Mr. Fitzmorris, he at the time was a candidate for Governor; he was running—he was a Lieutenant Governor running for Governor, and that the only approach that Hauser and the agent made to Fitzmorris was to have Fitzmorris help them write contracts with the City of New Orleans, Avondale Shipyards, and the riverfront laborers, three entities over which Fitzmorris had absolutely no control whatsoever. A perfectly legitimate quest, a perfectly legitimate transaction.
>
> The next day, on September 27, as a result of the meeting between Marinello, the undercover agent, and Fitzmorris, ten thousand dollars was given to Marinello, and Marinello gives that as a political contribution to Mr. Fitzmorris. The government prosecutors claim that that was a bribe. Evidence will be crystal clear that, in fact, it was a political contribution."

The government's case, consisting primarily of the tapes, was presented through the testimony of Wacks, Montegue, and Hauser. In some respects, the tapes had the positive effect of humanizing the defendants, especially Carlos. Instead of depicting him as a stereotypical "Godfather," talking about murder, extortion, drugs, robbery, or loansharking, the tapes revealed him to be a grandfather ruminating about life in general. For example, Carlos on real estate:

> "Dat's something they can't make no more—land. It's disappearing all the time. Especially around cities—New York, New Orleans, and Lafayette. . . . They make babies every day and every time a baby born, twenty-four years from now, they looking for a lot. They don't stay with their Mama and their Daddy."

Carlos on Old Metairie:

> "I hadda' move outta' there. They aristocrats and think they somebody. Their wives get drunk and got nothing for their husbands when they come home . . . a lotta' times they puttin' on because they don't have no money."

Carlos on the Metairie Country Club:

> "You gotta' die before you can get in there!"

The weakest link in the government's case was Hauser, of course. We brought out that as a result of his cooperation, he had received no additional jail time for the Phoenix conviction. In the vernacular, he had "walked." Also, he had received some seventy-five thousand dollars in "support" payments from the government during the course of the undercover operation. Our strongest attack, however, was based upon the fact that he clearly had manufactured evidence by pretending on occasion to talk on tape with someone who was actually not present. Mike Fawer dubbed these as "Hauser's soliloquies." For example, on one occasion, when Hauser had left Carlos's office to go to the bathroom, he had said:

> "Carlos, I'm listening. And I'm reading the papers. Okay. I'm gonna' read what you're showing me. So in a sense what you're saying is that you're taking over the whole family. Oh, then we can write business throughout the country. I'm—I'm reading. Okay, I'll read it. Lemme' finish reading this. You mean to tell me something like this they distribute in the mail. Oh, I see. By messenger. . . . I never realized numbers were such a big game."

Hauser had engaged in the same despicable conduct in order to falsely incriminate Louis Lambert when he had received his campaign contribution from the federal government. As the two met in the candidate's office, the following occurred:

> Lambert: "What do you want to contribute to my campaign?"
>
> Hauser: "I want to give you $10,000 in cash right now."
>
> Lambert: "And I'm gonna give you, let me tell you what I'm doing so you can just. . . . Wait right here 'til I get some tickets."

Hauser: "Oh, leave me alone, give them to L.G. Moore, leave me alone."

Lambert: "You take the goddamn tickets and then we've done it the right way."

Hauser: "Okay."

Lambert: "That scares you, but you just have to learn we've got a new policy."

After Lambert had walked out of the room, closing the door behind him, Hauser had continued to talk into his hidden tape recorder:

> "I want it understood one thing. That's part of the business. I—I call it a kickback, you can call it anything you want."

Feigning surprise when we discovered the "soliloquies," the government resisted our mid-trial motion to dismiss, and the Judge, although condemning the conduct as reprehensible, refused to dismiss the case.

There was also comedy on the tapes. On one occasion, Aubrey Young had attempted to arrange a meeting between Carlos and Roemer at the Holiday Inn. They had discussed the Holiday Inn in Baton Rouge, the Holiday Inn in Port Allen, and the Holiday Inn in Lafayette. At the appointed time, however, Roemer went to the Holiday Inn in Baton Rouge, Carlos went to the Holiday Inn in Lafayette, and the FBI agents went to the Holiday Inn in Port Allen. And this is the same Carlos Marcello who some claim orchestrated the Kennedy assassination.

There is an advantage to having Mike Fawer on a dragon hunt. One never has to worry about standing in the immediate line of fire—Mike always volunteers for the job. This case was no different. He and the Judge had many fiery exchanges and at one point, the Judge stormed out of the courtroom. Mike then said to the court reporter, "Let the record reflect that the judge has just left the bench," as he proceeded to dictate into the record the reasons for his objection. When the Judge discovered that the proceedings were underway without him, we almost spent the night in jail.

During my cross-examination of Hauser, I continued to emphasize the distinction between the Fitzmorris contribution and the payments to Roemer:

Lemann: "Now at this particular time you knew that Lieutenant Governor Fitzmorris was, first of all, a broke politician. Correct?"

Hauser: "Yes."

Lemann: "And Marinello told you that Fitzmorris put the state first?"

Hauser: "That is correct."

Lemann: "Marinello also told you that Fitzmorris had no influence in terms of the Edwards administration, the present administration that was running the State of Louisiana?"

Hauser: "That is correct."

Witnesses aren't hard to cross-examine in tape cases as long as one doesn't get greedy and is satisfied with what the witness must give:

Lemann: "In other words, the point I want to focus on is this: At this particular time, even with your impression, the transaction with Fitzmorris was different from that which you had with Roemer, correct?"

Hauser: "Definitely."

Lemann: "With Roemer, you felt that there was a commitment. Whether you were right or wrong, that was your impression?"

Hauser: "Definitely."

Lemann: "But at this particular time you didn't have a feeling that there was any commitment on the part of Fitzmorris to do anything?"

Hauser: "I did not."

Besides having had no commitment, the Fitzmorris transaction had been based upon a number of contingencies:

Lemann: "And the contingency plan at this particular point, you're talking about giving Fitzmorris more money?"

Hauser: "Uh-huh."

Lemann: "That was one contingency?"

Hauser: "Uh-huh."

Lemann: "Two, it would be if he would promise to help you?"

Hauser: "Uh-huh."

Lemann: "Three would be if he got into the second primary; and four would be if he was elected governor?"

Hauser: "Sure."

Lemann: "A lot of 'ifs.'"

Hauser: "A lot of 'ifs,' correct."

And of course, the jury knew that none of the "ifs" had ever materialized. Monsignor Gubler would have been proud of me.

What the jury didn't know, however, was that Fitzmorris had denied receiving the ten thousand dollars. Although Vincent had told Carlos and Hauser that he had "delivered the newspaper," Fitzmorris had not listed it in his campaign disclosure report. As a matter of fact, Fitzmorris had told the FBI that he had not received any money from Vincent. Since this was inconsistent with the government's theory of the case, the prosecutors decided not to call Fitzmorris as a witness.

After the government rested, Judge Sear directed a verdict in favor of Aubrey Young. For the rest of us, it was time to put up or shut up. Davidson and Roemer testified. On the other hand, Carlos felt that testifying, even in one's own behalf, was equivalent to "ratting"—and that he would never do.

I was in a real quandary. Should we call Fitzmorris as a witness, have him deny having received the contribution and, in effect, argue to the jury that the only crime Vincent had committed was a theft for which he was not on trial? Or should we put Vincent on the stand, have him say that he had delivered the money, and thereby set up Fitzmorris as a rebuttal witness for the government?

While Vincent was articulate and personable, he didn't have a long attention span, he was easily confused and, to say the least, he hadn't served on the Law Review. After hours of rehearsal, I knew that there was no way to limit him to short answers and that he would ramble on and on, creating fodder for the cross-examiner. After much anguish, and holding on to Dulcinea for sustenance, we decided he shouldn't testify. Had we done otherwise, the trial might still be on today.

As it was, it lasted for nineteen weeks. Toward the end, we started receiving good vibes from the twelfth juror, an expressive young lady who was doing everything but winking at us. Then one day Judge Sear abruptly halted the proceedings and sent the jury home early. We were called into chambers and instructed to return in two hours. Oddly, we were told to return via the judges' private elevator in the courthouse basement. We were also instructed not to discuss this cloak and dagger plan with anyone. Slim had to lead Mike Fawer out of chambers before he twisted himself into orbit.

Upon our return, we were ushered into a closed courtroom, and on the witness stand before us sat a man with a paper bag over his head. "What the fuck is this about," Mike whispered as he began to quake again. Judge Sear informed us that an FBI undercover agent, the man with the paper bag over his head, coincidentally had been in a cocktail lounge when he had overheard the twelfth juror say the government's case was weak. Of course, the government was now moving to disqualify her. Mike orbited.

At least we would be given the opportunity to cross-examine the man with the paper bag over his head and, desperately trying to compose ourselves, we were about to embark on this strange new experience when suddenly loud pounding came from the locked courtroom doors. Two news reporters were demanding access. Judge Sear became apoplectic. He demanded to know who had violated the secrecy order. We all proclaimed our innocence. Upon questioning the news reporters through closed doors, the Judge learned that while they had been eating at the Bon Ton the reporters had spotted Al Winters, with his six-foot, six-inch, two hundred fifty pound frame, crossing Magazine Street with a man with a paper bag over his head! Big Al, mostly a drug and gun man, had acted too quickly.

Still without reporters (and almost without Big Al), we commenced cross-examining the man with the paper bag over his head. The tale became even more bizarre. Admitting that the encounter with the twelfth juror had not been his only one, the man with the paper bag over his head incredibly claimed that he had seen her unexpectedly on other nights in other barrooms, one of which was located clear across town. This had been an undercover operation all right, one designed to disqualify the twelfth juror. When the defense engages in this kind of conduct, it's called jury tampering. Most of us were shell-shocked. Carlos, the calmest person in the courtroom, watched with resigned bemusement.

The twelfth juror finally was brought into the closed courtroom and told of the government's accusations. She was devastated. She denied having made any such statements, and swore her impartiality. Judge Sear denied the disqualification motion and, instead, allowed us to decide whether she should continue to serve. We decided to keep her, but undoubtedly the government's outrageous conduct irretrievably intimidated this juror.

At last, we reached closing arguments. Eads Hogue closed for the government: "Mr. Marcello and Mr. Davidson had no qualms about corrupting Mr. Roemer, and Mr. Roemer had no qualms about being corrupted. And the majesty of a state office was sold." Tom Dyson argued that Davidson was out of the loop after introducing Hauser to Carlos. Mike argued that Roemer never intended to commit a crime, that he was only stringing Hauser along to get campaign contributions and that, in the end, Roemer "outfoxed the fox." Russell Schonekas argued that Carlos was the victim of entrapment and selective prosecution.

I began closing argument by reminding the jury of the importance of their role in the administration of justice:

> " . . . all of you in the course of your lives have made decisions which are very difficult decisions and very important decisions, such as deciding whether to marry, deciding on the kind of a career, the kind of job you might want. All of those are very important decisions that you have been called upon to make, but they are decisions that you yourself at any time can reverse. They are not irrevocable decisions. The decision, however, that you will be called upon to make as a juror in this case is unlike these other decisions because once you make it, you cannot reverse it. You cannot come back the next day and say to yourself or to anyone else, 'I may have been mistaken.' It's a decision that is final. It's a decision that is irrevocable and, for that reason, it's a decision that the law requires that you make under the standard of law that the judge will tell you about, and that is, that before you can convict, you must be convinced that the government has proved its case beyond and to the exclusion of a reasonable doubt."

I then emphasized the difference between the government's sting operation in this case and the typical undercover case:

> "An undercover agent of the FBI masquerades himself as a convict, as a dope pusher, and he goes up to the suspected person and he says, 'I want to buy some dope,' or 'I want to sell some dope,' and the target individual then gets himself involved. But the difference is that the approach to the individual, the first come-on, is a come-on of criminality. . . . That was not the situation here. The come-on was with legitimate people, and, 'We represent Prudential, and we're willing to put money in the outstretched hands of people who rightfully and legitimately have their hands out.' . . .

For example, if you have a beggar on the street starving and a Sunbeam truck driver drives up and the Sunbeam driver in the uniform gets out and he says, 'You want some bread?' And the guy says, 'Yeah,' and he puts some bread in his hand and the guy eats it and then the Sunbeam driver says, 'Oh, wait. I'm sorry. You're under arrest. I'm really not a Sunbeam driver. This is really not Sunbeam bread. This is stolen bread and you're possessing stolen bread,'—that is the kind of technique that was utilized in this case."

A good defense concedes its weaknesses and, consequently, I admitted that Vincent was not an innocent babe in the woods:

> "Marinello's motivation for what he did was ambition, and there's no question about it. And when you look at the very first tape of the first office meeting between Marcello and Marinello, you do see Marinello there with ambition. He wants to get ahead. He wants to raise money for his candidate for governor, Fitzmorris. He wants to make Brownie points. He wants to be solid with Fitzmorris. Ambition. The kind of ambition that many lawyers have had historically. Lawyers become judges, lawyers become prosecutors, lawyers become state attorneys as a result of their involvement in the political world. It's by raising money. It's by currying favor . . . and that is what Marinello was doing. He was involved in the raw whirlpool of politics. And what Marinello did in this case you may not think is right and you may not approve of it. And Marinello's conduct doesn't have to be right and I don't have to approve of it in order to represent him, just like it does not have to be right in order for you to acquit him, because the question before us is not whether or not you condone Marinello's activity on a moral basis or a political basis or on an ethical or on a societal basis. The only issue is whether or not the government can convince you beyond a reasonable doubt that when Marinello did the things that he did, that he had the specific intent to violate the law."

Dragon slayers, like basketball coaches, know the importance of the home court advantage. I reminded the jury that we were the "local boys," and that the undercover operatives were the "outsiders":

> "You see what these people have attempted to do! They have attempted to put the political system of Louisiana on

trial. . . . They ought to go do it in California. They don't have to come and do it here. And Fitzmorris says, 'I'll be glad to get in touch with some of my friends.' And they're going to suggest something sinister! 'Look,' Fitzmorris says, 'I hang on a two-way street. I hang on a two-way street. You scratch my back; I'll scratch your back.' That's the way the world operates. Not just politicians do that, not just businessmen—nuns and bishops do the same thing, FBI agents do the same thing among themselves."

And, of course, I kept the searchlight on Hauser:

"You know, if you folks return a verdict of guilty—and I suggest that you won't—there'll be some sadness and some tears over here (indicating the defense tables). If you return verdicts of not guilty, there'll be some sadness and disappointment over here (indicating the government's table). But no matter what you do, there's only one person who is going to smile either way, and that's Hauser. Hauser is going to laugh all the way to Switzerland, because Hauser has accomplished the greatest con job of his career, because Hauser has conned the government. He conned them into believing that by them allowing him an unlimited amount of cash to go put in the hands of people running for Governor, he had them hoodwinked into believing that he was catching criminals. And he got himself out of jail. He made himself $75,000 as a result of it. And no matter what you do, Hauser is going to laugh all the way to Switzerland. . . . He is the super con of the case, and he conned the government."

Throughout the trial, whenever we had suggested entrapment, the undercover agents had been quick to respond that all they had done "was offer the defendants an opportunity to do wrong." This notion had to be placed in its proper perspective:

"In the Old Testament, that's exactly what the devil through the serpent did; he tempted Adam and Eve to take of the forbidden fruit and the Old Scripture writers, when they wrote that, they didn't write that Satan, the Serpent, offered the opportunity or created the opportunity for these people to do wrong. He tempted them, and that's what it's called, the Temptation and Fall of Mankind.

He tempted them and for that, he was condemned to

crawl on his belly and to eat the dust of the earth for eternity, which is what Hauser ought to be doing right now."

I ended on the high note:

> "Let me tell you what this case really—when you get right down to it—what this case is really all about. These folks—the technique that they utilized—it would just be like . . . if a rake and a rogue described himself, disguised himself as a gentleman and sought out to seduce a lady, and he courted her, caroused her, cajoled her, persuaded her, enticed her, entreated her, wined and dined her, made her promises, bought her jewelry, told her it was legitimate, told her it was honorable, promised that he'd marry her, then he seduced her, and then he jumps up, takes off his disguise as an honorable person, and points his finger at her and says, 'Harlot! Whore! Prostitute!' That's what they're doing in this case. They don't understand that what makes a lady a lady is what she thinks about herself and not what some sun worshiper from California thinks. They don't know the difference. They put the money in these people's hands. They're telling them it's a political contribution, and then they want to scream 'crime.' Hogwash! You can't buy this. It turns the stomach of a civilized person if you condone this kind of activity on the part of your government. And believe me, I know it's hard. All of us love this country. We all are law-abiding people. But the point is, you have a duty. You have the power and control in this case to tell your government, 'Don't be giving away political contributions in some make-believe game. Go out and catch the murderers and rapists and muggers that are plaguing our streets, but not this kind of hogwash."

After two hours of deliberation, the jury sent a message that they had reached a verdict. We were shocked. When we arrived in the courtroom and the jury was brought in, they had only reached a verdict as to one defendant. Wisely, Judge Sear decided not to publish the verdict at that time, and he sent the jury back to deliberate further. After two more hours, the jury reached another verdict for another defendant. Again, we didn't know which defendant's fate had been sealed. The jury then deliberated for three days before reaching verdicts on the remaining defendants. It was the longest three days of my life.

When the jury came into the courtroom with their final verdicts, we sensed trouble. Some of them, including the twelfth juror, were crying. The verdicts were: Marinello, not guilty; Davidson, not guilty; Roemer and Marcello, guilty of conspiracy.

As we left the courthouse, we were besieged by reporters. Asked for his reaction, Vincent said, "I'm very happy for myself and family, but I'm also saddened by the verdicts for my friends," then added, "I can't understand it. I'm just as guilty as they are!" At that moment, I knew that the smartest decision of my legal career had been keeping him off the witness stand.

After the verdicts, the Monday morning quarter-backing began. Did Roemer bring down Carlos, or did Carlos bring down Roemer? My two cents is that Russell and Henry made a terrible mistake in relying solely on the entrapment defense. With that defense, one concedes guilty knowledge and, in effect, the commission of the crime. The truth of the matter is that Carlos never understood that he was committing a crime. Indeed, in one of the tapes, he had explained to the undercover agents the difference between a bribe and a legitimate business deal. To him, a bribe was paying money to a sheriff to turn his head while one did something illegal, like gambling. On the other hand, paying a politician to do something good for the State—such as saving one million dollars in insurance premiums—was not a bribe. In Carlos's words, "It was a tip."

That Christmas, Slim sent Big Al a gift package labeled "Secret Witness Kit." Inside was a paper bag with eye holes. Vincent went back to practicing law at La Louisiane. During the trial, he had instructed his secretary to tell pestering clients that "he was tied up in a big federal case." He no longer had that excuse. We remained friends. I never asked him what really happened to the ten thousand dollars he received for Fitzmorris. On occasion, I would hear him in La Louisiane talking about another big deal, another fast buck.

On June 24, 1991, Vincent Marinello was found dead behind the wheel of his car in a deserted parking lot near his home in Mandeville. He had been shot once in the back of the head. A professional hit. No one has been arrested.

NINE

The Knight in Hollywood

Sam Sciortino was an alleged member of the Los Angeles Mafia, at least according to Aladina James "The Weasel" Fratiano, a well-known government informant. In February 1978, Sciortino was indicted in a federal racketeering case in Los Angeles, and the case was allotted to Judge Harry Pregerson, a liberal judge well-respected by the criminal defense bar. The Judge dismissed the case on two separate occasions because of irregularities in the grand jury proceedings. Coincidentally, the prosecutors in the Sciortino case, James D. Henderson and Bruce J. Kelton, were the two Justice Department lawyers supervising the Brilab investigation.

Sciortino's cousin, Phil Rizzuto, lived in New Orleans. He owned and operated a barroom on the corner of Bourbon and Iberville streets in the middle of the French Quarter. It was a great location, around the corner from La Louisiane and catty-corner to my favorite restaurant, Galatoire's. There is always a line in front of Galatoire's since it doesn't accept reservations, and a part of the waiting-in-line ritual is to buy Bloody Marys from Phil's bar before having lunch at Galatoire's. Phil was a good businessman and also a friend of Carlos.

On October 3, 1979, in the middle of the Brilab investigation, Phil mentioned to Carlos that his cousin was awaiting trial in California before Judge Pregerson. Unbeknownst to Phil and Carlos, the Judge had been nominated to the Ninth Circuit Court of Appeals, and his confirmation hearing in the United States Senate was occurring that very day. A small article appeared the next day in the *Times-Picayune* about Judge Pregerson's confirmation hearing and, seeing the article, Carlos was struck by a comment attributed to the Judge that, "he would not follow the law in ruling on a case if the law required a decision that offended his conscience." Impressed by the comment, Carlos called Phil to tell him about the article.

Later that morning, Carlos also mentioned the article to Hauser in a telephone conversation. Quick to seize any opportunity for self-aggrandizement, Hauser told him that he knew " . . . the man personally," adding that he was " . . . one of the nicest, most liberal judges . . . " and not like " . . . the cocksucker that he went before."

When Hauser reported this conversation to his federal handlers, Henderson and Kelton, they immediately directed him to pursue the topic, and approximately three hours later, Carlos was saying to Hauser that he " . . . might want to talk to you about something . . . " because he had " . . . some people ah, goin' to bat . . . " in California.

"Anything you want me to do?" Hauser asked.

"Ain't nothing you can do," Carlos replied.

"There's a lot of things that I be able, may be able to do," Hauser insisted.

Carlos then called Phil to tell him to "sit tight" because he had "somebody in California who knew the man personally."

By the following week, the government had created George Ashley, a fictitious friend of Judge Pregerson's. Hauser then phoned Carlos and told him, " . . . one of my boys . . . has a very, very close friend who's a friend of the judge that you mentioned," adding, "we took the man out to dinner." Hauser again asked, "What do you want me to do with the judge?"

"Ain't nothing you can do. I've learned that all my life if you've got a federal judge, money ain't gonna' do no good. You ain't gonna, I don't care . . . unless you got your brother in there. But they ain't. You can't give 'em enough money to take it, anything like that, you understand. They ain't gonna do it. I got uh, I know half, half of 'em right here, right here, they're personal friends of mine. I better not ask for something like that, they'd get insulted. Because they got a lifetime job," Carlos said.

Although Carlos clearly showed no predisposition to bribe a federal judge (in fact, just the opposite), Hauser and the undercover agents nonetheless persisted relentlessly. The following day, Hauser furnished Carlos with a detailed background of the Judge: the year of his birth, the year of his wife's birth, the law school he attended, the fact that his wife taught microbiology at Pierce College, and that his son was an assistant district attorney. All of this information supposedly came from Ashley when, in actuality, it had come from the FBI's background file on Judge Pregerson. Hauser concluded by telling Carlos how much they "love" him and that " . . . they would do anything that can be done . . . " with the Judge.

Finally, a meeting was held in New Orleans. It was the first and only meeting between Hauser and Phil and between Sam and Carlos. Sam began the meeting by telling Hauser, "if everybody told the truth, I'd be home free."

Hauser responded by saying that his friend Ashley was "like this" with the Judge, clinching two fingers together, and that, "Whatever you want I will do for you."

"If someone mentions something to him, he may disqualify himself," Sam said with concern.

"What would be wrong with going to the Judge and laying out the facts?" Hauser asked.

"How could he do that? If he could do that, could you do that and still maintain? . . ."

"Maintain what?" Hauser asked.

"Honesty, I mean in other words, if everything was honest here, Joe, I'd walk. Now there's no bullshit about this. If it was all honest, I'd walk," Sam said.

Towards the end of the meeting, Sam told Hauser, "I'll tell you right now. I wouldn't even make an attempt to try and say here, offer the Judge—ah—because first of all, I wouldn't; I know he's a fine man. You understand me. You, you, you, no way anybody could and I don't want to. I wouldn't have no idea that that's the way to go."

The end result of the New Orleans meeting was that Carlos, Sam and Phil all made it abundantly clear to Hauser that Ashley shouldn't say anything to the Judge that might be considered improper. As Carlos said to Hauser, "You got to use your own judgment."

Not content with simply offering an opportunity to do wrong, Henderson and Kelton then decided to commit what amounted to Article III treason by creating a corrupt judge, one who would extort a bribe from Sam as the price for not going to jail. And so, Hauser was instructed to tell Sam that Judge Pregerson, according to Ashley, had previously accepted a bribe in a drug case, that the Judge disliked him (Sciortino), and that for a one hundred twenty-five thousand dollar painting, the Judge would guarantee that he wouldn't go to jail. Truly an offer that Sam couldn't refuse. When Hauser told Carlos about the painting for the Judge, Carlos said he would "stand good for it."

However, despite repeated efforts to get Sam to meet Ashley and to buy the painting for the Judge, nothing happened. Again, the government ran into a problem with the pragmatic Carlos, who began to say that it was a "bad deal," and that he was "finished with it." Unfortunately, Carlos said this not for reasons of good citizenship, but rather because, in his words, "Man, people gonna' be askin' da Judge where he got da picture from. Just give da Judge cash money, man, and leave him buy his own picture."

Although a painting was never given to the Judge, the government had two good reasons for being satisfied with the conspiracy to give him one. First, Henderson and Kelton achieved what Sam had dreaded the most, the recusal of Judge Pregerson from his pending case. After the prosecutors informed the Judge that he was the object of a bribery attempt, he had no choice but to recuse himself. Although he would bitterly complain to the Attorney General, after discovering that the prosecutors had portrayed him as a corrupt judge, nothing would come of it. The second reason for the government's satisfaction with the conspiracy was that it unleashed a second dragon against Carlos, this one on the heels of the New Orleans dragon.

After winning Vincent's case, Carlos wanted me to represent him in the California case. Vinny Mosca and I were off to Hollywood. My mother stopped calling Carlos the "damn Dago," and instead started saying novenas for him. Aunt Delta referred to him as that "noble Roman."

Because Judge Pregerson had been the object of the alleged conspiracy, his former colleagues on the district court bench recused themselves *en masse*. Also, because the Judge was now on the Court of Appeals, those judges recused themselves. This all led to the Chief Justice of the United States, Warren Burger, taking personal charge of the case. From that point on, I knew we were in trouble.

The Chief Justice hand-picked his old friend, Tom Devitt, to preside over the trial. Judge Devitt was a famous judge from St. Paul, Minnesota, who had co-authored a well-known treatise on jury instructions. He was a towering figure. He was slender and had silver hair and a resonant voice to accompany his charming personality. And like Judge Rubin, he knew how to protect the record from reversible error.

Our first move was to attempt to have the case transferred to New Orleans. Our stated reason for requesting the change of venue was that most of the activity had occurred in New Orleans and that most of the witnesses lived there. The real reason, however, was because we felt that Carlos would receive a fairer trial in New Orleans. In spite of his recent conviction, I suspected the jury really hadn't wanted to convict him. After all, we have a tendency in New Orleans to romanticize our villains and Carlos, like the pirate Jean Lafitte, was a Robin Hood character. Judge Devitt, however, wasn't about to let us try the case at home. He denied the motion. This time, we would be the outsiders.

Ensconced in the Beverly Wilshire Hotel, Vinny and I worked hard preparing the case for trial. We spent a lot of time with Carlos and got to know him well. A good client, he trusted his lawyers absolutely and, though essentially uneducated, he was smart and very wise about human nature. He loved to tell stories and to give fatherly advice. For instance, he explained to Vinny, who in the main was unschooled on the subject, the art of love-making, "You got to lay on 'em 'til they satisfy theyselves."

Carlos also loved to eat. Each night, we went to a different Italian restaurant. And each night, it was de rigueur for Carlos to begin dinner by announcing that he would "eat light tonight." He would then feast upon antipasto, soup, bread, salad, and always "clams and linguine." After a rich dessert, coffee, and Strega, he would say without fail, "Dat's da best damn spaghettis I ever had, man."

When the government ensnares a defendant into wrongdoing by engaging in conduct so outrageous that it shocks civilized notions of fair play, the government should be barred from prosecuting the case regardless of a defendant's predisposition to commit the crime. Theoretically. We filed a motion to dismiss on this ground, but the Judge deferred ruling on the issue until after the jury decided the merits of the case.

The trial lasted six days. Again, Hauser was the government's star witness and, again, the tapes told the whole story. With little room to maneuver, all we could do was harp on the entrapment theme. In closing argument, I explained:

> "Entrapment historically developed in England where the king had all the hunting land, and bounty hunters and game wardens would induce people onto the king's property, the peasant would shoot the deer, and then he would be arrested; and the policy of the law is that when the government entices, seduces, tempts, encourages, and engages in that kind of activity, then it is against the policy of the law to find an individual like that guilty unless the government proves that he was predisposed to doing it."

But I had to concede that:

> "It's true that Marcello is not saying—doesn't come out and say, in moralistic terms—'What you're doing is wrong.' That's absolutely true. But I suggest to you that the law doesn't require that. Marcello is saying, 'I don't like this deal because I might get caught,' and he doesn't want to get caught doing anything wrong.
>
> Now that may not be the noblest, loftiest reason for rejecting what the government was trying to do, but I submit to you that it is legally a good reason."

I concluded by telling the jury that Carlos was "just like the bass who is rejecting the lure; he doesn't strike because he doesn't want to end up in the soup."

After deliberating for three days, the jury came back with a message that they were hopelessly deadlocked. We moved for a mistrial, but the Judge responded with the dynamite charge, the bane of every dragon slayer. Under this instruction, jurors are told that they must reexamine their respective positions, especially those espousing the minority viewpoint. After the dynamite charge, most juries come back with guilty verdicts. This one was no different. We lost in Hollywood.

PELICAN PUBLISHING COMPANY, INC.

Palo Alto, the home of the Lemann family, in Donaldsonville, Louisiana.

My father, the Squire.

My mother, who would sit me on the potty and give me books to read about knights in shining armor on white steeds rescuing distressed damsels from fire-breathing dragons.

Jacob Lemann,
my first known ancestor
on my father's side.

The B. Lemann & Bro. Building, located in Donaldsonville, Louisiana, built in 1877 to house the mercantile business started by Jacob Lemann in 1836.

Sooner or later, my mother and Aunt Delta will trace my lineage back to Ivanhoe.

With much love Pud Nov. 1994

from Dee

with reservations as to who you lend this to — Read first — (I have not read it, but know about many of the incidents I guess that will be in here)

Aunt Delta forging history.

R.A. and the corporal
who would never be a general.

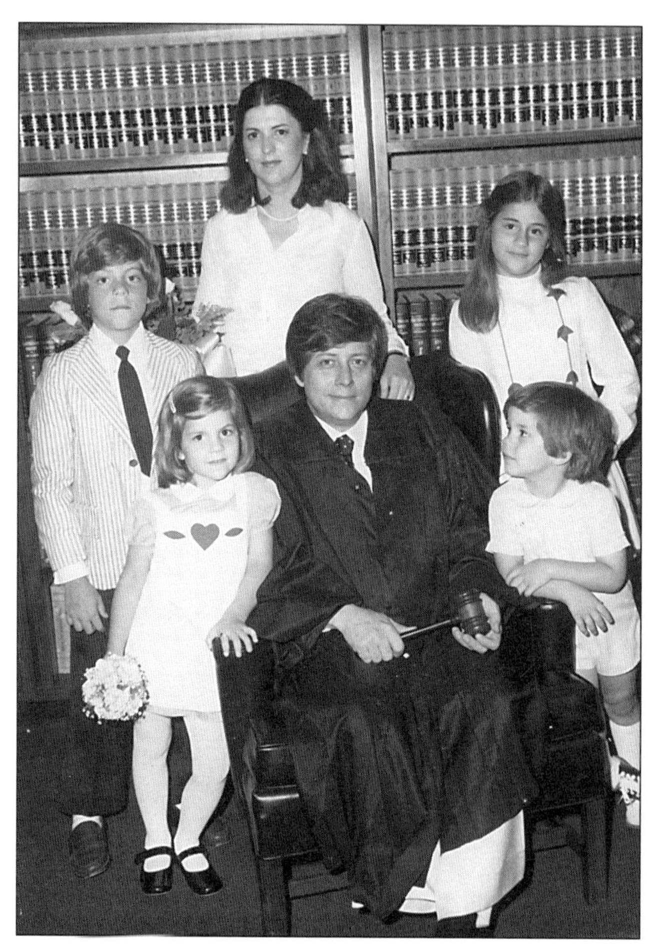

The Wizard of Magic Court with R.A., Rachel, Jonathan, Amy, and Arthur IV.

One of the denizens of Magic Court.

PHILIP GOULD

Slim, my Della Street.

COURTESY OF JOHN DILLMANN/NOPD

Dr. Mark Sheppard,
who got his thrills from bedding down
with black street hustlers.

COURTESY OF JOHN DILLMANN/NOPD

Candy Smith, the hustler, who made the ultimate gamble that his confession would prove his innocence.

AP\WIDE WORLD PHOTOS

Byron de la Beckwith, the kind of white knight one might find with a sheet over his head.

AP\WIDE WORLD PHOTOS

Delores, Vincent Marinello and his mother. In a Mandeville mirage, I gazed at Dulcinea sunning herself under a Castilian sun.

AP\WIDE WORLD PHOTOS

*Losing in Hollywood was hard,
almost like flunking a screen test.*

Dr. LeChasney's castle in Atlanta.

Dr. LeChasney's bear that ain't talkin'.

Kirksey McCord Nix, who made more money in prison than most people make out of prison.

"I know how you call the hogs in: 'Sooey, sooey, sooey.'"

Ten

Coram Nobis

It is always hard to lose, but losing in Hollywood was harder, almost like flunking a screen test. There was also trouble on the home front. Adolescence hit my oldest daughter Rachel like a hurricane on Grand Isle. Rachel, a free spirit, wore wool in the summer and cotton in the winter. If a blind man held onto her, he wouldn't know if it were day or night, summer or winter. Her hormones were in a turmoil, and as my father said, referring to my rowdy childhood, "The chickens come home to roost." But R.A. was the one who had to weather these domestic storms. I hunted the fields.

Judge Sear sentenced Carlos to seven years in prison, and to make matters worse, Judge Devitt imposed a ten-year consecutive sentence. That meant Carlos, in his seventies, was facing seventeen years in jail, and he would not become eligible for parole until he had served one third of the sentence.

Vinny and I appealed the New Orleans conviction. Along with Roemer's new lawyers, Jack Martzell and John Reed, we attacked the RICO conspiracy on the basis that there is no legal distinction between two individuals conspiring to commit, for example, mail fraud and two individuals conspiring "to associate as an enterprise" to commit the same mail fraud. No court has ever satisfactorily explained this distinction. Nonetheless, on April 11, 1983, the Court of Appeals affirmed the conviction in a two-page opinion that didn't even address our arguments.

Three days later, the government moved to revoke Carlos's bond because some confidential informant said he was planning to flee the country. Utter nonsense. The government had been trying to deport Carlos for thirty years, and once, in the 1960s, it actually "kidnapped" him and flew him to Guatemala, only to have him sneak back into the country. It was not his style. Carlos would never flee.

He was in my office when we received the news that the government was seeking to revoke his bond. I went to Judge Sear's courtroom to argue that he should remain free pending our application to the

Supreme Court for supervisory review. It was useless, and the Judge ordered his immediate incarceration. As I left the courtroom, at least six FBI agents followed in order to arrest him at my office in front of TV cameras. Furious, I returned to the courtroom and argued that he should at least be allowed the dignity of self-surrender. To his credit, the Judge ordered the agents to remain in the courtroom until I returned with him.

Carlos had left home that morning without a thought of going to prison that day. A stocky, powerfully built man, he usually hid his hardness behind a warm smile and laughing eyes, but when the mood struck, he could stare down a gang of thugs on any night on any dead-end street in New Orleans. I didn't know what to expect. I had just given Judge Sear my word that he would self-surrender and, already nervous about that, I returned from court to find that my father (of all days) was in the office conducting family business. In one room, I had Carlos going to jail; in another, my father discussing sugar cane tonnage.

When I told Carlos that he had to go to jail, he threw back the blinds in anger and looked out of the window as though gauging an escape or plotting some retaliation, but only for a few seconds. Composing himself, he told me to call his wife Miss Jackie and then we walked together to the courthouse to surrender. Carlos was very stoic, determined to maintain his dignity. In hindsight, I believe that had Carlos known he was going to prison that day lunch would have been the only thing done differently. He would have insisted on clams and linguine at La Louisiane, instead of a ham po-boy at Mother's, the little neighborhood restaurant on Poydras Street.

Carlos was taken to the Community Correctional Center, the main prison in New Orleans, which also serves as a temporary holding facility for federal prisoners. When I arrived that night to visit, he was in the "medical" suite along with Norman Johnson, an eccentric millionaire in jail for income tax violations. They each had a private bedroom and bath and they shared a living room fully equipped with TV and kitchenette. Meals were brought over regularly from La Louisiane; brocilone, cabrito, and cucuzzi were some of his favorites.

Carlos's suite mate Norman was married to a beautiful girl, who once had worked in the French Quarter. She would later become a New York City socialite. They were still married but separated at the time, and Carlos tried to console the love-sick Norman by telling him, "Man, I remember da broad when she usta' sell macaronis on Bourbon Street."

Of course, the New Orleans conviction was only half the problem, the other half being the California conviction. In the summer of 1983, we had a break when H. Edward Tickel, a renegade FBI agent, was indicted for theft. He also happened to be one of the FBI's top "black box" operatives, and he wanted to talk. We went to his home in the Virginia countryside; according to Tickel, he had been sent to New Orleans from FBI headquarters on January 2, 1980, to illegally break into Carlos's fishing camp in order to secure information for a subsequent wiretap order. Naturally, the illegal break-in had not been disclosed to the court.

We presented a motion for a new trial to Judge Devitt in Minnesota on the ground that the unlawful break-in was additional proof of outrageous governmental conduct. Unfortunately, the Judge denied the new trial motion and, ultimately, the Court of Appeals affirmed the California conviction.

The unexpected then happened. In 1987, the Supreme Court decided that the mail fraud statute applied only to a property loss and not to a loss of intangible rights, such as the citizenry's right to honest government. Carlos and Roemer had never been accused of causing a property loss; indeed, the whole concept behind the scheme had been to save the State of Louisiana money through reduced insurance premiums. Thus, our case was a classic example of the federal government's use of the mail fraud statute to impose its brand of honest government on the citizens of a sovereign state, precisely what the Supreme Court said it could no longer do.

We filed a writ of coram nobis to set aside the conviction. Judge Sear, who displays in his office a framed "CM" which was made from the wire used to bug Carlos's office, could not bring himself to undo the trial of his lifetime. But on June 23, 1989, the Court of Appeals vacated the convictions of Carlos and Roemer, meaning they had served time in a federal penitentiary for conduct that was not a crime. Finally, one dragon was down.

People often ask me whether Carlos was a member of the Mafia. I don't know. Of course, I didn't know him during the 1940s and 1950s when illegal gambling was rampant in New Orleans and some sheriff might have taken money to look the other way. But I do know that after listening to some thirty-five thousand taped conversations from the 1980s, the only evidence of criminality on those tapes were the conversations that had been scripted by the government. I also know that descendants of money-taking politicians live today on St. Charles Avenue, while a seventy year old Carlos Marcello went to jail for attempting to save the State of Louisiana a million dollars a year in insurance premiums—not a crime—and for attempting to protect a friend from a fictitious corrupt judge created by the FBI—also not a crime. In America, we call this justice.

After Carlos was released from prison, his son brought him to see me. I knew then that it was too late. The surviving dragon had ravaged his mind with Alzheimer's disease. Carlos Marcello died on March 22, 1993, at home with his family around him. And with style.

ELEVEN

The Wounded Knight

By the fall of 1982, Slim and I had moved from the old Commerce Building in the central business district to the new Pan American Building on Poydras Street. With the Superdome on one end and the Riverwalk on the other, Poydras had become the fashionable street in downtown New Orleans. Progress had left Airline Highway. Federal Court had moved from the French Quarter and was located on the corner of Camp and Poydras streets, across from our new office building.

We shared office space with Walter Stuart, a smooth-talking, ambitious, young business lawyer, who had formed a partnership with a New York law firm and served as its resident partner in the New Orleans office. The very conservative Louisiana State Bar Association viewed this kind of alliance as a threat to the old-line legal community.

Walter and I were regulars at Friday afternoon lunches at Galatoire's. In fact, Walter would send a court runner to stand in line on Friday mornings at eleven-thirty in order to hold a table until the rest of us arrived between two and three o'clock in the afternoon. Galatoire's is a proper place for proper people to act improperly. Once, the very proper wife of a very proper client beat him unmercifully with a loaf of the magnificent French bread served at every table. After the incident, their waiter no longer brought French bread to their table, not wanting "to arm the natives." The incident also demonstrates that the code of conduct at Galatoire's is much looser than the one at La Louisiane. This is because Galatoire's customers feel more secure with their stations in life, the dirty work having been done by great grandfathers.

The food at Galatoire's is good but the food is good everywhere in New Orleans. What makes Galatoire's special is the waiters. Everyone has to have his own waiter at Galatoire's. It is an extremely intimate relationship. As with spouses, fidelity is a cardinal principal. One waiter, for example, whose wife was transferred to Miami, commuted from Florida so as not to desert his customers. And like spouses, customers and waiters often look alike. Fat customers have fat waiters, thin customers have thin waiters, loud customers have loud waiters, and so forth. Aunt Delta's waiter looks like a Scottish butler from a Gothic novel. Mine is a cagey Cajun.

During the rest of the week, mind you, we worked hard at what we did best—the courtroom for me, and for Walter, the recruitment of new clients for his "national" law firm. Walter's upscale, yuppie image, however, was not always enhanced by some of my clients. In fact, he went to great lengths to avoid even meeting Carlos. Indeed, the only time one ever found Walter in the law library was when Carlos was in the office.

One of Walter's law partners, Steve Dwyer, was also more comfortable putting business deals together than actually representing clients in court. His grandfather had been a friend of Carlos, and when one of Steve's investment properties burned under mysterious circumstances, we nicknamed him Torch.

One afternoon, Torch, a civil lawyer, wanted me to see one of his clients urgently. I agreed and was introduced to T. Windle Dyer. In his mid-thirties, prematurely gray, heavy-set, and extremely mild-mannered, Windle was originally from North Louisiana, and he spoke with a faint southern drawl. He was a member of the New Orleans City Planning Commission, an agency which recommended zoning adjustments to the City Council.

After the introduction, Torch excused himself and Windle told me he had twenty-five thousand dollars in his briefcase that he had just received from Guy Olano, a former Law Clinic student. After graduation Guy had struck out on his own and had made a lot of money in personal injury cases. He then became involved with a Savings & Loan Association, and before long he had become its president and chairman of the board.

"How did you get the money from Guy?" I asked.

"Well let me say this. I may have said some things that don't sound right, but you have to believe me, Buddy, I didn't intend to do anything wrong."

"Tell me about it," I said, my dragon antennas on alert.

"I have a company, Square Twenty Corporation, which owns some land on Algiers Point that I've been trying to develop. Well anyway, my partner and I had a falling out and I was looking to replace him, and that's when I first met Guy," Windle said.

"Was Guy interested?"

"Yes, he said he was."

"Were you on the City Planning Commission then?" I asked.

"No, not at that time," Windle responded.

"So what's the problem?" I asked.

"Well you see, Guy owns this condominium on St. Charles Avenue called La Maison Charles that he's been trying to convert to a time-share project. Now to do that, he needs to get zoning approval from the City Council, and the City Council only acts on the recommendation of the Planning Commission."

"What happened next?" I inquired, sensing the reason Torch wanted him to consult with me.

"Well the City Planning Commission denied Guy's request for a zoning change. Again, that's before I was on the commission," Windle emphasized.

"So what's the connection," I asked, again wondering what the problem was.

"Well you see Buddy, at my first meeting on the commission, we voted to reconsider Guy's application and this time it passed, and then the City Council accepted our recommendation and granted the zoning change," he drawled.

"Did you vote for it?"

"It was my motion."

"Did he give you anything for your vote?" I demanded, thinking like a prosecutor, which dragon slayers must do at times.

"No, not exactly," Windle said.

"What do you mean, not exactly?" I barked.

"I'm gonna' be honest with you Buddy, he never gave me anything but I was certainly hoping that if I scratched his back, he would scratch mine and help me with my Algiers Point project."

"And did he?" I asked.

"For a while I thought so," he admitted.

"In what way?"

"Well I later got a commitment letter from his S&L to finance my project," he acknowledged.

"Does Torch know about this?" I asked.

"Yes of course. Torch has been working with me and Guy trying to put the deal together."

At this point I reflected on what Windle had told me. While raw politics and hard-nosed business tactics had been engaged in, no crime had been committed in my opinion, at least not until we got to the briefcase.

"Windle, I think I understand what you've said so far, but how does all this fit in with the twenty-five thousand dollars in your briefcase?"

"This is the thing, Buddy. Guy kept putting us off. Every time he was supposed to sign our partnership agreement, he would come up with some bullshit excuse or further demand. He kept draggin' things out. I was gettin' pissed off and losin' patience. The commitment letter was about to expire and we hadn't put the deal together yet. I started demanding money and yesterday, he gave me a twenty thousand dollar check and five thousand dollars in cash. He also wanted to know if I could help him get to the mayor and Councilman Jim Singleton, since he was still having problems with his time-share project."

My dragon antennas reacted again. Why cash? Why not simply a check for twenty-five thousand dollars? And why the talk about the mayor and a council member? "Was Torch with you when Guy gave you the money?" I asked.

"No."

"Was he with you when you and Guy discussed the money?"

"Not this twenty-five thousand dollars. Only when we were talkin' about the overall financing of the project."

I had heard enough. "Windle," I said, "you have to do three things. First, you have to assume that Guy is wired and actin' in an undercover capacity. Second, you have to give the money back. And third, you have to stop talkin' to him."

At this point, Torch came back into my office and I repeated my advice to him. We then discussed how to return the money. I suggested simply mailing the check and depositing the cash into Guy's checking account. Torch then asked, "Should we write a letter explainin' why we're returnin' the money?"

"Only if you can do so in the context of a legitimate transaction," I replied.

The next day, Torch wrote a letter to Guy, stating:

> " . . . I am returning to you a voided check No. 452 drawn on your special account for $20,000. In addition, I have deposited $5,000 to your special account No.3607-045-0 at Jefferson Bank & Trust Company. These are sums that you had tendered to my client as part of the advancement on the Algiers Point Condominium project at your meetings on last Monday and Tuesday."

Two nights later, around midnight, Slim and I were in the office working on Carlos's brief when the phone rang. It was Windle, whispering hysterically that, "Two FBI agents are at my house to arrest me."

"What for?" I asked.

"They say extortion," he cried.

I had been right about Guy. What I didn't know was that Windle had not followed all of my advice. Instead, he had talked to Guy again over the telephone and had told him that he had been conducting his own private investigation into corruption. I was furious. He couldn't have it both ways. Either he had accepted the money to "test" Guy, or he had accepted it as an "advance" on a legitimate business transaction.

After his arrest, Windle went behind my back and attempted to convince the United States Attorney that he hadn't done anything wrong. Naturally, John Volz wasn't the least bit interested in hearing his protestations of innocence. Rather, he wanted Windle to wear a hidden body mike and, ostensibly on behalf of Guy Olano, approach the mayor and a city councilman with an opportunity to engage in wrongdoing. To his credit, Windle refused to do so.

When Windle told me of his secret meeting with John Volz, I was furious again, and this time I threatened to discontinue representing him.

On his knees, he begged me not to abandon him. Reluctantly, I agreed to stay on his case, but as it turned out it would not be for long.

After Windle's arraignment, I was talking to John Volz one day on the telephone when he mentioned to me that in his opinion the letter returning the money constituted an obstruction of justice. Dropping my shield momentarily, I said, "What the fuck you talkin' about, John. I told Windle to return the money and I knew about the letter before it was sent." In foolishly believing that my advance knowledge of the letter would convince the United States Attorney that no obstruction of justice had been intended, I was just as naive as Windle had been in meeting with him. John the Dragon responded with both nostrils ablaze. The first stream of fire was a motion to disqualify me from representing Windle on the ground that I was a witness to a material fact—i.e., the letter returning the money. The second fiery blast was grand jury subpoenas to Torch and me in connection with an obstruction of justice investigation.

A federal statute provides in part that "whoever knowingly . . . engages in misleading conduct . . . with intent to . . . delay . . . the communication to a . . . judge . . . of information relating to the . . . possible commission of a Federal offense . . . constitutes obstruction of justice." For all practical purposes, this statute outlaws the practice of criminal law. Indeed, under its sweeping provisions, a "not guilty" plea at an arraignment can be broadly interpreted as "misleading conduct" designed to "delay" the communication to a judge of the "possible commission" of a federal offense.

We filed a motion to quash the subpoenas on the grounds of the attorney-client privilege. The government argued that the privilege didn't apply because Torch and I either had been conspiring with Windle, or we had been duped into unwittingly advancing his unlawful scheme. Thus, Torch and I were either criminals or just plain stupid—not a very envious position for lawyers to be in. And to make matters worse, the trial court, after reviewing the tapes between Windle and Guy Olano, found that the government had made a prima facie showing that the crime and fraud exception applied and ordered us to testify before the grand jury. We appealed.

Although the trial court did not disqualify me, I was still concerned that the public's perception might be that I was refusing to testify before the grand jury in order to protect my own hide rather than that of my client. To eliminate this possible misperception, I voluntarily withdrew from representing Windle, and Mike Fawer replaced me.

In deciding the legal issue, the Court of Appeals wrote:

> "The tapes support the district court's finding that Dyer consulted with Dwyer for the purpose of obstructing justice by the creation of false evidence; that the government made a prima facie showing that the advice concerned future wrongdoing. There is no evidence, however, that

> the consultation with Lemann on the preceding day was with such a purpose. It is the letter written the day after consulting with Lemann that creates the prima facie case. That letter was written by the civil lawyer Dwyer. There is no evidence of any illegality in connection with Lemann. For all the record shows, Lemann could have given the sound and legal advice to return the money. That the return was made the next day with a phony explanation of a different lawyer is not enough as to Lemann. It follows that Dyer's communication with Dwyer concerning the November 16 letter is not privileged, but the communication with Lemann is."

I was off the hook but Torch had to testify before the grand jury. The whole matter became moot, however, when Windle pleaded guilty to mail fraud pursuant to a plea agreement.

This was not my only close call. Once I was charged with criminal contempt for having a time-of-day conversation with a discharged alternate juror, not anticipating that the alternate would have dinner that night with a juror before the verdict was returned the next day. Nonetheless, I had to defend myself on a baseless charge that carried with it the insinuation of jury tampering. And of course, I was tried by the same judge who brought the unfounded charge in the first place. Ironically, I was found not guilty because the judge was "not convinced beyond a reasonable doubt."

The Windle Dyer case was also not the last time the government would seek to disqualify me. Recently, prosecutors tried to disqualify me from representing different clients in separate cases in separate states because one client was the alleged unindicted co-conspirator of the other. Make no mistake about it, the government truly wants dragon slayers either out of business or in jail. It is a dangerous, risky business. Show me an unscarred dragon slayer, and I'll show you an impostor.

There is an old saying at the criminal defense bar that it is the clients who go to jail, not the lawyers. The lesson from the Windle Dyer case is that if a lawyer must go to jail, make sure it's a civil lawyer.

TWELVE

THE CRUSADERS

Riding the elevator to my office one morning in the Pan American Building, I ran into Mo on his way to Walter Stuart's office. No longer dean of the Law School, he had become a partner in Walter's law firm. In worldly dress and whistling a Handel tune, he appeared to be about three inches taller and not quite as haggard-looking. I never got the straight of it, but I heard his leaving the Law School had something to do with the Jesuits and Christian goals. I suspect the same dogs he had unleashed on me came back to bite him.

Now lest you be misled, understand that Mo wasn't altogether a new man. He was still a papist, albeit no longer in the direct line of duty. And he continued to be somewhat haggard because he was now, so to speak, in Spain and expected to speak Spanish. In other words, having been dean of a law school, he was eminently unqualified to practice law. Nonetheless, he tried hard and even went to Galatoire's on Friday afternoons. Fleta went back to looking like a nun.

Occasionally, I returned to the Law School as a guest lecturer, and for the final exam one semester I posed several hypothetical questions, all centering around a single theme: an undercover Jesuit priest masquerading as a law student as part of a papal sting operation. The undercover priest exposed a whole series of crimes allegedly committed by thinly disguised law professors. Here is a sample:

"***The Crow's Nest***

> Colonel William Logan Raven was a proud man. After the war, he returned to the red clay hills of Ouachita and, with hard work and determination, built a cotton empire that stretched into the horizon. Already an old man—perhaps even senile—when in Philadelphia to see cotton factors, he took as his bride the dark and lovely Eleanore, making her the mistress of his beloved Raven Nook

plantation. Half his age, Eleanore devoured the old man's body with her loin and created for him his only son, Somemore, who fed upon her dark and lovely breast, nursing, as some of the town folk said 'the damn Yankee blood' that forever cursed the Raven family. Somemore, indeed, could not stop nursing, and having gone through practically every Ouachita tit, he took to the bottle and drank at least one for every stalk of the old Colonel's cotton that he lost to the Red River Bank and Trust Company. Drunk and destitute, Somemore died in the arms of his wife, Esther, a sharecropper's daughter who raised their only son, Evermore, from the meager wages of a depot clerk for the Missouri-Pacific Railroad Company. It may well have been that midnight whistle in the soul of Evermore that caused him to leave the red clay hills of Ouachita in search of a better way, a search that carried him to the train station at Port Allen and across the Mississippi River on the 'George Prince' ferryboat to the green-wave ravished shores of Baton Rouge and on through the cowwalks of the LSU campus to the portals of the Law School. There, Evermore excelled and went on to become a judge and then law professor at Loyola Law School during its golden age, and finally, contender for the presidency of LSU—at long last, it seemed, a phoenix in the sunshine history of Louisiana. But for Eleanore's curse, that ancestral affliction for dark and lovely Yankee women. Evermore fell madly in love with a freshman student at Loyola, Sarah, a Jewish princess from Philadelphia. Secretly they touched and made love in every hidden nook of the Law School. And then the trap. Caught in the arms of Sarah by Sam Judas, seemingly a freshman law student, worldly and corruptible, but actually a novitiate and operative in a Rome based undercover investigation designed to ferret out decadence in Jesuit institutions.

(In each of the following questions, assume you are the prosecutor. State each offense, if any, that you would consider and explain fully the charges you would bring.)

*Evermore is in his office waiting to see Sam, who has been summoned there after discovering Evermore and Sarah the night before in the love tryst on the third floor of the library. Evermore, unaware of Sam's undercover role, has decided to use academic coercion to guarantee Sam's silence. Soon after the meeting begins, however,

Sam reveals his true identity. Evermore panics, knowing that the scandal will ruin his chances with the Preen Administration to become president of LSU. Evermore immediately picks up the bronze bust of 'Charlie Mac' that he keeps in his office and crushes Sam's skull. Sam dies.

*Evermore is in the rear parking lot of the Law School when Sam discloses his undercover role and his plan to report the incident of the previous night. Evermore rushes to his car and pulls out his 'forty-four.' Meanwhile, Professor Keith 'Bush' Wetterschnitzel is in his automobile in the front of the Law School approaching the corner of Loyola and Calhoun Streets. As is his custom, Wetterschnitzel intends to turn right onto Calhoun and then proceed to St. Charles Avenue. However, unknown to Wetterschnitzel, a prankster has reversed the one way sign on Calhoun so that it points in the opposite direction. Pausing only so long as it takes for his Teutonic genes to overcome the habit of turning right, Wetterschnitzel obediently follows the sign and turns away from his destination onto Calhoun heading in the wrong direction. At precisely the time that Wetterschnitzel's automobile becomes adjacent to the rear parking lot, Evermore begins to unload his forty-four into Sam. Five shots hit Sam, but the sixth one misses and slams into Wetterschnitzel's hairy neck. Both Sam and Wetterschnitzel die.

* * * * *

*Evermore confides in Professor Kathy Lothario. They agree that Lothario will seduce Sam and that Evermore will appear at the climactic moment with a camera. Sam would then be blackmailed into silence. However, unknown to Evermore and Lothario, their whispered conversations are overheard by a member of SUN, a secret interfaculty organization of radical do-gooders who plan to take over the Law School's administration. After Lothario succeeds in compromising Sam and Evermore takes the incriminating picture, the SUN professors barge in and threaten to reveal both scandals unless Evermore and Lothario agree to support a SUN professor for the deanship. Completely overwrought by these occurrences, Sam and Lothario run off together to Paraguay, and Evermore hangs himself in the belfry of the neighboring

> church. At his lifeless feet lay the suicide note. Quoth the Raven, 'Nevermore.'"

The students thought the exam was hilarious, but when the grades were posted, those making D's and F's bitterly complained that they had been unable to concentrate because the exam was too funny. Naturally, this resulted in a marathon faculty meeting, and as though it were an argument before the Supreme Court, the non-practicing professors rose to the occasion. After four hours of debate, the faculty voted to publicly censure me for giving an exam that was inconsistent with Christian goals. The notice of censure, which was tacked on the bulletin board, granted the students "psychologically traumatized" by my exam an opportunity to re-take another one from a different professor. Uncle, who was Professor Wetterschnitzel in the exam, reported to me that there were only two dissenting votes: his—because of his loyalty to me; and the one from Professor Lothario—who felt that public censure wasn't a strong enough sanction.

I wrote the faculty to offer a more practical solution. Obviously, the pure-hearted students had been the ones "traumatized" by the exam, while the evil-hearted ones had been undaunted. To be consistent with Christian goals, the faculty should simply reverse the grades: those with F's and D's should be awarded A's and B's, and vice versa. That way, the meek would truly inherit the earth. Thus ended my career as a law professor.

The Windle Dyer case was my last one with Walter. Having clients in the office with briefcases full of cash from questionable sources was not compatible with the image he wanted to project. So I decided to build my own Monroe & Lemann, only this time, the Lemann name would come first. Not realizing that law firms are built on the backs of clients, I went instead with chemistry. After all, Sam Spade had Miles Archer and Iva. Who else but O'Grady? He had left the Law Clinic and was in private practice with a small firm. The third partner was William Mills. Like O'Grady, Mills had gone to law school after serving in Vietnam. He had been editor-in-chief of the Law Review and after graduating had clerked for a federal judge. He then had worked for a time with an insurance defense firm and, afterwards, had established a small personal injury law firm. We thought it would be commercially sound to diversify into the personal injury field, and so began Lemann, O'Grady & Mills. Except, Lemann, O'Grady & Mills was never a law firm. We were an outfit.

O'Grady and Slim got along well from their days together at the Law Clinic. But Mills and Slim hated one another instantly, and their fights became legendary. In fact, their fights were so raunchy that at this very moment she refuses to type any account of them. Suffice it to say, I spent half my time breaking up the fights and the other half looking for O'Grady, who was either bullshitting, drinking, fucking, or all three.

The outfit moved to Lafayette Street, a small street in the warehouse district which had been widened and beautified into a showplace as a result of the World's Fair. Near the federal courthouse, it had become a prime location for new, expanding law firms.

Aunt Delta and her "manservant," Gilmore, decorated our new offices. Aunt Delta was no stranger to my office, having come by at least once a month to change her will whenever she became angry at one of her grandchildren. In the days before word processors or computers, this was quite a burden. There is a thing called a codicil, which is like an amendment to a will, but Aunt Delta doesn't favor amendments, especially the Thirteenth. Now that everything is done by computer, Aunt Delta simply calls Slim to rearrange the destiny of her grandchildren.

Aunt Delta decided my new office should be done in a Napoleonic motif, owing to the fact that it fit my personality. She and Gilmore hung all kinds of Napoleonic memorabilia on the walls, the one exception being a framed copy of President Jefferson's appointment of my great, great, great, great grandfather as a federal judge for the Mississippi Territory. She also purchased an antique tray table which looks as though it belonged to Napoleon's butler. Finally, she found a concrete eagle from somewhere, the "imperial symbol," she said, and she mounted it high on a pedestal, where it perches like a white Maltese falcon and makes a good rack to hang my hat on every morning. After they finished decorating, Aunt Delta and Gilmore drove off in her twenty year old black Cadillac in the wrong direction on Lafayette Street.

Somehow, Lemann, O'Grady & Mills grew and prospered, at one time reaching a grand total of eight lawyers. Always searching for order and stability, we recruited a fourth partner, Paul Donald White, another former Law Clinic student. Don was a large man with a booming voice. He was from Alexandria, the same town that Bobbie Gail moved to when she found out about Ann Goette before Ann Goette found out about R.A. Don was married with children and he was also a Deacon in the Episcopal Church. In fact, he was so holy we called him Bishop. Significantly, Bishop was a business lawyer and my father felt that we had, at last, a "real" lawyer in the outfit.

Across the street from us was the Ernst Cafe, an old establishment which also had been resurrected by the World's Fair. Close to the courthouse, it became the federal equivalent of the Miracle Mile. It was also the outfit's annex. After video poker machines were added, Slim was over there as much as Mills and O'Grady.

Mills was a cowboy from Texas, and every year he went on a cattle round-up. He also got into fights like a cowboy. He fought with everyone but especially with policemen—and I don't mean courtroom fights. Once the police handcuffed him to a chain-link fence while they beat him, and on another occasion during Mardi Gras, I found him under a gurney sheet at Charity Hospital after a police whipping. But he was a quick draw and good to have on a dragon hunt.

After his trip to Mexico with the beautiful law student, O'Grady and Maddie divorced. Then, at a New Year's Eve party, Judge Marullo married them again. This was right after Elsie Flowers entered O'Grady's life. He met her while on a law firm retreat at the Grand Hotel in Alabama. The retreat had been Bishop's idea, a time for strategic planning and goal development. After a day of this, we retreated to a local country and western saloon. O'Grady dropped us off and went to park the car. Inside, I looked across the horseshoe bar and I saw this blonde facing the door as O'Grady limped in to join us. Their eyes met, locked, and that told the difference. For the next two hours, I searched the horseshoe in vain for Jane Fonda, Mills fought with the bartender, and Bishop prayed; O'Grady left with Elsie.

O'Grady was like that. Nondiscriminating. Once, at the Law Clinic, he had a menage a trois with the two ugliest law students on campus, "Left" and "Right," we called them, after their respective bedtime positions. Now don't get me wrong, while O'Grady may have caught the 3-M syndrome from me, he had receptive genes for the malady. As a matter of fact, his uncle, Judge MacHardy O'Grady, had married three college roommates; and all three women remained friendly, sharing recipes, family stories, and the like. Indeed, Uncle Mac and his three wives always spent Christmas together.

O'Grady's stump was the bellwether, at least according to Maddie. She loved to say that word, and everything was stump this and stump that. Whenever someone called for him at home, instead of just saying he was busy, she always went out of her way to say, "Oh, Sean is soaking his stump. He'll have to call you back later." So whenever she talked kindly about the stump, we knew all was well with the marriage. When we didn't hear about the stump, however, we knew he was straying.

O'Grady's drinking became progressively worse. He would go to Ernst for lunch about eleven-thirty and never return. Finally, his old commanding officer made arrangements to have him dry out in a V.A. facility on the Mississippi coast. Maddie was delighted with the diagnosis: post-traumatic stress syndrome. She thought the doctors, at last, had discovered the cause of his problem. Then one night after a conjugal visit, she realized that she had forgotten something and, returning to the V.A. facility unannounced, she found O'Grady leaving for the weekend with a nurse. The doctors had to explain to Maddie that he was there for "sobriety, not chastity." After the cure, O'Grady switched from Jack Daniels to vodka, and we rode together in quest of dragons.

THIRTEEN

The Strawberry Ruby

Lil' Henry DeFraites was six feet, six inches tall and weighed three hundred fifty pounds. He was called Lil' Henry to distinguish him from his father, Big Henry, also known as the Colonel. The Colonel was a very fine man who had worked hard all of his life to build a very successful business—a lumber company right off Carrollton Avenue. Lil' Henry, on the other hand, was a scoundrel. When the Colonel died, his partner continued to operate the lumber company. On every other Friday, Lil' Henry walked into the lumber company and declared a dividend by cleaning out the cash register. A fight soon developed over the Colonel's estate between Lil' Henry, the partner, and children from another marriage. O'Grady said it would be the only will probated at Tulane and Broad.

Lil' Henry, however, hadn't come to see us about probating the Colonel's will. He had a different problem. He'd sold a ruby to a lawyer for twenty-five thousand dollars, having told the lawyer that although the ruby was worth seventy-five thousand dollars, he'd let him have it at the lower price because it was "hot." The lawyer, being more concerned with the ruby's history than with its authenticity, had checked it out with a friendly FBI agent. Indeed, a ruby of the same size and shape had been stolen in New York. Believing he was on to a good deal, the lawyer had then taken the ruby to a jeweler in the Royal Orleans Hotel, who had said, in Lil' Henry's presence, that such a stone, if genuine, would easily be worth seventy-five thousand dollars. Satisfied, the lawyer had paid Lil' Henry twenty-five thousand dollars for the ruby. Much later, the lawyer had sent the ruby to be scientifically tested and, lo and behold, it was a fake. When Lil' Henry had refused to return the money, he had been arrested and charged with theft.

The case was allotted to Judge Rudolph Becker. Rudy was one of my favorite judges. His father had been a judge and he had grown up in uptown New Orleans. Like me, he had gone to a military high school and was generally considered the only blue-blood on the Tulane and Broad bench.

Not only did everyone smoke cigarettes in those days, but everyone smoked in the courtroom. I had a three-pack a day habit and Rudy's addiction was at least as bad as mine. When I tried a case before him, we couldn't see one another through the thick clouds of smoke.

As a general rule, dragon slayers don't favor judge trials. Most judges are former prosecutors and, therefore, favor the State. However, on occasion, as in this case, I will waive a jury for a judge trial, especially when relying on a technical point for the defense.

The prosecutor's case against Lil' Henry was very simple. The State called the lawyer, who testified that after visiting the jeweler, he paid Lil' Henry twenty-five thousand dollars for the ruby. Next, the prosecutor called an expert witness in order to establish that the ruby was a fake. The State rested. Everyone expected me to put on a defense, but I rested. You could hear a pin drop in the courtroom, although you couldn't see it because of the thick clouds of smoke.

Of course, the State was required to prove beyond a reasonable doubt that Lil' Henry knew the stone was a fake. Yet the only evidence in the record on this point was the lawyer's testimony that "they" were told by the jeweler that such a stone, if genuine, would easily be worth seventy-five thousand dollars. By resting and not putting the defendant on the witness stand, the prosecution was denied the opportunity to develop the facts and circumstances surrounding Lil' Henry's acquisition of the ruby—the facts and circumstances which might have given rise to an inference of guilt. Judge Becker, blowing smoke, found Lil' Henry not guilty.

The next morning, I received a hysterical call from Maddie. She wanted R.A. and me to come over to their house right away. When I asked why, she reported that on the previous evening Lil' Henry had delivered part of our fee: two diamond rings and two Rolex watches. One of the diamonds was a marquis, the kind she had always coveted, and she had spent a sleepless night debating whether to offer first choice to R.A. or to keep it for herself. Of course, her anxiety had been wasted—the fee, naturally, was fake. Making do, however, our son Arthur was the big man on the Holy Name Elementary School playground the next day with his Rolex wristwatch.

Over the years, I have learned not to ask certain clients certain questions. In the Darwinian school of criminal defense lawyers, of which I am a member in good standing, good defenses evolve over time in any event. For example, during Lil' Henry's trial, I was assisted by Mike Bewers, a young associate in our office. Mike was a bright young lawyer—but also very naive. Standing in the hallway at Tulane and Broad after the trial, he looked up at Lil' Henry and asked innocently, "Mr. DeFraites, where did the ruby come from?"

"Son, I eat strawberries and shit rubies," Lil' Henry said with a half grin.

FOURTEEN

The Saint

I love St. Bernard Parish. It's a defense lawyer's paradise. Located in the marshes on the outskirts of New Orleans, St. Bernard is the home of fishermen, oystermen, trappers, and smugglers. The descendants of the pirate Jean Lafitte and his crew must all live in St. Bernard. On election days, the busiest precinct in the parish is the one where the cemetery is located—a precinct where the registered voters outnumber the live population. I once represented a group of poll commissioners after an election in which the "cemetery vote" made the difference. Indeed, the government charged that some "ghosts" even voted twice. The cemetery precinct is also a very wealthy precinct. In another of my cases, millions of dollars in bank loans had been made to residents of the cemetery. In short, St. Bernard is a place where dragons love to feed.

Duggie Robin was from Ysclosky, a small fishing village in St. Bernard. His ancestors, like some of mine, came from the Canary Islands and he grew up speaking Spanish like everyone else in Ysclosky. Duggie looked like a pirate: small, compact, muscular, tanned and weathered; the only things missing were an eye patch, a red bandanna and a knife between his teeth. He cut a dashing picture. Rumor has it that Duggie's father used to smuggle supplies to German U-boats at the mouth of the Mississippi River during World War II.

Duggie had three brothers—Corky, Booby, and Ronnie. With their father, they established the Robin Seafood Company. After their father died in the early 1970s, Duggie and his brothers had a bitter falling-out. Duggie left his wife Doris and their four sons and moved to Honduras. There, he started a new seafood business with his second wife. Tasha was pretty, at least twenty years younger, and looked as if she had been rescued from a Caribbean island. Duggie and Tasha started a second family. Then disaster struck in 1979. A hurricane destroyed his two fishing boats so Duggie and his new family returned to St. Bernard.

Duggie and his four sons from his first marriage, Pete, Chris, Brad, and Don, reestablished the Robin Seafood Company. They worked very hard together, and every day they had their noon meal, called dinner, at "Mama's." Tasha and the younger children would also join them for dinner at Doris' home. Duggie was quite a man!

In the meantime, Duggie's brothers had been convicted of drug smuggling. Of course, the scuttlebutt was that Duggie was also a drug smuggler. Supposedly, as a diversion, he had tipped off the DEA about his brothers' load in order to successfully land his own load on the same night.

In September of 1984, Duggie and Brad were arrested and charged with conspiracy to import marijuana. The case was what is called an historical case, since they had not been arrested in the act of importing any marijuana. The government's principal witnesses were Lynn Breeland and William White, two admitted drug smugglers, who claimed that Duggie had been involved with them in importing two loads of marijuana in 1980. There was another witness, Ernie Stein, an undercover agent who had infiltrated the Robin clan and had secretly taped some of their conversations.

Although Duggie was arrested in September, the indictment had been returned under seal the previous month. During this one month interim, the government outfitted Breeland with a body mike and she recorded a long conversation with Duggie. Always the ladies' man, he flirted, drank, and talked with her about drug smuggling. However, the conversation only related to future drug smuggling, and no mention was made of the two loads they allegedly had imported in 1980.

I represented Duggie and O'Grady represented Brad. The case was allotted to Judge Adrian Duplantier. A trial before Judge Duplantier was never a pleasant experience but that was true for both sides since he was equally hard on everyone. A smart judge who didn't tolerate bullshit from anybody. O'Grady would be at a disadvantage. But then, right before trial, O'Grady and Maddie took a long Caribbean cruise on his sailboat. It seems that saltwater, particularly Caribbean saltwater, soothed the stump. Mills had to replace him at the last moment.

We filed a motion to suppress the Breeland tape on the grounds that it violated the right to counsel since it had been made after the return of the indictment. The Judge agreed and suppressed the tape.

Most lawyers fear hearsay. It is generally inadmissible as evidence because of its intrinsic untrustworthiness. It's like gossip and rumor. In this case, however, I embraced hearsay in my opening statement:

> " . . . the evidence will show . . . that because of his three other brothers having been involved in smuggling, because of the rumor mill that you find in small localities, because of the fact that they are fishermen, we will show you that the Federal Government—and this is no secret—the Federal Government clearly suspected Duggie and his

sons of being involved in drug smuggling. We will show to you the fact that they have been under constant surveillance. Their boats have been checked, the trucks that they use to ship the seafood out have been checked, and never have they even been arrested with any marijuana found in their possession or, for that matter, any drug . . . no prior criminal record whatsoever except for the fact I think Duggie might have shot too many ducks on one occasion, which is not uncommon in that area."

I also conscripted the government's undercover agent as my own, another unorthodox tactic:

"For one whole year during this two and a half year period of the conspiracy charged by the government—for almost a whole year—the government had an agent, one of their own agents, masquerading as a friend of the Robins. He was tape recording. And he spent almost a year watching them, having been accepted into their confidence. And it is true that there were some conversations where there was some discussion about importing or bringing in large amounts of marijuana, that the undercover agent brought up; and there were discussions, but nothing ever came of it. Nothing. Nothing at all."

During its case-in-chief, the government presented a parade of convicted drug smugglers, all of whom testified that Duggie had imported marijuana with them. On cross-examination, I used these witnesses to illustrate the typical profile of a drug smuggler: the millions of dollars in cash, the fancy cars, the heavy gold jewelry, the big mansions, the lack of a legitimate source of income. In our defense, we showed the jury photographs contrasting Duggie's two hundred fifty dollar per month apartment with the big houses of his brothers. We also put on the testimony of the company's CPA in order to demonstrate that he was involved in a legitimate seafood business.

I then played my Ace: the Breeland tape. Howie Peters, the prosecutor, went berserk, but the fact that the Judge had suppressed the tape due to the government's misconduct did not prevent us from using it in our defense. And in spite of the Judge's legalistic explanation, I suspect it appeared to the jury that the government had withheld something from them. Precisely the image we wanted to create.

In closing argument, the Breeland tape became our most important piece of evidence:

"Now you have to ask yourselves if the government is so satisfied with the testimony of Lynn Breeland and William

White—they want you to believe them, they get up here and tell you they are good witnesses—you ask yourselves this question: If they are so satisfied with those two witnesses, why, why, after the indictment has already been returned . . . did they feel it necessary to send Lynn Breeland and William White with secret tape recorders on them to go down and try to get incriminating testimony against Duggie Robin? Why? Why? They went there secretly recording him like a bounty hunter. They went there to get evidence on Duggie and, as you will remember, that tape was played by me, and I submit to you it may be a little hard to hear, but I submit to you that that tape, which took place just in September of '84, that tape patently proves the innocence of my client, and I will tell you why.

Now it is true in that tape—it's a three-hour conversation—that Duggie is drinking. This is his friend, Lynn Breeland. They are flirting; they flirt together. She is talking about wanting to marry him when he becomes a millionaire. She brings up this cocaine deal.

Listen to that tape. She brings it up. She has got to explain the whole thing. You will become convinced that she is not talking to a schooled drug smuggler. It is like she's talking to a first grader, explaining to him what a kilo is, how many ounces, how much it costs, how much you can sell it for. She dominates the tape, and it is true that she does get him talking about, ' . . . okay, yeah, that sounds good; we're going to do it, Baby; we're going to do it, Baby; anything you want, Baby.' Then he changes the subject. She brings him back to it, and she brings him back, but he said, 'no question about it, we're going to do it, Baby,' and they're drinking, and he takes her to a restaurant, and they're talking about all kinds of things. And she wants to try to get him to come up with a hundred thousand dollars. This is the telltale of this tape.

* * * * *

Now you ask yourselves. These conspirators—supposed to be conspirators with William White and Lynn Breeland—meeting to do a deal over a three-hour period of time, trying to get him to come up with the hundred thousand dollars; in view of their own testimony, is it reasonable that during that whole period of time there is not one reference to the so-called past events, that five years later, four years later, we are in a courtroom trying to defend? You ask yourselves, is that reasonable, and I submit to you that it is not. I submit to you that the absolute proof of his innocence is in that tape that the government made—that the government secretly made to get further damaging evidence against him because they are not satisfied with their own witnesses; and it boomeranged, and it backfired, and I want you to listen to that tape, and keep in mind, also, nothing ever came of it. Nothing ever came of it. There was never any hundred thousand dollars. There was never any cocaine. Nothing ever came of it."

The difficulty with defending a conspiracy case is that one can be found guilty even though the object of the conspiracy is never accomplished. Indeed, in a drug conspiracy, it's not even necessary for an overt act to have been committed in furtherance of the conspiracy. It's a very far-reaching crime, and for that reason, it's known as the "darling of the prosecution." Legally, it's the closest thing to guilt by association. The only thing separating the two is an agreement, a state of mind. Here is how I explained it to Duggie's jury:

"Conspiracy punishes group thoughts and, because of that, it's extremely important that you pay very close attention to the facts and to the duty that you have, because no one can deliver to you a picture of the inside of a person's mind. In a conspiracy, conspirators don't sit down and write up a big agreement and sign it and have it notarized; they don't do that. So that you, as the finders of fact, will be called upon to decide whether or not, in the mind of this man, there was a criminal thought that matched the criminal thought in another person's mind so that there was an agreement.

Now intent—thought—as I said, no one can give you a photograph of it, but you're entitled to infer a person's thoughts from his words and his actions, so you're going to have to sit down and consider evidence of what was said and what was done, and through that infer whether or not there was a criminal conspiracy—a crime of group thought.

Now my suggestion, my analogy is this. If you can remember the old Saturday afternoon westerns, the scene where you have the bad guys in their hideout and they sit around and they discuss and decide that they are going to go into town and rob the bank. They all get on their horses and ride into town and rob the bank and go back to their hideout. I would suggest to you that you could find from those facts, (a) a conspiracy, and (b) a violation of the substantive crime of armed robbery.

Now let's suppose that that bad gang is sitting up in their hideout in the hills and they decide—they case this town, they know that on every Thursday afternoon the sheriff leaves town and he goes fishing. So, they decide that they're going to rob the bank, they're going to do it on a Thursday afternoon when the sheriff is out of town. They ride into town, get off their horses, each take their stations, put on their masks, pull out their guns. All of a sudden, the sheriff rounds the corner, so they all jump on their horses and flee back to their hideout.

I suggest to you that from such evidence you can find no substantive violation. The bank was never robbed, but you could, you could infer and find a conspiracy because there was a discussion and there was activity, and from the words and from what was done—from the putting on of the masks, the pulling out of the guns, seeing the sheriff and then fleeing—you could infer from that that there was group criminal thought, and you could find them guilty of a conspiracy.

Now, on the other hand, if in that same atmosphere, in the same movie you have got a bunch of cowhands who work hard all day long, they come into town on Friday night, sit down at the saloon and get drunk; they talk, they have a good time. They're talking about all sorts of things. There's this macho thing about them, and they draw up an elaborate plan to commit the perfect crime. The perfect crime: they're going to rob the bank, and it is a perfect plan. Then they all go home drunk, go to bed, get up and go to work the next day and the next day and the next day. Then they may come back to town the next Friday night, get drunk, come up with another elaborate plan, go home drunk that night, and come back to work the next day. I submit from such evidence that you can conclude that there was no conspiracy. They talked about it, they drew plans, but you could infer from the fact that they were talking, that they were drinking, the fact that they were cowpokes, the fact that they were hard workers, the fact of their life style, from all of that, and from the fact that they didn't do it, you can infer from that that there is no group criminality—no group thought criminality.

Take it even further. You have got the cowhands. They come in and sit around the saloon, and they talk about it, and there's Bell, a beautiful girl, and some slick sidekick of hers, and she tells him, 'Man, you really ought to rob that bank, because we ought to get a lot of money and go to San Francisco and have a high life.' And maybe the next morning one young fellow or two old fellows, they may even go and look at a cave and say that would be a good place to hide the loot, and they may sit down in the dust and draw a map of how to get in town, how to get back to hide the stash in the cave, but then nothing happens. It would be up to you, the jury, to consider what was said, to consider how it was said, to consider what was done and what was not done. You can, from the fact that it was not done, infer that in this man's mind there was not really a sealed agreement to join group thought—criminal thought."

The jury found Duggie not guilty. Now Duggie wasn't my best paying client, but he brought us an awful lot of seafood. Years later, a frozen body was found in a St. Bernard bayou, and rumor was the body had been stored in the freezer at the Robin Seafood Company. When I told this to R.A. and the children, they never again ate seafood from a client.

FIFTEEN

The Blue Knight

Stephen Rosiere always wanted to be a cop. After high school, he went into the Navy and then returned to New Orleans and entered the New Orleans Police Academy. After graduating from the Academy, he worked as a policeman for fourteen years. He loved it. His wife Madeline, on the other hand, hated his job. She didn't like the long, irregular hours, the low pay, the danger. During holidays, when good husbands were at home, Steve wasn't there with their two young daughters. She hated the job so much that she hounded him into quitting and selling insurance for two years. She was happy; he was miserable. On July 14, 1983, Steve rejoined the NOPD. He couldn't help it; it was in his blood. He was assigned to the Sixth District, which is known as "Fort Apache" because of its high crime rate.

Six weeks later on the night of August 30, Steve and his new partner, Fred McFarland, were assigned to Car 608, a "hot" car—one that responds to problems in progress, as distinguished from a one-man unit that handles follow-up investigations. Around midnight, the partners were driving on Louisiana Avenue toward the river when they noticed a motorcycle speeding in the opposite direction. McFarland made a U-turn and gave chase to the motorcycle down Louisiana Avenue, Toledano Street, Washington Avenue, across Carrollton Avenue, and finally onto the Palmetto Street overpass.

The motorcycle was being driven by Raney Brooks, a young black male, and the sixteen year old passenger sitting behind him, Gerard Glover, ironically, was the son of a policewoman. During the chase, with blue lights and siren on, the cops followed the motorcycle through red lights and stop signs, around tricky curves, and over bumps and potholes, reaching speeds of ninety and ninety-five miles per hour. At the foot of the overpass, the cops screamed over the police radio:

> "608, shots fired. (Pause) What's your location? (Pause) 608, what's your location? (Pause) . . . (unclear to

> Reporter) . . . (Pause) Got a 108. 608, give me your last location. (Pause) Subject on Palmetto overpass, shots fired. (Pause) Your last location is Palmetto, headed toward J.P., 108, shots fired. (Pause) 608, keep me advised. (Pause) 2564, I'm in plain-clothes."

A single shot fired by Steve out of the passenger window of Car 608 hit Gerard Glover in the back, knocking him from the motorcycle and causing him to roll up the overpass to its crest. Raney Brooks sped away as Car 608 reached the top of the overpass. The partners exited their vehicle, examined Gerard, and McFarland then resumed the chase in Car 608. A few minutes later, he radioed to the dispatcher that he had lost the motorcycle on Bamboo Road, and he rejoined Steve at the top of the overpass. By this time, other police officers and medical technicians had arrived on the scene. The partners then drove to the other side of the overpass, by Bamboo Road, where Steve supposedly "found" a gun without a clip in it. Later that night, Gerard Glover died in Charity Hospital.

Since a shot fired by a policeman resulted in a death, the NOPD automatically conducted a criminal investigation. Also, the Office of Municipal Investigations (OMI), an independent watch dog agency, conducted its own investigation. Statements were taken from Steve and McFarland. The partners said that when they reached the foot of the overpass, they heard "pops," saw "flashes," and, believing that they were being fired upon, they radioed the "108" distress signal. The partners maintained Steve returned fire only after seeing the outstretched arm of Glover pointing toward them.

The black community was in an uproar. Shortly before, some white police officers had been indicted for killing a black man in the so-called Algiers incident. The black leadership was convinced that Glover's death was another example of white policemen executing an innocent black youth. It was a very tense time in New Orleans.

Detective Dave Morales took charge of the investigation. A few days after the shooting, he reviewed the transcript of the radio communications between Car 608 and the police dispatcher. Something didn't ring true. At one point, McFarland said he had lost the motorcycle on Bamboo Road, yet at another point he said he had lost the motorcycle at the foot of the overpass. Detective Morales confronted him with the discrepancy.

After the confrontation, McFarland met with Steve at a Tastee Donut Shop and told him that Detective Morales suspected them of not telling the truth. The partners decided to change their stories. Still maintaining they were fired upon, the partners agreed to say that Steve's gun accidentally discharged when Car 608 hit a bump. Under the revised version, Steve admitted he planted a "drop gun" on Bamboo Road because they hadn't found a weapon at the scene.

Admitting the drop gun naturally created a public outcry. The partners were immediately suspended, and a grand jury investigation got underway. Steve went before the grand jury and testified in accordance with the Tastee Donut version. Without his knowledge, however, McFarland retained a lawyer, received immunity from the DA, and completely changed his story. In exchange for the immunity, he told the grand jury that the 108 distress signal was made after, not before Steve fired his weapon; that he never saw any pops and flashes; that he lied to the dispatcher when he said shots were being fired at them; and that he was never in fear of being harmed that night by the subjects on the motorcycle. In an about-face, he swore that as they approached the overpass Steve pulled out his weapon and said, "I'm going to shoot." After firing, Steve said, "I missed," but then, "Oh, fuck, I hit him," as "the subject on the back of the bike fell off." According to McFarland, they then exited the police car and at this point they hatched the cover-up plot by making it appear, through the phony 108 distress signal, that they had been fired upon. After leaving Steve alone on top of the overpass, McFarland said, he resumed the chase as a pretext, purposely allowing Brooks to escape because "he could collaborate [sic] that no shots were fired, and that there were no weapons." Finally, after rejoining Steve, McFarland claimed, the two of them drove back to Bamboo Road where Steve took a gun from his briefcase in the trunk of the car, dropped it and, a few moments later, pretended to find it while other officers were nearby.

Under the terms of McFarland's deal, he was not charged with any criminal offense—not even malfeasance—and he was permitted to keep his job as a policeman. Steve, on the other hand, was indicted for second degree murder.

As his defense counsel, Steve retained Joe Meyer, who had left the DA's office for private practice. Because of the tremendous amount of racial tension in New Orleans over the case, Joe moved for a change of venue. Then a new twist developed. All of the Tulane and Broad judges recused themselves because Steve's stepmother had been a court employee for more than twenty-five years. Because of this development, the Supreme Court appointed Judge John Covington of Baton Rouge to try the case. Since Judge Covington did not have to run for reelection in New Orleans, Joe withdrew the change of venue motion, waived a jury trial, and tried the case before him. In hindsight, a big mistake. The Judge found Steve guilty of second degree murder and sentenced him to life imprisonment at hard labor without the benefit of parole, probation, or suspension of sentence.

Joe filed a motion for a new trial on the grounds that the DA had failed to disclose to the defense two pieces of critical evidence. First, the DA had not given Joe a statement the police had obtained from William Helfand, a reserve police officer and Tulane law student. According to Helfand's statement, he and his girlfriend, Donna Oakleaf, were driving in the opposite direction on the overpass when they saw the chase in progress. Hearing the 108 distress signal over his police radio, he made a U-turn to join the pursuit, and arriving at the scene almost immediately after the fatal shot had been fired, he got out of his car as " . . . the two district men were just getting out of their car, and one of them yelled to me that the man on the ground had a gun."

The second piece of critical evidence that had not been disclosed to Joe was a statement the OMI had obtained from police officer Michael Glasser. According to Glasser's statement, he was in his car at the intersection of Washington Avenue and Broad Street at approximately twelve twenty-five when he saw the motorcycle, followed by Car 608, pass by at a high rate of speed. He immediately joined the pursuit, and while Car 608 was still in the chase, he heard the 108 distress signal over his police radio. At that point, he advised the dispatcher, " . . . I was 2564, I'd be with them in plainclothes." He arrived on the scene immediately after Helfand.

The statements of Helfand and Glasser were obviously inconsistent with the State's case. Both said they heard the 108 distress signal while the chase was still in progress, thereby contradicting McFarland's claim that it was a part of the cover-up the partners concocted after examining Glover's body and not finding a weapon. In spite of this inconsistency, however, the Judge denied the new trial motion.

I was hired to do the appeal and, ultimately, the Supreme Court granted a new trial because of the DA's nondisclosure of the exculpatory evidence. Fortunately, Steve would have a second chance.

Judge Patrick Quinlan would preside over the second trial. New to the bench, Quinlan didn't have the long-standing employee relationship with Steve's stepmother that the other judges had at Tulane and Broad. As a former Assistant Attorney General, however, he had been consulted by the DA's office over McFarland's immunity. And so he offered to recuse himself for that reason, but I declined, believing him to be a fair judge with the strength and character to do the right thing. He was my kind of judge and my kind of man.

What we needed most in the case was a change of venue. Tulane and Broad juries are mostly black, and a black jury in New Orleans would no more acquit Steve Rosiere than would a black jury convict O. J. Simpson years later in Los Angeles. This is not racism; it's reality. As any dragon slayer knows, the fox sees the world differently than the hen.

Joe Walker, the pollster who helped us in Dr. Beasley's case, did a survey in order to determine whether Steve could receive a fair trial in New Orleans. Prospective jurors, like people in general, don't always tell the truth during the selection process, sometimes for evil reasons but more often than not simply to avoid embarrassment. Through the Walker survey, we were able to demonstrate that the feeling in the black community against white policemen was so deep and pervasive at that time and place, that *voir dire* alone could not assure a fair trial. Judge

Quinlan did the right thing and changed the venue to Lafayette. As I said, my kind of judge.

I once argued a case before the Supreme Court in which a defendant made a confession in Lafayette without the assistance of his lawyer. It appeared that the sheriff, believing the lawyer was drunk, would not allow him in the jail to consult with his client. During argument, Justice Marcus asked whether it wasn't true that the founding fathers had assumed a "sober lawyer" in guaranteeing the right to counsel. I replied, "Not in Lafayette, Your Honor." In fact, Lafayette has some great restaurants and night spots and, undoubtedly, Judge Quinlan had that in mind when he moved the trial there. As I said, my kind of man.

Having the right venue, we now needed the right team. O'Grady, with his scientific bent, would handle the forensic witnesses since I never advanced beyond arithmetic or high school biology except to learn that a man and woman have the same number of ribs. We also needed to know the lay of the land, and Julie Conlin, a lawyer working in the Lafayette area, joined the team. Finally, we needed a good investigator. My old foe, John Dillmann, had left the police force to become a private investigator and, although we had fought each other hard in the Candy Smith case, we had a mutual respect for each other. He joined the defense and it was good having him on the right side this time.

Dillmann, as an ex-policeman, worked well with Helfand and Glasser, the two friendly police witnesses. Additionally, he located two other witnesses who lived near the overpass and who heard more than one gunshot that night. This evidence was inconsistent with McFarland's story that the only gunshot that night came from Steve's weapon. We also reenacted the high-speed chase. With O'Grady driving as fast as he could and with Dillmann hanging out of the car's sunroof with a video camera, we tried to cover the same distance in the same amount of time as Car 608 had covered on that fateful night. Although we were never able to match the time and speed, the video reenactment would provide dramatic proof to the jury of the overwhelming eeriness of the chase.

Eventually, we moved into the Lafayette Hilton to continue our trial preparation. Steve was extremely nervous and cried a lot. He had not testified in the trial before Judge Covington and we were determined to have him ready to testify this time. Dillmann spent most of his time rehearsing him. In the evenings, we met at the hotel bar for before-dinner drinks—except for O'Grady, who was still having after-lunch drinks. One night when he didn't show and the phone didn't answer in his room, an alarmed Dillmann obtained an extra room key from the front desk. As he opened the door to the room, O'Grady's leg floated out on a wave of water. Suspecting mayhem, the ex-homicide detective was relieved to discover that O'Grady had merely passed out in the tub with water running, while he soaked the stump.

I called Maddie to tell her we had found him and she, too, was relieved to know it was all stump-related. R.A. and Slim never understood how she brought such misery upon herself by sticking with him but, to my way of thinking, Maddie was a nurturing woman, a good woman, and we stayed on the phone that night for a long time.

As trial approached, we realized the most important piece of evidence in the case was the police tape of the radio dispatcher. And like Detective Morales, we too realized something didn't ring true. The timing was all wrong for McFarland's version. To demonstrate the point, we prepared a transcript of the tape with time differentials marked off between the key events.

After the jury was selected, I laid out the defense in the opening statement:

> "So Rosiere stays at the top of the overpass with Helfand. McFarland then proceeds to go and look for the driver of the motorcycle. Before he leaves, he says—one, two, and you'll hear this on the tape, he says three times—McFarland said three times on the radio: 'The subjects are popping caps at us.' Popping a cap is police jargon for shooting a weapon. So McFarland is on the radio. He's on the radio within eleven seconds after the 108 is kicked in. McFarland is on the radio saying this because at this time the car is stopped. He now can talk on the radio and he is telling the dispatcher shots were being fired. Caps were being popped at us. He then goes and attempts to find the driver of the motorcycle.
>
> Within about twenty-six seconds after he leaves, he comes on the radio and he says, 'I've lost the subject on Bamboo Road.' When you go over the overpass, you then get into this real desolate area back over here. It's not really on this map, but right in there is a very—it's almost like a little lane and it's full of bamboo and it's called Bamboo Road. Twenty-six seconds after McFarland leaves here, he radios in that he's lost the subject.
>
> Now what actually happened is that McFarland at this point knows that the subject has been hit. He knows that there's no gun in the area where they stopped to examine the young man. Helfand is immediately on the scene. McFarland then goes off by himself. So McFarland is by himself on Bamboo Road. McFarland knows that Rosiere has in his briefcase in the trunk of the car that McFarland is driving—he's got the keys—he knows that in Rosiere's briefcase is a gun, a drop gun. He takes the weapon and he drops it in this area on Bamboo Road. He then comes back and joins Rosiere, Helfand, the fallen subject, and by

> this time there's police cars all in this area.
>
> He then tells Rosiere that he couldn't find the subject, he couldn't find a weapon, so that he dropped a weapon back in the area of Bamboo Road. Well Rosiere has a fit. See, number one, why would someone drop—I mean, the shooting occurred at the top of the overpass. This is where the fallen body was. Why would someone drop a weapon way over here on Bamboo Road. Number one, he shouldn't have dropped the weapon at all. Number two, if you're going to drop a weapon, why would you drop the weapon back on Bamboo Road.
>
> What then happens is Rosiere decides to get McFarland to go with him because Rosiere wants to retrieve the gun. You will see from the tape that before they leave the top of the overpass . . . you will hear McFarland on the radio four minutes and twenty-two seconds after the 108 . . . telling the dispatcher: 'By the way, I want you to know that when I was back here on Bamboo Road a couple of minutes ago looking for the fleeing subject, the driver of the motorcycle took shots at me.' They then—McFarland and Rosiere—go to the Bamboo Road area. McFarland shows Rosiere where he put the gun. Rosiere goes, picks up the gun. At this time, there are other police officers all in this area and one policeman sees Rosiere with the gun and says, 'Oh, you found the pipe,'—which is another police word for a weapon. And Rosiere then made his first horrible mistake of that night; he said, 'Yes, I found the gun.'"

The State's lead witness was Raney Brooks, a real punk. Dressed in leather with gold necklaces and earrings, Brooks corroborated McFarland's version: no shots had been fired at Car 608, and his motorcycle had not backfired. On cross-examination, I brought out his criminal record and the fact that the motorcycle had been stolen.

Of course, McFarland was the State's principal witness. Not only was he a weasel, but he looked like one. Small, bespectacled, with a wimpish voice, he recounted his tale of the cover-up and the drop gun. During cross-examination, with a large blackboard behind me, I had him identify each of his earlier assertions to the police that he now claimed was false. They were so numerous, I had him simply raise his hand for each lie, and each time he raised his hand, I put a mark on the blackboard. At one point, the following occurred:

> Lemann: "Excuse me. Excuse me, do you want to raise your hand?"

McFarland: "For what?"

Lemann: "Are you telling the truth right here?"

Reluctantly, he held up his hand like a schoolboy. Altogether, when the cross-examination was over, there were forty-one marks on the blackboard, more than the symbolic thirty pieces of silver I was hoping for.

For our defense, we called a motorcycle expert who had been hired by the OMI to reenact the chase. According to the expert, when his motorcycle hit a bump at the foot of the overpass, he accidentally hit the "kill" button, causing the motorcycle to backfire. We called an OMI investigator who had found a spent bullet at the crest of the overpass. It was not the type used by the NOPD and supported our theory that someone other than Steve had fired a gun that night on the overpass. We called Helfand and Glasser and the witnesses who had heard more than one gunshot. We played our video reenactment of the chase and, lastly, we put Steve on the stand. Having a former cop on his team did wonders for his self-confidence and he made an excellent witness.

In closing argument, I told the jury:

> " . . . we've demonstrated to you that Raney Brooks is completely untrustworthy. He claims that he had no knowledge, first of all, that the motorcycle that he was on was a stolen motorcycle. There's no question that the motorcycle was stolen. We've proved that and the State stipulates to that. The question becomes: did he have knowledge of the fact that it was stolen? Well he had keys that only operated the ignition. The license plate on the motorcycle disappears. . . . Well the reason that there was no plate on the motorcycle was because Raney Brooks ditched it—threw it away—because he knew it was stolen; and the reason he was fleeing that night was because he knew he was on a stolen motorcycle, and for a man to say that his good friend who was riding as a passenger on the back of that motorcycle and who ultimately died because of this high speed chase, that that young person entered into a mutual agreement with him to flee from the police to avoid a traffic citation for the passenger is absolutely incredulous and you cannot place any weight on the testimony of Raney Brooks. Had Raney Brooks done what anyone of us in this courtroom would have done if a police car was behind us and put on a blue light, had he pulled over on the side of the road, had he taken his traffic ticket like anyone of us would have done, none of us

> would be here today and young Gerard Glover would be alive today."

But my main target, of course, was McFarland:

> "September 6 is the mirror into the soul of McFarland. I should say the mirror into the black soul of McFarland because there you see Judas at work. This Judas who sold his forty-one lies for thirty pieces of silver of immunity. There you see the kiss on the cheek. McFarland is brought in. He's confronted. He's the one who lied on the radio. Morales has done the same thing that I invite you to do. He's a trained homicide detective. He did exactly what I invite you to do. Go to that tape. That's the evidence in this case, that tape. See who lies on that tape. McFarland is the one who lies on that tape and he's confronted and he's accused and what does he do? He takes this sparrow, this simple, gentle, unthinking, not too bright man, he takes him to the Last Supper. He takes him to get coffee and doughnuts and he brings him back and he delivers him on a silver tray. Take him. That's what he did. He served up his partner. He served him up. He sold him for thirty pieces of silver. That's what he did. He delivered him and he still continues to lie."

McFarland's story that the gun was planted by Steve after the two of them drove to Bamboo Road was simply not supported by the tape:

> "And this, ladies and gentlemen, was the first lie on that tape. Three minutes and thirty-seven seconds after that 108, McFarland says, '608 for additional. I was driving over the overpass. The subject had stopped the motorcycle and continued shooting at me as I was coming over.' Now when you analyze what was said . . . this is the first reference by McFarland that someone shot at him three minutes ago. Now three minutes ago doesn't sound like a lot of time, but you know that's why I kept eliciting that testimony about a policeman and his radio. You know a policeman and his radio is no different than an airline pilot and his radio when his plane is crashing and it's no different from a soldier and his radio in a foxhole when he's being fired upon. You don't lie to that radio. This call about the additional information was the first non-simultaneous communication and it was the first lie. This is like a pilot in a crashing plane lying to his radio or it's like a soldier who says on his radio, 'By the way, when I was down the mountain by

myself, the Nazis were shooting at me.' Three minutes under fire is an eternity. This is when the lie begins. This is the first non-simultaneous conversation. It's the first lie and it's the lie of McFarland because he knew after Rosiere told him, 'What the hell are you doing planting a gun a mile away,' he knew that he had to cover up for what he did; so he gets on the radio and says, by the way, three minutes ago they were firing at me on the other side of the mountain. That just doesn't fly. That's your lie."

There was yet another reason why I was convinced McFarland had planted the gun:

> "I'm going to tell you something else that's the proof of what I'm telling you. There were only two people that night who knew that Rosiere had a gun in his briefcase in the trunk of McFarland's car. McFarland knew it and Rosiere knew it, but only one of those two people knew that the gun didn't have a clip in it. Only one knew that it didn't. That was Rosiere. So McFarland goes and drops a gun thinking that it's a functional weapon when it doesn't have a clip in it. Now why—why—would any sensible person who's going to drop a gun, number one, drop a gun a mile away from where the shooting occurred, and number two, drop a gun that didn't have a clip in it? And when the police find the weapon and they see that it doesn't have a clip, McFarland is the one who says the subject must have thrown it in the woods. 'Go look in the woods.' So he's got the policemen scurrying off going through the woods looking for a clip that Stephen Rosiere knew all along was never in the gun. McFarland planted that gun. Stephen Rosiere committed malfeasance in office in not reporting him and in continuing to cover up McFarland's error in judgment. The proof is on the tape, ladies and gentlemen. It's on the tape as plain as day."

Unquestionably, Steve and McFarland were both guilty of malfeasance and, as such, unworthy of being police officers. The DA might have been justified in charging Steve with negligent homicide, but not with murder. The charging decision had not been grounded in justice, but rather, in politics:

> "Look at the results of this. You've got one good policewoman who lost her son. You've got one good policeman who's standing on trial for his life, and you've got a rotten policeman still on the beat."

Turning into the home stretch, I told the jury:

> "A one-man judgmental call in the course of human events often results in error. . . . This is so even in the quiet decorum of a studied courtroom and this, of course, is far removed from a judgmental call made in the chaos and cacophony of squealing sirens, flashing lights, roaring engines, cascading down swerving roads through blind spots and darkness, across unsuspecting and uncontrolled intersections at terrifying speeds, all the while feeling the loneliness and despair of being on the wrong end of a 108. The racing heartbeats, the sweating hands, the tingling backbones, the red, bulging face of a mind bursting from an adrenaline overflow pumped incessantly by the hunter's mission and the fear of the unknown, inevitable, final strike of the pursued. The pop and the flash at the end of the chase.
>
> Policemen know that one-man judgmental calls are seldom made during the chase syndrome. Partners act in an unarticulated unison. Rosiere's shot was no more single-handed than was McFarland's acceleration of the vehicle after Rosiere unholstered his weapon. . . . When he rolled down his window, McFarland had his foot on the accelerator; when he leaned out of the window, McFarland had his foot on the accelerator; when he took aim, McFarland had his foot on the accelerator; and when he pulled the trigger, McFarland had his foot on the accelerator.
>
> The only truly one-man judgmental call made in this case was McFarland's cowardly decision to seek immunity to escape joint responsibility for the wrong decision made—not when the shot was fired but at the end of the chase. For planting the gun, both partners should suffer. But to send one to prison for life would be a miscarriage of justice. . . .
>
> For three long years, he's been accused of being a murderer. Three years. He can't look in his children's eyes or call their names without weeping in shame."

As he had done during his direct examination, Steve began to sob at this point—and some of the jurors began to cry. I smelled blood:

> "Now Stephen Rosiere, this gentle man, this blue knight, will never again wear the marshal's star, but you, ladies

> and gentlemen, you need to restore to him a badge of honor. You need to unshackle the handcuffs of despair. You need to let him hear again the sirens of freedom, and I ask you to do this not just for him, not just for his wife, not just for his children. I ask you to do this for all good policemen who everyday put their lives on the line for you and me for little pay, scant thanks, and no glory. You must return a verdict of not guilty."

When I turned around to walk back to the defense table, I saw John Dillmann in the back of the courtroom wipe a tear from his eye. I knew then that if I could reach the heart of an ex-homicide cop, I had struck deeply. The jury found Steve not guilty.

Unfortunately, the dead dragon had a twin on the prowl. The United States Justice Department indicted Steve for the murder of Gerard Glover as a civil rights violation and, if convicted, he could receive a life sentence. The new indictment also meant the federal trial would take place in New Orleans. Because the federal district encompassed a thirteen parish area, it would be impossible to make the same kind of showing we had made at Tulane and Broad for a change of venue.

The case was allotted to Judge A. J. McNamara, a tough judge, but a fair one. That was good enough for me. What we needed in the case was a meaningful *voir dire*. Relying upon the Walker survey to demonstrate how sensitive the case was to many people, the Judge conducted an individualized *voir dire* in chambers and permitted us to question each prospective juror in a meaningful manner.

The FBI was now involved in the case along with prosecutors from Washington, D.C.—one even in a wheelchair; but I still had O'Grady on his cane. More importantly, the evidence didn't change. Stephen Rosiere was found not guilty for a second time. The twin dragons were dead at last.

SIXTEEN

THE CHOCOLATE KNIGHT

I was at Palo Alto when I received a call from my former law school classmate, Manny Fernandez, now Counsel to Governor Buddy Roemer. Manny asked if I would be willing to represent the State of Louisiana in a multimillion dollar lawsuit filed as a class action by the Children's Rights Project of the American Civil Liberties Union (ACLU). I was nonplussed. Why would a criminal defense lawyer and card-carrying ACLU member, like me, want to represent the State against poor little foster children? Manny knew, however, that the State needed someone accustomed to defending unpopular causes—and he knew that a dragon slayer can never walk away from a challenge. After all, even Goliath is entitled to a lawyer. I took the case and became a special assistant attorney general.

The Children's Rights Project of the ACLU targets states with poor child welfare statistics and seeks to accomplish social reform through litigation. Their legal team was headed by Marcie Lowery, a renowned children's rights advocate in New York City.

The Louisiana lawsuit was brought on behalf of the State's six thousand foster children and sought both damages and injunctive relief. It alleged the failure of the State to provide necessary services to prevent the need for foster care; the failure of the State to provide adequate services to protect children in foster care; and the failure of the State to provide adequate services to remove children from foster care in a timely fashion. If the ACLU were successful in the case, the reforms would cost Louisiana approximately twenty-five million dollars annually.

Once in the case, I quickly realized it was one without villains. Everyone sympathized with the children, and rightfully so, as many of them presented truly tragic figures. For example Flemming G came into state custody at six months of age when his mother abandoned him. He had twenty-four placements during his twelve years in state custody. These placements included institutional settings, foster homes, specialized foster homes, and group homes. He was placed in pre-adoptive homes several times, but all of them disrupted. He was identified as needing psychiatric treatment but didn't receive it until a year later, only to have the therapeutic relationship broken—against the advice of his therapist—in order to effectuate a foster home placement. At ten years old, he began to run away. Indeed, he ran away on four separate occasions and actually, he was on runaway status at the time of trial.

On the other hand, I also realized the state officials in charge of the foster care system were not Simon Legrees but, in the main, were bleeding hearts who really wanted the best for the children. And while the difference between the ACLU and the state officials was philosophical, it was as vast and deep as one might expect, given that the subject matter was how best to raise a child. The ACLU advocated a more structured approach with unbending time lines, while the state officials adopted a more pragmatic, result-oriented approach.

When I entered the case, the State had already moved to dismiss the damage claims on the grounds of qualified immunity. Public officials generally are insulated from money damages as long as they do not violate clearly established constitutional or statutory rights. Otherwise, public officials could not be expected to perform effectively the discretionary acts required of them. The motion to dismiss, however, had been denied by the trial court and, therefore, my first task on behalf of the State was an interlocutory appeal—that is, an appeal before the actual trial on the merits.

Ironically, my old foes on the Court of Appeals now became my allies. Most appellate judges are extremely conservative and have a very narrow view of constitutional rights, precisely what I was looking for in this case. I argued that the due process clause does not embrace a right to avoid the status of foster care. Despite this brilliant (and cold-hearted) argument, the Court of Appeals affirmed the trial court; but on the strength of a very strong dissenting opinion from a very conservative judge, the State was granted a rehearing *en banc*—a seldom used judicial proceeding whereby all of the judges on an appellate court reconsider a decision of a three-judge panel. Among the federal courts of appeals in the country, ours is one of the more conservative, and the ACLU became very concerned over the national implications of a bad precedent. To avoid this prospect, the ACLU decided to voluntarily dismiss its damage claims against my clients. It was the beginning of the end.

Without the damage claims, the ACLU was left with only the equitable remedy of an injunction to prevent future wrongs. Injunctive relief, however, is not directly concerned with past misconduct and, accordingly, any past abuses in the foster care program were only indirectly related to the remaining issue of whether my clients were presently acting in good faith.

By this time, I'd had sufficient opportunity to assess my opposition. Unquestionably, on legal issues the ACLU lawyers were unbeatable—they lived and breathed child welfare law. However, there is more to good lawyering than knowing the law. In fact, it became apparent to me that the ACLU lawyers were not trial lawyers at all; rather, they were social reformers and, more aptly, zealots. While the Children's Rights Project had never lost a test case, neither had it won one after a full-blown trial. On the contrary, its so-called victories had been the result of settlements or consent decrees, and this was because the lawyers who had represented the child welfare agencies in the other states were also bleeding hearts.

I also had the home court advantage of knowing the judge and, in this case, the judge was none other than the Honorable Morey Sear. Let me tell you a secret about Judge Sear. There is a big difference between "having" court and "holding" court. Most judges "have" court each day and then go home for the evening. Judge Sear, on the other hand, "holds" court each day and takes it with him wherever he goes. Judges who have court, "preside"; judges who hold court, "reign." The zealots didn't know this secret.

Judge Sear had become quite a majestic figure on the bench or, as some might say, on his throne. In New Orleans, Jews don't participate much in Mardi Gras. It's a pity because Judge Sear would make such a marvelous Rex. Unlike many judges who don't like administrative work, he viewed it as part of his courtly duties, and, undoubtedly, he would revel in the opportunity to reign over the revamping of the Louisiana foster care program. This would be the next card I would play.

Brenda Kelley, lawyer, social worker, and the career bureaucrat who ran the Louisiana foster care program, was a crackerjack. She and I went to Judge Sear and suggested that, with his guidance, we could confect a consent decree which would put Louisiana on the cutting edge of child welfare. Predictably, he liked the idea and he mandated the drafting of a settlement plan by Brenda and the ACLU's local expert. Working diligently, they crafted a settlement plan that was acceptable to us but, as expected, the zealots rejected it even though it had been drafted in part by their own expert and approved by the Judge. Dragon slayers would never have made such a mistake.

It was now time to prepare the case for trial before the not-too-happy Judge. Mary Widmann, a lawyer with the Louisiana Department of Social Services, knew the foster care system better than anyone else, and she began the long, arduous task of teaching me. I wasn't a very good student, partly because I'm not very child-oriented—at least according to R.A. For example, our youngest child, Jonathan, was born at the same time as our neighbors' baby girl, who, unbeknownst to me, was at our home one morning having her diaper changed by R.A.; as I rushed out on my way to court, I stopped momentarily to do my parental duty, coochey-cooed the child under the chin, and said, "Good morning, Son." As I was saying, Mary began the long and arduous task of giving me lessons on the law of child care.

The social work experts used by the ACLU usually took very extreme positions. Foremost among them was the nationally renowned Dr.

Albert Solnit, the Yale University professor who had co-authored the famous book, *In the Best Interests of the Child*, with Sigmund Freud's daughter. Mary and I went to Yale to take Dr. Solnit's deposition. Professorial, arrogant, and inflexible, he was a firm believer in what is called the psychological parent. In his view, whenever a conflict arises between the psychological parent and the biological parent, it is always in the child's best interest for the psychological parent to prevail. Carried to its logical end, this meant, according to Dr. Solnit, that custody of a child should be awarded exclusively to the psychological parent, and that parent alone—without court intervention—should decide whether the biological parent has any rights at all, including the right to visit the child. I knew that this extreme viewpoint, which obviously encroached upon traditional judicial turf, wouldn't sit well with Judge Sear.

After taking Dr. Solnit's deposition, Mary and I got stranded in a New York City snow storm and spent the night at the Plaza, not the usual haunt of child welfare lawyers. But, as I said before, I had become addicted to Dr. Beasley's lifestyle. When we returned to New Orleans, we began to develop a trial strategy unlike any used before in similar cases.

Louisiana has a very elaborate legal system to oversee children in foster care and—unlike other individuals who are in state custody involuntarily, such as prison inmates or the mentally ill—each foster child is permanently assigned to a state court judge who periodically reviews the status of the child. Consequently, many of the child-care decisions at issue in the case actually had been approved by these juvenile court judges. Although other states had similar procedures, no one seemed to have focused upon this aspect of foster care.

Judge Sear loved being a judge and he respected other judges. Of course, everyone knows federal judges are the grandest of them all but, in spite of this, there is an institutional bias among judges to favor the decisions of other judges. Playing upon this theme, we decided, in effect, to put the juvenile court judges on trial instead of my clients. To focus on the point, we hired a retired state court judge, Tom Tanner, a folksy, "good ole' boy," as one of our experts, and we had him review the volumes and volumes of records relating to the ongoing juvenile court cases of the plaintiff-children. During the trial, Judge Tanner recounted the alternatives that had been available to the juvenile court judges who had made the decisions at issue and the reasons supporting those decisions.

Although everyone obviously sympathized with the plight of the children, many of them in truth were little rascals and, not wanting this fact to escape Judge Sear, I illustrated the point through cross-examination of the ACLU experts. For example:

> Lemann: "Now the record reflects, however, that the grandmother in 1983 called the agency up and said, 'come and take this child.'"

Witness: "That's right."

Lemann: "Is that right?"

Witness: "That's what happened."

Lemann: "And the grandmother, the record reflects the grandmother did this because, among other reasons, Leroy stole $500 from her."

Witness: "That was alleged, right."

Lemann: "And how old was Leroy?"

Witness: "Almost seven."

Lemann: "And he ran away from home?"

Witness: "Right."

Lemann: "And he cut his sister with a knife?"

Witness: "That was our report, right."

Lemann: "So the grandmother said, 'come and take Leroy'?"

Witness: "Right."

Lemann: "Now the record also reflects that Leroy has had a number of attempted placements in foster homes."

Witness: "That's right."

Lemann: "And have they disrupted?"

Witness: "That's right."

Lemann: "And the record reflects that Leroy likes to set fire to things?"

Witness: "I read that, yes."

Lemann: "Is that correct?"

Witness: "Yes."

Lemann: "And Leroy is—I don't want to use the phrase 'a bad kid'—but Leroy has some real specialized behavioral problems, doesn't he?"

Witness: "Yes."

Lemann: "Now part of the time that Leroy was in foster care the mother was in jail."

Witness: "That's right."

Lemann: "Now do you know the ramifications of what happens when a child's mother or a child's parent is incarcerated?"

Witness: "No, I do not."

Lemann: "Do you know how that may impact upon the agency's ability to terminate the child for abandonment?"

Witness: "No, I do not."

* * * * *

Lemann: "Do you know of the various problems that that may cause in terms of having parental rights terminated?"

Witness: "No."

Lemann: "Do you know that there is by statute in Louisiana a five-year waiting period before you can terminate when a child's parent is incarcerated?"

Witness: "I did not know that."

An example of the extreme positions taken by the ACLU experts is that, to them, every child is adoptable no matter how physically, mentally or emotionally handicapped. Utopia, not reality, as I tried to demonstrate:

Lemann: "What's the goal of this child? Long-term foster

care, I believe. Is that correct?"

Witness: "That's right."

Lemann: "And he has been in custody of foster care for a long time."

Witness: "He has been in care nine—seven years."

Lemann: "And his goal is long-term foster care?"

Witness: "Yes."

Lemann: "And he has never been freed for adoption?"

Witness: "That's right."

Lemann: "And you fault the agency for that?"

Witness: "Well I think as a goal, a permanent plan, that could have happened. He could have been terminated and could have been available for adoption."

Lemann: "And you fault the agency for that?"

Witness: "That's right."

Lemann: "Now let me show you what I have marked as Exhibit 10-E. I will show you that. Then I will ask you a few questions.

The juvenile case of Leroy E is presided over by Judge Lagarde. Is that correct?"

Witness: "That's correct."

Lemann: "And you know, do you not, that in addition to freeing a child for adoption by way of abandonment or termination, that another way is by voluntary surrender?"

Witness: "That's correct."

Lemann: "And that the agency can seek from the parent the parent's voluntary surrender and the child can thereby be freed?"

Witness: "That's right."

Lemann: "Without an adversary proceeding?"

Witness: "That's correct."

Lemann: "By the way, you do understand, do you not, that in an abandonment proceeding the child is represented by a lawyer. Is that correct?"

Witness: "Right."

Lemann: "And the parent is represented by a lawyer?"

Witness: "Right."

Lemann: "And the same is true in a termination proceeding. The parent is represented by a lawyer. The child is represented by a lawyer. It is an adversary proceeding."

Witness: "Okay."

Lemann: "Now that can be avoided by voluntary surrender. Is that correct?"

Witness: "That's right."

Lemann: "And have you had a chance to review that?"

Witness: "Yes, I have."

Lemann: "And it's true, is it not, that in that order—when is that order dated, or judgment?"

Witness: "It is dated September 7, 1988."

Lemann: "And it is true that in that order the judge ordered the defendants not to accept the surrender of the mother or to seek the surrender of the mother. Is that correct?"

Witness: "I see that, yes."

Lemann: "You see that?"

Witness: "Uh-huh."

Lemann: "Do you also know that Leroy had four or five siblings from the same mother?"

Witness: "All right."

Lemann: "Who were in foster care."

Witness: "At one time, right."

Lemann: "And all of them are out of foster care."

Witness: "Okay."

Lemann: "Is that right?"

Witness: "I didn't have any records on them, and the record I did have indicated that her children were with her."

Lemann: "And that this mother is parenting three or four other children. Is that correct?"

Witness: "Yes."

Lemann: "I mean the record reflects like with Del and Brendolyn that, unfortunately, this mother doesn't like Leroy as much as her other children, correct?"

Witness: "Correct."

Lemann: "And Judge Lagarde, however, is apparently dead set on not letting her surrender him. Is that right?"

Witness: "I think you need to read the next part. The testimony revealed he is not an appropriate adoptive candidate and my concern would be who said that."

Lemann: "The judge is saying that."

The Court: "It said that the judge said that."

Witness: "Because the judge said that the testimony that he had heard on this child indicates that the child is not an appropriate candidate, but somebody said that in testimony."

Lemann: "Or said certain facts which led the judge to the conclusion that, perhaps, a kid who likes to burn things and cut his sister and do things like that may not be an appropriate candidate but you, as a social worker—and I understand it and I respect you for it—you don't agree with that. Is that correct?"

Witness: "Right."

Lemann: "And you bring that mindset to your testimony."

Witness: "Correct."

Precisely the point I wanted Judge Sear to ingest. In reality, the ACLU wanted the Judge to second-guess experienced hands-on juvenile court judges on the basis of the radical views of its social work experts.

The ACLU had another disadvantage. Judge Sear, like myself, had grown up in a different era, during a time when religious organizations had carried the burdens of what we then called orphans. We both knew a number of orphans who had been brought up in the New Orleans Jewish Orphanage and who had become lawyers and doctors. We were totally unfamiliar with the modern-day phenomenon of crack babies and the like. This old-fashionedness, or perhaps backwardness, was apparent in the following exchange:

Lemann: "Now this child has been put in what? Twenty different placements?"

Witness: "Twenty-four."

Lemann: "Twenty-four?"

Witness: "Right."

Lemann: "In the last—"

Witness: "Twelve years."

Lemann: "In the last two years he has probably been a runaway longer than he has been in our physical custody."

Witness: "That's right."

Lemann: "And they disrupted?"

Witness: "Right."

Lemann: "For among other reasons the record reflects that he, the child, struck a foster father. Is that correct?"

Witness: "Right. I remember."

Lemann: "The child set fire to a foster father. Is that—"

Witness: "I don't remember seeing that. I think I would have remembered."

Lemann: "Set fire to the foster father's coat while he had the coat on. You don't remember that?"

Witness: "No, I don't."

Lemann: "Do you remember that at one point he covered his body—his own body—with mousse?"

The Court: "With what?"

Lemann: "Mousse."

It was not until after the trial that Slim explained to me that mousse was a kind of hair styling product. During the witness' testimony, the picture I had in mind and, I suspect, the one the Judge had in mind, was that of a child covered with chocolate pudding.

When the Judge rendered his decision, a local newspaper reported:

> "U.S. District Judge Morey Sear concluded in a 56-page opinion that the state did not violate the Adoption Assistance & Child Welfare Act of 1980 and that, in fact, the state 'substantially complied' with the act regarding the thirteen children named as plaintiffs in the so-called 'Del-A' suit.

> New Orleans attorney, Steve Scheckman, who represents the ACLU of Louisiana, said Sear's decision will be appealed to the 5th Circuit Court of Appeals.
>
> The case ultimately may reach the U.S. Supreme Court, he said.
>
> Scheckman said the 'cries for help' from Louisiana's foster children 'are obviously going to go unanswered, at least for the time being.'
>
> New Orleans lawyer, Arthur Lemann III, who represents the state in the suit, said he is confident Sear's 'wise' ruling will be upheld.
>
> Lemann said the ACLU has been 'sincere' but 'overzealous' in its pursuit of the case."

Surprisingly, the ACLU decided not to appeal the case, perhaps fearing bad precedent, or perhaps realizing that zealots are no match for a dragon slayer.

SEVENTEEN

The Bear Ain't Talking

Dr. Charles LeChasney was a malevolent genius. In the first place, he wasn't a doctor at all. Secondly, his name wasn't Charles LeChasney. His real name was Himberto Figueroa; he was a Cuban who came to this country when he was fourteen years old. Dropping out of college after one year, he worked as a used car and insurance salesman in Houston until the mid-1970s when his true calling surfaced. It was then that he changed his name, awarded himself a Ph.D. in psychology from the University of Paris and began to treat patients at two hundred dollars an hour until, becoming bored with his practice, he became a financial consultant and founder of The First Church of Tomorrow, which he established to acquire real estate as a non-profit organization.

In the summer of 1980, Dr. LeChasney decided to leave Houston and move to Quebec because he thought it would soon become a new country after separating from Canada. But, running out of money, he got only as far as Atlanta where he parked his car at the airport and lived for the next four months by eating at happy hour buffets in nearby hotels and sneaking into rooms in the early mornings to sleep and shower before check-out time. Finally, he landed a job as a clinical psychologist but, as in Texas, he found financial consulting more to his liking. Within a few years, he became so successful he bought the Callan Castle, a huge mansion in Atlanta once belonging to the founder of Coca Cola. He married and rubbed elbows with the political and financial elite of Atlanta. He became a big fund raiser for the Republican Party and even had a new town named after him in Alabama.

Dr. LeChasney's litany of lies was unending. He claimed to be friendly with Richard Nixon and Henry Kissinger; he claimed to be a former ambassador and diplomat; and he claimed to be in line for an appointment as an under-secretary of state. He fashioned a noble pedigree for himself almost as distinguished as that of my mother's and Aunt Delta's. His family allegedly owned a castle in France and a country estate in

Spain. Among his many business successes, he included producing the movies *Urban Cowboy* and *Romancing the Stone*.

In January of 1987, Dr. LeChasney met Amato Hernandez, another native Cuban. This time, however, Dr. LeChasney would be the one outfoxed by a Cuban. Hernandez, like Joseph Hauser in the Marcello case, was an agent provocateur for the federal government. Working for the IRS, his mission was to approach innocent businessmen with the proposition that he represented a drug cartel with millions of dollars in cash that needed to be laundered. The IRS, through Hernandez, offered a six percent commission to launder what in actuality was taxpayers' dollars.

Dr. LeChasney was soon taking Hernandez around the country to launder tax dollars for the six percent commission. The two were truly a match made in hell. They eventually ended up in New Orleans, where Dr. LeChasney previously had met David Levy, a ne'er-do-well former classmate of mine from law school. David had been a marginal student and after law school he maintained an office at the Town & Country Motel, drifting on the outskirts of disaster by functioning as in-house counsel to Carlos Marcello. Like Vincent Marinello, David would spend eight hours to figure out how to avoid an hour's worth of work. The connection to Carlos assured him countless opportunities for get-rich-quick schemes. He was enamored with the easy buck. Naturally, he went for LeChasney and Hernandez's deal.

David usually laundered money for Hernandez by purchasing cashier's checks in amounts of less than ten thousand dollars and by returning the proceeds via his trust account. On one occasion, he attempted to launder the money by giving fifty thousand dollars to Elmo Pitre, one of his clients in the seafood business. Pitre, a Cajun, in turn gave his company's check (less the six percent commission) to one of Hernandez's dummy corporations. But this time, the Cajun outsmarted the Cuban. Elmo's check bounced and the IRS was out fifty thousand dollars.

Another of David's clients, A. P. Marullo, was Judge Frank Marullo's cousin. When Frank and I were law students, we would visit A.P. and his family on Grand Isle. Located on the Gulf of Mexico about one hundred miles south of New Orleans, Grand Isle was a run-down, decrepit resort area that had seen better days. Like Airline Highway, it was one of Carlos's favorite places, and he kept a fishing camp there until he died. During prohibition, Grand Isle had been a key location for smuggling liquor into the country from Cuba. Allegedly, A.P.'s father, "Uncle Tony," had been involved in this industry and had spent time in the penitentiary. It didn't strike any of us as unusual that Uncle Tony's brother, Frank's father, was a cop.

Following in the footsteps of Frank's father, A.P. also became a cop. However, he soon grew tired of that life-style, so he went into the restaurant business, opening the French Market Seafood Restaurant on Decatur Street and making it into a very successful business.

A.P. was very fond of David and was aware that he had a drinking problem. He tried to help by giving him minor legal work. They spoke on the phone frequently, not knowing that David's phone had been tapped as a part of the IRS undercover investigation.

Around this same time, David, A.P., Judge Marullo, and an entrepreneur by the name of Lebo Mancuso had formed an investment group to purchase an abandoned shipyard. In the course of seeking financing, David had introduced the group to Dr. LeChasney, the whiz-kid consultant from Atlanta. After he had hooked up with Hernandez and during one of their trips to New Orleans, Dr. LeChasney went with the investment group to a New Orleans bank to assist them in obtaining a loan. After the meeting with the bankers, Dr. LeChasney and David took Lebo to Hernandez's room at the Marriott Hotel in the French Quarter while A.P. and Judge Marullo stayed in the hotel's lounge. Hernandez then explained to Lebo that his principals had lots of money available for financing the shipyard project, all the while secretly taping the conversation. Hernandez deftly steered the conversation into how the shipyard could be used to import drugs and, with his typical mendacity, Dr. LeChasney volunteered that a judge was also involved in the investment group—a fact which, according to Dr. LeChasney, would serve them well if problems arose with law enforcement.

After Elmo's check had bounced, David told A.P. that Elmo owed him money and, being a mutual friend, A.P. agreed to intercede. As they spoke, the government secretly recorded the conversation:

David: "Still waiting to hear from the crazy Cajun down the bayou."

A.P.: "Oh, yeah."

David: "Yeah."

A.P.: "You didn't hear from him at all?"

David: "No, not over the weekend at all."

A.P.: "Well you wanna' go pay him a visit?"

David: "I think we gotta' pay him a visit."

A.P.: "Alright, well I'll go with you. I can probably go, you know, ah, this afternoon or tomorrow."

David: "Alright."

A.P.: "I wouldn't tell him you're coming though."

David: "Oh, no indeed, absolutely not. Absolutely not, my man. . . ."

The next day, David, Dr. LeChasney and A.P. drove to Grand Isle and, not knowing where Elmo lived, they stopped at the local police station for directions. After locating Elmo, A.P. asked him to sign a note and mortgage for the money owed, but the "crazy Cajun" wouldn't agree to pay and, ultimately, David and Dr. LeChasney had to repay Hernandez (and the IRS) with money from other sources.

David also introduced Dr. LeChasney and Hernandez to other notable New Orleans characters, including Stephen "The Dog" Migliore, a truly honorable hustler who later said he would "rather be a dog in jail than a rat on the street!" And, always puffing his connection with the Marcello family, David introduced Dr. LeChasney and Hernandez to Sammy Marcello, Carlos's youngest brother, who in turn introduced them to Nick Popich, a real estate developer with holdings in Louisiana and California.

On January 26, 1988, a complaint was issued for the arrest of David, his wife Becky, Nick Popich, Sammy Marcello, Lebo Mancuso, Steve "The Dog" Migliore, and Elmo Pitre. A.P. was not on the list.

Dr. LeChasney was arrested at the airport in Washington, D.C., where he was returning from a trip to China that had been sponsored by the state department. He had been so active in the money-laundering deal that he ended up indicted in Atlanta, Washington, D.C., Puerto Rico, and New Orleans. Indeed, in the Atlanta case, Congressman Pat Swindall eventually was convicted for his dealings with Dr. LeChasney and Hernandez.

Naturally, with all of these cases pending against him, Dr. LeChasney decided to join forces with the government. Even though A.P. had never met Hernandez and had not laundered money for him, Dr. LeChasney told the government that A.P. had joined the conspiracy as "an enforcer" by attempting to collect the money from Elmo. And so, A.P. was added to the indictment on October 31, 1989. Of course, I agreed to represent him.

The tapes made it crystal clear that David had laundered what he had believed to be drug proceeds and so, attempting to develop the reverse sting defense, he claimed that he had been conducting his own investigation and that he had tried to report it by leaving telephone messages for AUSA Howie Peters. After his arrest, he asserted this defense in a statement to the IRS, saying:

> "Levy is aware that A.P. Marullo launders money through casinos. Marullo goes to a casino with cash, gets chips, then turns the chips into casino checks. Marullo had lined up someone from Las Vegas to come down and discuss the money laundering idea with Hernandez.

> Levy and A.P. Marullo had gone to Grand Isle to see Elmo Pitre concerning the money owed by Pitre.
>
> Levy had gone to Aruba with Marullo to gamble and look over the casino. Marullo mentioned that they could launder money through the Aruban casinos by using a Miami bank."

Thus, in addition to Dr. LeChasney, we had to worry about David.

Eddie Sapir joined me in defending A.P. As a young man, Eddie had served in the Louisiana Legislature before becoming a city councilman. A consummate politician but with long hair worn in a page boy style, he had looked more like one of the Beatles than a city father. His district included the Garden District—the most aristocratic part of New Orleans—and yet, the blue-bloods had reelected him each time without fail. Eventually, he became a Municipal Court Judge, where he was allowed to maintain an outside law practice; he rendered invaluable assistance to A.P.'s defense through his clear thinking and cogent analysis of the evidence and legal issues involved.

While the case was of the utmost importance to A.P., it wasn't the only thing on his mind at the time. There was the matter of "Lil' Frankie." Actually, there were three Lil' Frankies in A.P.'s life. There was the Judge, who was called Lil' Frankie to distinguish him from his father, the cop. There was the Judge's son, who was called Lil' Frankie to distinguish him from the Judge and the cop. And there was A.P.'s youngest brother, who was also called Lil' Frankie—but that's not what distinguished him from the others. Rather, what distinguished this Lil' Frankie from the other Lil' Frankies was the tone of A.P.'s voice when he mentioned his name. Whenever A.P. said, "Lil' Frankie" with despair in his voice, you knew he was referring to his younger brother.

This Lil' Frankie "stayed by his Mama's" in Grand Isle. It wasn't that he was a Mama's boy, mind you, it was because no one else would have him. You see, this Lil' Frankie had a terrible temper. Once, in a rage over an annoying call, he tried to shoot "the motherfucker" through the receiver of his Mama's phone. Blinded in one eye from an old gunshot wound, Lil' Frankie looked like a mad and crazy Roberto Duran in an alleyway.

In the middle of trial preparation, Lil' Frankie, on a high with his girlfriend, wrecked his boat on an oil rig in the Gulf. The Coast Guard rescued them and, once on board, Lil' Frankie told the captain he wanted to be dropped off at Cheramie's Wharf. Apologetically, the captain told him regulations required that all shipwreck survivors be taken to the Coast Guard Station. With that, Lil' Frankie pulled out his forty-four and, sure enough, he and his girlfriend were dropped off at Cheramie's Wharf. A few days later, United States Marshals hit Grand Isle like Marines on Iwo Jima. Lil' Frankie was arrested for hijacking a Coast Guard cutter, and after serving a jail sentence, he was banished from Grand Isle as a condition of his parole. A.P. would have to figure out what to do with Lil' Frankie.

The prosecutors in A.P.'s case were two of the most obnoxious, mean-spirited AUSA's I had ever encountered. Jim Letten and Steve Irwin would have overqualified for Hitler's SS troops, and what made them so dangerous as prosecutors was the fact that they appealed to white, blue-collar juries—the kind one often gets in federal court. We would have a tough time ahead.

Not all of the defendants made it to trial. Sammy Marcello, Nick Popich, and Elmo Pitre pleaded guilty. Then the judge, the late Veronica Wicker, a real sweetheart, became ill in the middle of the trial and the case was transferred to Judge Duplantier. He did two things immediately: first, he effectively took me out of the case with the judicial muzzle; and secondly, being even-handed, he did the same to Letten and Irwin. There would be no dog fight in his courtroom.

The government's chief witness, Hernandez, was damaging because his testimony was corroborated by the tapes. Fortunately, A.P. had never met or spoken to him. Our main threat was Dr. LeChasney. His lifetime of deception, however, made cross-examining him a lawyer's dream. Because of my being practically benched by the Judge, Lebo Mancuso's lawyer, John Reed, an excellent lawyer and more the boxer, took the lead in cross-examining him, parading before the jury all of his past lies and catching him in a lie on the witness stand. At first denying he had ever applied for United States citizenship, he had to change his testimony because his immigration file plainly showed he had applied unsuccessfully. He simply couldn't resist lying—even in front of Judge Duplantier.

My cross-examination of Dr. LeChasney was short and sweet. I wanted to demonstrate how he had taken a totally innocent person, Judge Marullo, and had falsely portrayed him as corrupt:

> Lemann: "Now later on—and I am now on page forty-nine of the transcript of that meeting—the conversation between you and Levy and Hernandez—and at that point Mr. Mancuso had gone up to the room—turned to talking about the port, is that correct?"
>
> LeChasney: "Yes, sir."
>
> Lemann: "And it turned into a discussion about the possibility of the port being used to import drugs, is that correct?"
>
> LeChasney: "Yes, sir."

Lemann: "And during that conversation—in that context when that was being discussed—you say, do you not, on page 49, that 'this judge can handle anything in the state.' Do you remember saying that?"

LeChasney: "Yes."

Lemann: "Now in making that statement, were you implying that Judge Marullo had an understanding that this port was going to be used for cocaine and that, if anybody got in trouble, he would be available to take care of it? Wasn't that the impression you were seeking to make at that time?"

LeChasney: "Yes, sir. Some of that, yes, sir."

I also wanted to set him up for closing argument:

Lemann: "Now Mr. LeChasney, all of the other lawyers have asked you a whole bunch of questions this morning about your various lies, and I'm not going to get into that. You do use the word at some point, do you not, that what you're attempting to create and to do through telling these falsehoods was to make yourself into a more reputable person, is that correct?"

LeChasney: "Yes, sir."

Lemann: "And you did that because you wanted people to believe in what you were saying, is that correct?"

LeChasney: "Yes, sir."

Lemann: "So that people would trust in what you were saying, is that correct?"

LeChasney: "That's correct."

Lemann: "And in addition to all other falsehoods that you told, one thing that you talked about was the fact that you created for yourself a historical family, is that right?"

LeChasney: "Yes, sir."

Lemann: "A family with a long background, is that correct?"

LeChasney: "Yes, sir."

Lemann: "For example, I think you said that your great grandfather was a gentleman who fought with Napoleon, is that correct?"

LeChasney: "Perhaps I said that at one time, yes."

Lemann: "And you also said, did you not, that another ancestor of yours killed a polar bear with the Czar of Russia? Do you recall that?"

LeChasney: "I don't recall saying that, no."

Lemann: "Well let me—"

The Court: "Is it important?"

LeChasney: "I would not deny it, sir."

Lemann: "Do you know whether or not you ever said that?"

The Court: "I'm sure he did."

LeChasney: "I probably did."

Lemann: "May I approach the witness?

Let me show you Government Exhibit 309. This is the photograph, the brochure, is it not, of the castle in Atlanta that you lived in?"

LeChasney: "Yes, sir. It has the bear in it."

Lemann: "There is a picture of the bear there, isn't there?"

LeChasney: "That's correct."

Most of the defendants, including A.P., decided not to testify. With the evidence of guilt so overwhelming against some of them, we were very afraid A.P. might go down with the rest of them. Closing argument was critical:

> "These people were legitimately trying to buy a shipyard and when American businessmen try to buy property, often they need—if not always—to borrow the money; and they were looking for financing. Now, into this tranquil American scene of endeavor, enterprise, entrepreneurship, arises the IRS and the Cubans. They come in on the scene. These people are minding their own business. They are in a legitimate transaction. They have their hands legitimately out for money. They try to find funds to put together a legitimate deal.
>
> Now the first Cuban that the IRS brings in at the beginning of this rainbow of deception is Hernandez. Here's a man who has defrauded a bank of hundreds of thousands of dollars, who violated the law, who, in an effort to save his own hide, tried to cut a deal with the government. He first goes to the FBI and they turned him down. The FBI rejects him, but the IRS, they take him. They give him hundreds of thousands of dollars. They give him a free apartment. They give him a free house, and they direct him first, where? They direct him toward a den of drug smugglers that he, on his own, had acquaintances with and had hobnobbed with before he saw the light. So they direct him, properly so, to a den of thieves, to some drug smugglers, and he goes in to try to trap them. But what happens? He comes back with zero. He gets nothing. So of course he's desperate to try to do something to save his hide.
>
> So what does the IRS do? They then set him loose on John Q. Citizen. Don't need any suspicion that you're a bad guy or you're out violating the law; just turn him loose with a briefcase full of money, put the honey pot out and see who might be tempted to bite. The second Cuban, we know, started out on a different team, as the government is quick to point out. The second Cuban, of course, is the man you know by the adopted name he gave to himself. Dr. Charles LeChasney. I mean, here's a man who has deceived people all of his life. He has thrived on deception and lies. And as I told you in my opening statement, his lies weren't the kind of lies that someone

impulsively gives maybe to get out of trouble. His lies were always designed to get someone to trust him, to get someone to have faith in him, to build up his credibility so that he could victimize them. And here's this man charging $200 an hour providing services to people who legitimately had problems. Here's a man who starts a church.

The man is a genius, and his genius remains today because—where is he? He is now with the other Cuban, all on the same team with the IRS, and he's looking to get his pot of gold at the end of this rainbow of deception."

I ended on this note:

"The document which, from my perspective, tells the whole case is Exhibit 309, which shows the picture of the castle and, on the back, the polar bear. That's the polar bear that Dr. LeChasney says his great, great grandfather shot with the Russian Czar. And it's kind of humorous, but it tells a lot, because let me tell you—he always told lies which were hard to disprove. I mean, the great, great grandfather is dead . . . the Russian Czar is dead . . . and the bear ain't talking.

But you take an ordinary polar bear—you skin him, you make a hide, and you put him in a beautiful mansion, and you tell people that 'my ancestor skinned this with Russian nobility,' and all of a sudden, you have a stinky old bear rug becoming what? A symbol of great respectability, a symbol of power, a symbol of credibility: a tool of Dr. LeChasney to make a victim out of someone.

But you see, once you know the true story of Charles LeChasney, the bear doesn't have to talk because you know from Dr. LeChasney that the chances are overwhelming that this poor bear is a part of a fraudulent hoax perpetrated by this man, Charles LeChasney.

The same is true—that what he has done to that bear rug is what he is doing and has done to my client. He has taken an innocent trip to visit an old friend on behalf of another friend in order to get a note and mortgage, and stops by a police station, and he has made that into some sort of a criminal enforcer, a squeeze, an evil trip, all from the mouth of Charles LeChasney."

The jury found A.P. not guilty. As a bonus, he had promised to take us on a trip to either Sicily or Las Vegas. R.A. and I were dying to go to Sicily but, unfortunately, he felt so good about the victory, he decided Las Vegas was a much greater treat. Wanting at least to look the part, I bought some blue jeans and a gold necklace and, now being familiar with it, I put mousse in my hair. When we met at the airport, A.P. chuckled and told R.A. I looked like an uptown law professor.

EIGHTEEN

THE LONE KNIGHT

O'Grady's childhood friend Tom Tyrell was busted for selling drugs. Eventually, O'Grady got him a suspended sentence by delaying the case for so long the DA simply wanted the case to disappear. Delay was one of his strongest cards. No one could outdo O'Grady doing nothing.

Tom and O'Grady began a drug and alcohol counseling business. I had heard of reformers going into this line of work—but never activists. In any event, their business grew and they worked at it in the law office or, more often, at the Ernst annex. Indeed, O'Grady spent so much time at Ernst that a cocktail was named "the O'Grady," a double Jack Daniels on the rocks. Like O'Grady, Tom also liked women. But, unlike O'Grady, he liked only young ones (with O'Grady it made no difference). At times, Tom would have to excuse himself from the pinball machine at the annex in order to help his girlfriend write a paper in English 101.

When we returned from the firm retreat at the Grand Hotel in Alabama, Elsie Flowers followed O'Grady to New Orleans. After she found a job and bought a house, he moved in with her. Maddie took it well; Betty was furious. Betty was an O'Grady girlfriend who slept with him only when he and Maddie were together. Like Uncle Mac's three wives, O'Grady's three women eventually got along pretty well with one another. At times, Maddie, Elsie and Betty had lunch together to discuss life in general and the stump in particular. I suspected it all had something to do with the stump—that he had, so to speak, an extra leg up.

One night O'Grady and Elsie got into a drunken brawl at her house, causing him to fall out of bed and break the stump. Naturally, she dropped him off at Maddie's. Later, Elsie filed a lawsuit against him for mistreating her and he countersued, alleging that, as she performed oral sex on him, he became disoriented and fell out of bed and broke the stump. Ultimately, Elsie's homeowner's insurance company settled and paid him fifteen hundred dollars. The incident became known as "O'Grady's fifteen hundred dollar blow-job."

With the broken stump, Maddie (and Betty) were back in control. Maddie became convinced that he needed medical treatment for his 3-M syndrome. She persuaded Uncle Mac to intervene, and he made arrangements for us to meet with a doctor. Mac, Mills, Judge Marullo, I and a few other "impaired lawyers" were at the meeting. When the doctor inquired about O'Grady's whereabouts, I said he was working at his drug and alcohol counseling firm. That's when the doctor's pen hit the floor.

We put O'Grady away in a Lafayette hospital. When he finished the program, Maddie, who had been commuting daily to visit him, went to pick him up, telling him there were only three ground rules to their new life together: first, no drinking; second, no lying; and third, no women. Surprisingly, O'Grady complied with the second condition by telling her that the other two were deal-breakers and that, in any event, he was moving in with a woman he had met at the hospital. Maddie drove him to the home of the new girlfriend.

After the Stephen Rosiere case, O'Grady and I stopped talking to one another. I don't know whether it's a Southern thing, but it's not uncommon for law partners in New Orleans to stop talking to one another. Take Russell Schonekas, the lawyer who represented Carlos in the New Orleans case. He had a thirty-year partnership, but he and his partner never spoke during the last twenty years. Russell used to say if doctors ever cut his partner's head open, " . . . nothing but pussies would fly out." I said the same about O'Grady.

And so, Lemann, O'Grady & Mills never dissolved, we just rode off in separate directions. O'Grady went to Ernst for lunch one day and never came back. Bishop left to become a full time priest. Mills got sick from drink and died. He was forty-nine years old. We spread his ashes over Texas. Maddie went to the funeral—but not O'Grady.

During A.P.'s case, my brother, David, was stricken with cancer. Of all my brothers and sisters, he had the biggest heart.

David fought the cancer valiantly for four long years, undergoing three major surgeries and ending up without a tongue, without a voice, and without half of his neck. He couldn't eat and he couldn't talk. He would communicate by writing on scraps of paper. And when the morphine got heavy, the scribbling stopped. He died a silent, tortured death.

We were all devastated, especially my father. He and David had worked side by side for twenty-five years at the family business in Donaldsonville. They were best friends. One day at Galatoire's, my father broke down and told me he didn't want to go on living. Shortly afterwards, he went into surgery for a heart condition and never woke up.

My life would never be the same. This time, it wasn't the Church but God whom I would never forgive. I no longer wanted a partner.

Henceforth, I would fight dragons alone.

NINETEEN

The Rented Grail

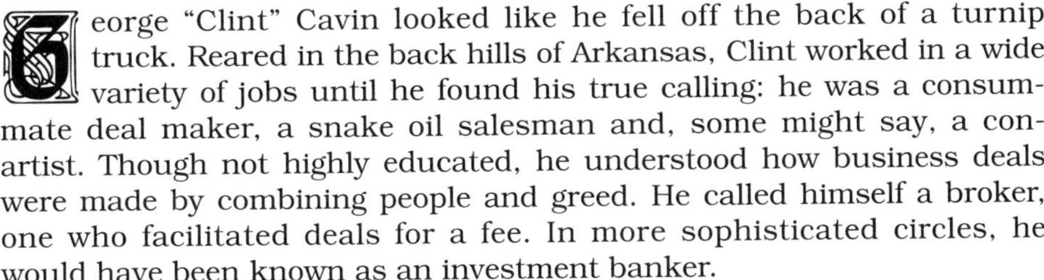

George "Clint" Cavin looked like he fell off the back of a turnip truck. Reared in the back hills of Arkansas, Clint worked in a wide variety of jobs until he found his true calling: he was a consummate deal maker, a snake oil salesman and, some might say, a con-artist. Though not highly educated, he understood how business deals were made by combining people and greed. He called himself a broker, one who facilitated deals for a fee. In more sophisticated circles, he would have been known as an investment banker.

Louisiana has been good to deal makers, and this was particularly true in the insurance industry in the late 80s and early 90s when many main line companies had stopped writing business and a host of new, smaller companies were attempting to replace them. In Louisiana, the insurance commissioner is elected (as are most of our public officials, from recorders of vital statistics to coroners). During these turbulent times, at least two of them had gone to jail for accepting bribes. Business as usual in Louisiana.

In order to retain a license, insurance companies are required to maintain a certain ratio between net worth and sales. Thus, insurance companies need "admitted assets" to stay in business and to increase sales. At that time, the Insurance Code did not specifically prohibit the use of so-called "rented" assets, a term embracing any number of transactions which have in common the use of a third party's asset on an insurance company's balance sheet. Usually, they involve the acquisition of an asset in a credit transaction by a holding company which, in turn, contributes the asset to its insurance company. What made such transactions feasible was the fact that the commissioner didn't require holding companies or their subsidiaries to file consolidated financial statements. Therefore, an asset could appear on an insurance company's financial statement without showing the off-setting liability on the holding company's financial statement. These types of rented asset transactions were accepted by the commissioner so long as the asset was at risk. In other words, if an insurance company went into receivership, the so-called rented asset had to be available for liquidation by the commissioner. A rental fee was paid to the third party to compensate him for placing the asset at risk. This was the kind of smoke and mirrors that deal makers, such as Clint, thrived upon.

Earl Krenning was the president of Sovereign Fire & Casualty Insurance Company, Inc., a small insurance company that was struggling to retain its license. Robert Bishop was the president of Falcon Pipeline Company, Inc., the owner of an abandoned pipeline in North Louisiana. Clint knew that Krenning's insurance company needed an asset and that Bishop's company had an unused asset. And from the "five loaves, and two fishes. . . ."

Here is how the deal worked. Sovereign Holding Company issued a one million dollar note in order to acquire a one million dollar note from the Falcon Pipeline Company. The Falcon note was secured by a mortgage on the pipeline, since the pipeline itself would not qualify as an admitted asset. Sovereign Holding Company then donated the Falcon note and mortgage to the Sovereign Insurance Company, thus increasing the insurance company's net worth by a million dollars. The other side of the transaction is what made it worthwhile for Bishop. The Sovereign Holding Company note paid a higher rate of interest than the Falcon note, and the difference in the cash flow represented the fee Bishop received for putting his asset at risk. For his part in brokering the transaction, Clint received a twenty thousand dollar fee.

Ultimately, Sovereign Insurance Company went into receivership. The feds got involved, and by using the mail fraud statute, the grand jury in New Orleans returned an indictment against Clint, Krenning, and Bishop. The legitimacy of the whole transaction, of course, depended on whether the abandoned pipeline was worth one million dollars.

After the indictment, Clint and Rose, his very bossy wife of thirty years, became "born-again" Christians. They did an awful lot of praying. They prayed before court, during court, and after court. No amount of prayers, however, would make the indictment go away. They needed a dragon slayer. I took the case.

The case was allotted to Judge Edith Brown Clement, a Republican and former partner in one of the state's largest law firms. Her husband had been president of the Louisiana State Bar Association. Judge Clement had grown up in uptown New Orleans and she was a Sacred Heart Academy girl but let me tell you, not the kind with a bleeding heart. She had a sense of humor, and it was a generally pleasant experience to try the case before her.

Peter Strasser and Marvin Opotowsky were the two prosecutors. Peter was a soft-spoken, well-mannered, southern gentleman from Virginia. In contrast, Marvin was a big, emotional, flamboyant character from New Orleans. Recognizing there are generally two ways to shoot down a defendant—one by rifle, the other by shotgun—Strasser and Opotowsky opted for the shotgun in arguing that the Falcon Pipeline transaction was illegal because: first, it involved a rented asset; second, the asset was not at risk; third, the asset was not worth a million dollars; and fourth, the paperwork had been back-dated. Any hit could be fatal.

During the case-in-chief, the prosecutors called an expert witness to testify that the pipeline was not worth a million dollars. Remembering my lessons from Monsignor Gubler, I ended my cross-examination thusly:

Lemann: "Now a pipeline in some respects is sort of like a dinosaur trap, isn't it? In the sense that it's only real economic value is to transport gas, just like the only real economic value of a dinosaur trap is to catch dinosaurs. . . . (Courtroom laughs)"

Manuel: "Right. (Courtroom laughs)"

Lemann: "And, I mean, if someone had built a dinosaur trap, some engineer could probably look at it and say, 'I estimate you paid X amount of dollars to build that.' Or, he could look at it and say, 'I estimate it would cost you X amount of dollars to replace that.' Isn't that true?"

Manuel: "True."

Lemann: "Now in your report here, you mention that there is a Michigan Wisconsin tap. What does that mean?"

Manuel: "That is the physical connection where the existing pipeline was physically connected to the Michigan Wisconsin Gas Company."

Lemann: "Now did that lead you to believe that at the other end of that pipeline was a company called Michigan Wisconsin, who had a contract to buy whatever was shipped through the pipeline? Did you know that or did that lead you to believe that?"

Manuel: "Yeah."

Lemann: "But you didn't go and check out to see exactly what that contract constituted, did you?"

Manuel: "No."

Lemann: "You didn't check to see that that contract is in existence until May 13, 1997, did you?"

Manuel: "No."

Lemann: "And, you know, as we said earlier, the only real economic value of a pipeline is if you have a supplier at one end and a buyer at the other end. Isn't that true?"

Manuel: "That's true."

Lemann: "Now unlike the pipeline, we all know, don't we, that there ain't no dinosaurs. Right?"

Manuel: "Yes."

Lemann: "But you don't know and you can't tell this jury, can you, whether or not there are reserves of gas to be pumped today, with Michigan Wisconsin at the other end committed to buy. You can't say that, can you?"

Manuel: "No."

Lemann: "Thank you."

So much for expert witnesses.

Almost nine years earlier, Clint had been convicted of a state felony and a federal misdemeanor for theft by trickery. More smoke and mirrors. Unfortunately, the Judge would not exclude this evidence on the grounds of remoteness and, fearing the jury would definitely convict if they believed Clint was up to old tricks, I decided to keep him off the witness stand. More prayers by Clint and Rose.

The prosecution makes two closing arguments to the jury, one detailing the government's proof and the other rebutting the arguments of defense counsel. Typically, where there are two prosecutors, they will divide the arguments and in this case, the two prosecutors were perfectly matched: Strasser, the more reasoned, would present the first argument, and Opotowsky, the more emotional, would make the rebuttal.

I began closing argument by first attacking the government's shotgun approach:

"Now—the lawyers have been talking to you about the difference between a criminal case and a civil case. Well I'll tell you one difference. A criminal case is the most serious kind of case you can get. And the government, in a criminal case, is supposed to come here and prove to you that the defendant did something and did it wrong—and they tell you, 'This is what you did and we're going to prove that's what you did, and that's wrong.' That's not what the government has done in this case. They've come here and they've told you, 'Well we have a bunch of different theories, and we want to test 'em all out on you—hoping that maybe you'll find one of 'em to your liking.' That's not what the government's supposed to do.

You know—let me tell you—the government's case reminds me of a television commercial—in the New Orleans area—some of you who are not from this area may not know about it—but it's, there's this little furniture store and I think it's called, F & J. It's on North Broad. And it's a little neighborhood furniture store but it's a very gutsy little store. I mean, they compete against the big furniture stores and they have a little advertising which is a low budget thing. It's the two partners, and that's it. And the thing starts with a female customer coming in the store—and the first partner, he's very calm. He's very reasonable. He's very serious. He's very staid and formal. And he presents her with all the different bargains. There's a bargain for everything. And then when he's got her hooked, she says, 'Well you know, I've just gone into bankruptcy,' or 'I just lost my job,' or 'I just got divorced.' And then the other partner comes in at the end, and he's expansive and big, and affable, and very emotional, and he says, 'Let her have it. Let her have it. Don't worry—throw caution to the wind.' Now why is the government's case like this? Well you see, Mr. Strasser got up and he gave the first of the closing statements and he's kind'a serious and formal, and he laid out to you all kinds of different theories about why this man committed fraud. And then when I sit down, Mr. Opotowsky's going to get up and he's—you know what—you know what he's going to tell you? 'Let her have it. Let her have it.'"

I then reminded the jury who the true villain was:

"First of all, we established from their evidence, from their witnesses—and the government's called all kinds of witnesses in this case. I mean, I've never seen anything like it. They called a lawyer who doesn't want to talk about law. They called a CPA who doesn't want to talk about accounting. They've called all kind of different witnesses. But it's clear from their witnesses that the Louisiana Insurance Commissioner only regulated insurance companies. It only required insurance companies to file those forms. It permitted an insurance company to be separately held by a parent company. Now, was that wise? No, that's not wise. It was stupid. But that's why we're here. In other words, it's just like in the opening statement. If I go to the bank and borrow fifteen thousand dollars and buy my daughter a car and give it to her—my fifteen year old daughter—her balance sheet's going to show an asset of fifteen thousand dollars unencumbered. Now if she needs to borrow money—if she goes into a bank and presents that balance sheet, what banker is going to rely on the balance sheet of a child without first of all saying, 'Bring your parent in here. Make him sign.' Or, 'Let me see his financial statement.' Then they would have seen the true reality of what was going on. But they didn't do that. And . . . that's not my client—who lives up in Little Rock, Arkansas—that's not his fault. That's not his fault. That's how they decided they were going to permit insurance companies to operate. And so this is what this whole case is all about. It's simply putting an asset in the insurance company and a liability in the holding company. That's it. Now does it look slick? Does it look fishy? Does it look sharp? Yes, it does. It does. Is it taking advantage of a loophole? Yes. Lawyers did it. You know it's going to be slick. Accountants did it. I mean, in other words, but it's not against the law in this country to take advantage of loopholes. It's not a crime to do that. If that was a crime, half the lawyers would be in jail—and the other half would be defending them."

At one point, while focusing on the weakness of one of the government's theories, the following exchange took place:

Lemann: "You know, that's like—I tried a case once—and the federal government was supposedly taking the position that one of its agencies had been defrauded. And they kept talkin' in that case, not about premium dollars. . . ."

Opotowsky: "Your Honor, I'm going to object. What

happened in another case is totally irrelevant to this case."

Lemann: "Well it's argument, Your Honor."

Opotowsky: "Oh, then I can do the same type of argument?"

Lemann: "Absolutely. (Jury laughs) Abso . . . let her have it. (Whole courtroom laughs)"

Opotowsky: "We will let you have it."

The Court: "Let him have it. (More laughter)"

And so, I let him have it:

> "See, that's another one of their theories—that the values were all wrong. Well you know, if it was a rented asset and the people didn't own it, then the values wouldn't make any difference. They only want you to look at the values if they say, 'If you don't like this furniture, this sofa, then look at, look at values.' Well we can talk on and on about value. You know, if you have a brand new Cadillac sittin' in your carport, it's got a book value, it's got a replacement value, it's got a salvage value—but if you can't afford to put any gasoline in it, it ain't got no value to you. Now it may be that the pipeline—if there's no gas running through it—may not have any value. But these are businessmen dealing with one another at arms' length. Everybody is trying to get the best deal for themselves. Now as for the broker, what evidence is there to lead you to believe that Clint Cavin knew anything about the value of the pipeline under the ground? How is he supposed to know the value of this asset? And if it turns out to be worthless, how can you pin that on him? They say another thing that made it all a crime was a side agreement. Well I mean, what evidence is there that Mr. Cavin knew anything about any side agreement? If you look at those side agreements, you don't see his signature on 'em. I mean, the government in this case is stretching and stretching and stretching, and they want to give you all kinds of different theories. That's not what a criminal case is supposed to be like. You can't just come in here and say, 'Let her have it. Forget reason. Forget reasonable doubt. Just keep searching for something that you're

> comfortable with.' That's not a criminal prosecution. It may be a good way to sell furniture, but it's a hell of a way to send a man to jail."

The jury agreed and acquitted Clint—but the war wasn't over. There was a second dragon lurking in the bushes. In the second case, the rented asset supposedly had been collateralized by government securities issued by the Federal National Mortgage Association, known as Fannie Maes. In fact, the Fannie Maes had been purchased on margin and, therefore, didn't have the stated value. This time, the jury concluded that Clint was aware of the shenanigans. He was convicted and sentenced to forty-two months.

A defendant convicted in federal court is not entitled to bail during the pendency of an appeal unless the trial court certifies that it probably committed reversible error. The Judge who presided over Clint's second case wasn't about to do that, although he probably is the most error-prone judge sitting in America today. And so Clint served fourteen months in jail before the Court of Appeals reversed his conviction and ordered a new trial. Since it made no sense to retry the case, we struck a deal with the government, and Clint was allowed to plead guilty to time already served.

Even though Clint was now a free man, he had to report monthly to a probation officer as a condition of parole. For some reason, this caused Rose to stop praying and to start bitching. There is an old saying in prison, "If you can't do the time, don't do the crime."

Curiously, Clint had done the time without Rose, he just couldn't do it with Rose. One day he disappeared. Rose believes he's running from the government. I believe he's running from Rose—the kind of dragon I don't mess with.

Twenty

The Stolen Grail

Lynn Paul Martin perpetrated the most colossal fraud in the history of Louisiana by stealing fifty million dollars in a Ponzi scheme. In a Ponzi scheme, the culprit robs Peter to pay Paul. Lynn did it by creating a fictitious business arrangement between his company, LPM Enterprises, and certain Las Vegas hotels. He then induced his victims into providing LPM with capital to purchase huge blocks of airline tickets for passengers on gambling junkets to these hotels. He represented to the victims that the hotels reimbursed LPM at the end of each month and paid a ten percent commission that he was willing to share with the victims. In exchange for certified or cashiers checks, he issued the victims two postdated checks—one purportedly representing the investment and the other purportedly representing the return on the investment. In fact, there were no arrangements with Las Vegas hotels. He was able to perpetuate the scheme for six years by paying the victims on the due date of the postdated checks with funds obtained from other victims in the Ponzi scheme.

By April of 1988, Lynn was depositing as much as eighteen million dollars a month into his checking account. But the stress and strain of the scheme—the constant need of finding new victims, or finding new money from old victims—became too much for him so he decided to throw in the towel and confess to the FBI. Ultimately, he pleaded guilty to federal racketeering charges and was sentenced to fifteen years in jail.

I never represented Lynn. Instead, one of his victims, Robert J. "Bobby" Guidry, came to see me. Bobby had grown up in Galliano, a small fishing village on Bayou Lafourche between Grand Isle and Donaldsonville. Working on boats since childhood, Bobby had ended his formal education with high school and, although he spoke French fluently, he spoke English with a thick Cajun accent. He had made a fortune in the maritime business with a fleet of tug boats that worked primarily in the oil service industry in the Gulf of Mexico. In short, he was a self-made millionaire and one smart coon-ass—until he met Lynn Paul Martin.

Bobby's background made him peculiarly susceptible to Lynn's scheme. As a rube businessman coming up the hard way, he had experienced the difficulties of obtaining bank financing and the necessity, at times, of having to take on a rich partner who would receive half the profits for simply supplying the capital. Now, he thought, it was his turn to be the rich partner of another struggling Cajun.

When the Ponzi scheme collapsed, Bobby was left holding some twelve million dollars in worthless checks from LPM Enterprises. About half of this amount represented "phantom" profits that he thought he had made in the deal and the other half represented his own hard-earned money that Lynn had stolen from him. But Bobby was not only enraged at Lynn, he was also furious with the banks that had enabled Lynn to get away with the scheme. And, of course, suing Lynn, who was in jail with the money either spent or stashed away, would be like trying to catch a greased pig at a county fair. No, it was the banks that Bobby targeted—and I thought I saw a couple of dragons on the horizon.

The term "Ponzi" is actually the last name of the swindler who perpetrated a similar fraud in the early 1920s. In that case, the victims had also attempted to recover from banks, but they had lost because, " . . . a bank cannot question the legitimacy of a depositor's checks on his bank account." However, a dissenting judge had written that "the community has a right to require high standards of banks and of their officers, and to expect them to discountenance, and when practicable to expose, fraud, and not directly or indirectly to sponsor it, in order to get deposits for their own profit—in this case the deposits of a mere thief." I decided to test the same judicial waters, hoping the dissenting viewpoint of the 1920s would have become the prevailing one in the 1990s.

The banking relationship between Lynn and the Bank of LaPlace (BOL) was not an ordinary one. Initially, he had conducted the scheme through his BOL account and another account at the St. James Bank & Trust Company (SJBT). Following a federal grand jury investigation in 1984, SJBT closed his account, but BOL kept him as a customer even though it was aware of the investigation. His account was overdrawn on virtually every day from April 22, 1986, when a special arrangement was entered into that allowed the bank to charge him interest on the overdrawn balance in addition to the customary per item charge for NSF checks. In effect, this constituted an extension of credit to Lynn of almost one million dollars per day. Because of this special arrangement, the LPM account became a significant profit center for the bank. By 1988, more than half of its overall revenue from overdraft fees came from this one account.

Following the 1984 federal investigation, bank examiners warned BOL about check kiting in Lynn's account and, consequently, the bank required him to deposit only certified or cashier's checks into his account, making him the only customer with such a requirement. Lynn would begin each day by calling BOL's bookkeeper to ascertain the amount of certified or cashier's checks he had to deposit before the close of business. Although the bank had the right to immediately return checks presented against insufficient funds, it extended to him an additional day to make the required deposits. On some occasions when he was unable to make the required deposits, the bank allowed him to decide which checks would be returned NSF. Also, if a victim's check could be returned for a more innocuous reason, such as an insufficient endorsement, the bank would do so, since having checks returned NSF obviously would raise red flags with the victims.

From the beginning, the bank understood Lynn's purported travel business. It understood that he had investors putting up capital to purchase plane tickets to Las Vegas and that the hotels were paying a commission at the end of each month. Yet, instead of showing the supposed legitimate side of the business, the checking account actually reflected only the Ponzi side—that is, money from victims being used to pay other victims. Additionally, not once was an LPM check ever used to buy plane tickets, and not once was a hotel check ever deposited into the account. On the contrary, the account showed LPM checks being used to pay Lynn's personal gambling debts at Las Vegas casinos. Indeed, between April of 1987 and April of 1988, over one million dollars in LPM checks was used to pay his personal gambling debts to Las Vegas casinos. Thus, the BOL account was a mirror of the pyramid scheme.

The other bank we targeted was the huge First National Bank of Commerce (FNBC) in New Orleans, BOL's correspondent bank. A correspondent bank furnishes banking services to a smaller bank. FNBC became involved with Lynn at least as early as April 11, 1985, when Kenneth Martinez, a vice-president, met with one of his customers, William A. Slatten, to discuss a two hundred thousand dollar investment in LPM. Although expressing concern over the fact that "detailed financial information" was not available and that the "dollars involved seem to be pyramiding," Martinez loaned the money to Slatten to invest in LPM.

On April 22, 1986, parenthetically the same day BOL and Lynn entered into their special arrangement, Lynn met with Martinez to obtain a line of credit from FNBC to cover "over line situations" at BOL. FNBC extended the line of credit in the name of Slatten, and Lynn also opened a personal checking account at FNBC. Under the line of credit, FNBC would give Lynn a one hundred thousand dollar cashier's check in exchange for two postdated checks drawn on the BOL account, one for one hundred thousand dollars payable to both FNBC and Slatten—representing a repayment of principal—and the other for Slatten's profits from the transaction. Martinez's secretary held the postdated checks in her desk drawer and, when they became due, FNBC credited the principal check against the line of credit and then issued a new cashier's check to Lynn. The cycle then would repeat itself. Since the LPM checks were always drawn against insufficient funds, the effect of the transaction was for Lynn to be able to exchange a worthless check for an

FNBC cashier's check.

Coincidentally, FNBC began to solicit Bobby as a bank customer during the summer of 1986. Ian Arnof, the top man at FNBC, took him to lunch at the Sazerac in the Fairmont Hotel and courted him as a bank customer, telling him that FNBC was a full service bank that could meet all of his business needs, including investment advice.

Bobby's first investment in LPM was on August 28, 1986. In conducting due diligence, Bobby spoke with a BOL vice-president by telephone and was told that Lynn had been a long-standing, good customer of the bank, that he was in the travel business, that he maintained a six figure account, and that there had never been any trouble with the account. Of course, it turned out that Lynn's account at BOL was in fact overdrawn by over three hundred thousand dollars on the day they spoke and that the bank had returned over four million dollars in NSF checks during the previous month.

Bobby met Martinez around this time and claimed that he relied primarily on Martinez's advice in deciding to invest in LPM. Both the timing and content of these discussions would become hotly contested. FNBC would claim Martinez only told Bobby that Lynn might go "east with the geese." In contrast, Bobby would maintain Martinez told him that he had known Lynn for a long time; that other FNBC customers were LPM investors; that FNBC loaned money to investors in LPM; that FNBC "could find nothing wrong with the deal"; and that it was a "good deal" for the investors. Martinez also gave Bobby information about LPM before Lynn did, such as the names of new hotels and new investors participating in the deal. All of this, when coupled with the fact that FNBC was BOL's correspondent bank and in the position to see both sides of the transactions, led Bobby to believe that FNBC endorsed LPM as a legitimate investment.

At this time, multi-parish banking was prohibited in Louisiana and, consequently, BOL was prohibited from operating a branch bank in downtown New Orleans. To make a deposit, a BOL customer had to either physically hand it to a teller in LaPlace or mail it there. All customers, that is, except Lynn. He was allowed to make deposits by taking them directly to FNBC in downtown New Orleans for simultaneous credit to BOL's account at FNBC and the LPM account at BOL. This highly unusual banking practice was permitted even though an FNBC employee warned her superiors that she suspected Lynn of money-laundering.

During the late fall of 1987, Bobby began to reduce his LPM investments. Then one day Martinez told him that LPM was a "bankable deal" and that some bank would replace investors as the source of LPM capital. Believing he had received important insider information from Martinez, he increased his investments from roughly two million to over five million dollars.

After the scheme collapsed, Bobby met Martinez for lunch at Kolb's Restaurant and secretly taped their conversation. Bobby reviewed the history of their LPM discussions and, instead of contradicting his version, Martinez apologized for the "miscommunication" and admitted he had been negligent: "I need to be clear and understanding with Bobby. I can't use fifty-cent banking terms . . . when maybe I should be talking on other lines."

We initially filed suit in federal court, alleging that the banks conspired with Lynn to conduct a racketeering enterprise and that the investment transactions constituted securities fraud. We soon learned the judicial waters had not changed much since the 1920s. In spite of the fact that we alleged exactly the same RICO enterprise used in the indictment against Lynn, and in spite of the fact that the SEC had obtained a judgment recognizing the investments as securities, the District Court dismissed our complaint. The Court of Appeals affirmed, but allowed us to proceed in State Court on State law claims.

Civil lawsuits are different from criminal lawsuits in many respects. For example, in civil lawsuits the defense lawyers are the bad guys, exactly the opposite in criminal cases. Also, since property is at risk in civil lawsuits, the law provides for full discovery, meaning a defendant can learn everything available about the case against him before it goes to trial. In contrast, in criminal cases, where only a person's liberty is at stake, the defense gets very little discovery and trial by ambush is the norm. Because of full discovery, defense lawyers in civil cases bombard the plaintiff's lawyer with paperwork. Also, defense lawyers get paid by the hour, while plaintiff lawyers usually get paid only if they win the case. Thus, it is standard practice for civil defense lawyers to prolong pre-trial litigation for as long as possible. The bank lawyers in this case were no different.

One of the bank lawyers (there were eight altogether) was Patrick Vance, a partner in a huge law firm. Patrick, whom I had known for many years, was married to Sarah Beth Savoia from Donaldsonville. Sarah, a lawyer too, had finished at the top of her class at Tulane Law School. She also had the blackest hair and the whitest skin of any girl in Donaldsonville, and I had had a crush on her since high school.

In the middle of these protracted proceedings, Sarah was in line for an appointment to the federal bench. I wrote a letter on her behalf to another old Donaldsonvillian, James Carville, who had been one of the chief architects of President Clinton's election. During the course of the FBI's background check, Sarah's father, a wounded World War II veteran endearingly known as "Cap," was going around Donaldsonville claiming to have a better war record than the President. I called Pat, a typically uptight, big firm lawyer, and told him that I had received an alarming call from Carville and that they had better "muzzle Cap" since the White House had "ears" in Donaldsonville. Pat was mortified, and I delighted in repaying him for the harassment I was getting from his gang of lawyers in Bobby's case.

Although suit was filed in 1989, we didn't go to trial until 1994. The jury was my kind of jury: predominantly black, blue-collar, street-wise—a cab driver, a black minister, a cook, a nurse—people who lived in the real world. I began by standing in front of them with a stack of dollar bills in one hand and a bundle of Monopoly money in the other, saying:

> "Robert Guidry gave over five and a half million of these to Lynn Paul Martin. In exchange, Robert Guidry got about twelve million of these—Monopoly money, funny money, phantom money. You must wonder that my client here must be pretty stupid. I mean, how can someone give five and a half million dollars for twelve million dollars of play money? That's what happened in this case. That's what we are going to spend some time explaining to you. What you will find out is that far from being stupid, Robert Guidry is not that. He's not well educated, but he ain't stupid, but what he did was he trusted the wrong people. He misplaced his trust and as a result of that, he got raked."

Anticipating the card I knew Pat and his gang of bank lawyers would play throughout the trial, I went on:

> "Now the bank lawyers are going to make a big, big, big point throughout this trial, I submit, about greed. . . . The evidence will show that there are two kinds of greed. There is a kind of greed where a man says: 'Look, I was born poor, I been lucky, but I have worked hard and I made money and I like making money and I'm going to make as much money as I can make'—and if that is greedy, then Robert Guidry is greedy. But there is another kind of greed that I suggest you will see in this case, and that is the greed of someone who says: 'No matter—maybe I may not make a lot of money, but I'm going to make it, and I'm going to make it by screwing somebody else over. I'm not going to play the rules right. I'm going to hurt people and run over people.' That is the kind of greed that Robert Guidry does not have."

I ended the opening statement discussing the Kolb's luncheon where Martinez apologized to Bobby for his negligence: "Well sorry don't count. What counts is the fact that we will prove through this case that this real money—some of it went over there," dropping a stack of dollar bills at Pat's feet, "more of it went over here . . . " dropping more at the feet of another bank lawyer, "some of it went to Lynn Paul Martin, and some of it went to investors who got out of the deal in time. We, however, got this. . . ," dropping all of the Monopoly money at Bobby's feet. "So," I concluded, "we are going to ask you today and in this trial for justice!"

The trial went well for us. Predictably, the bankers came across as stuffed shirts, while Bobby was magnificent on the witness stand. Explaining the trust he had placed in bankers, he said:

> "You see, I have been raised to believe that a banker—where I'm from . . . in Galliano—the smartest guy in the community was the banker and the priest. That was the smartest guy. You lived and believed in whatever the banker told you. Now that's the truth.
>
> I used to pass down the road with my dad when I was six years old, and I would say, 'Daddy, who lives in that big house right there?' 'That's Mr. Funderburk's, he's the guy that owns the Citizen's Bank.' You know what I'm talking about? And boy, that's a smart man, you know. My dad still feels that way about bankers, but I've changed my mind about them."

On cross-examination, when Pat challenged whether he really felt that way about priests, let alone bankers, Bobby stood up and, pulling a large rosary from his pocket, said that his mother had given it to him to carry always. A knock-out punch. The jury loved Bobby and identified with him, not with the bankers in their Brooks Brothers suits and Hermes ties.

As plaintiff's counsel, I had the opportunity, like a prosecutor in a criminal case, to make two closing arguments to the jury—a luxury usually not mine. And so, I parroted Peter Strasser in the Cavin case by keeping the first argument low-keyed:

> "Bobby may not be educated, but he's sharp. He's sharp as a fox because he invited the man to lunch, and he had a little Arab tape-recorder in his sock at Kolb's Restaurant, and that's where the man told him the things that he wouldn't tell him in front of his bosses. Look, you remember fifty-cent banking. Let me tell you, if your roofer tells you, 'I'm sorry, I did fifty-cent roofing for you,' you know what that means. It's going to rain in your house; and if your banker tells you, 'I'm sorry, I did fifty-cent banking for you,' you know what that means. There's a big hole in your wallet. And there's a big hole in Mr. Bobby Guidry's wallet as a result of the fifty-cent banking that he received from these banks."

After the gang of bank lawyers had made their final arguments, I came back like Marvin Opotowski with both barrels blasting:

"Let me talk a little ham and eggs law to you about this case. . . . You are going to hear the judge use a big term when he instructs you on the law, and he is going to talk to you about a fiduciary duty. A fiduciary duty. Let me talk to you about that.

You know, suppose a guy owned a bar and he is sitting at the bar and he is wiping the bar and he looks out of the window and he sees a guy rape a woman out there and he doesn't do anything. He just keeps wiping, just keeps wiping. He is not a very good citizen for doing that, but he doesn't break the law. He doesn't have to go out to try to rescue her.

Now if he goes out there and holds the poor lady's hands down, he is obviously aiding and abetting. But aiding and abetting ain't always that obvious.

Suppose the guy owns the bar and he's cleaning the bar and the bad guy is in there, and he knows the guy. The guy has been coming in there. He knows the guy's reputation. The man's been around there. He's done things before. He knows that he is abusive to women and he sees the man in there with a young lady and he starts giving the young lady free drinks and the young lady is drinking them and drinking them and she has too much to drink, and he's giving her more free drinks—the bar owner—and the man takes her out. She leaves with the guy and the man goes out and date-rapes her. This bar owner has aided and abetted. What is his motive? I don't know. He is sick. But what his motive is, I don't know. Maybe he just likes to listen to the bad guy come back the next day and boast about it. You don't need a motive. You're not going to hear the judge ever say, 'motive.' But the bar owner is aiding and abetting.

Let me tell you what is really like this case.

The man is in his barroom and the young lady comes to him. 'Mr. So & So, this guy over here wants me to go out with him. What do you know about this guy?' Well the bar owner can do three things. He can tell her the truth: 'I know this guy. This guy is trouble. Darlin', don't go out with this guy.' He could have done that. The other thing he could have done is he could have said, 'Miss, I am sorry. I can't talk about my customers. I can't talk about my customers.'

Or, the third thing he could have done: 'I've been knowing that guy for four years. He's a good guy. He's a good customer. A lot of my other customers have gone out with him. He's got a lot of money. Now he might die one day. He might go east with the geese, but I can't find anything wrong with the guy. As a matter of fact, he's marriage material. He's marriageable. He's marriageable.'

That's what happened in this case and when that happens, that's breaking a fiduciary duty. When you go to someone who's in the position to know—to ask for advice when you're trying to make an important decision—and that person gives you inaccurate advice, misleading advice, and you rely upon that advice to your detriment, that person has breached the fiduciary duty and that person belongs in jail with the perpetrators. That's what this case is all about."

During Pat's closing argument, he played the greed card as expected, saying "Greedy hogs get slaughtered first." I rode back on the boomerang:

"The only problem with the statement is that Mr. Vance doesn't decide which hogs are going to be slaughtered in this case. You folks are going to decide that, and you know, I know a little something about hogs, because I grew up in the country. I know how you call the hogs in: 'Sooey, sooey, sooey.' You bring them in.

Let me tell you what the facts of this case demonstrate.

The facts of this case demonstrate that Mr. Bobby Guidry is slopping the trough and the banks are in the trough with Lynn Paul Martin. And you know what the bank officers are doing? They're the ones hollering, 'Sooey, sooey.'"

The jury returned a verdict in Bobby's favor for over four and a half million dollars. But, unfortunately, the Court of Appeals reversed the verdict against the banks and left us with a worthless judgment against Lynn Paul Martin. It seems the judicial waters haven't changed much since the 1920s after all. While the jury obviously believed the banks were the hogs, the appellate judges believed the banks were still sacred cows.

Today, Lynn Paul Martin is out of prison, living in Florida and, incredibly, working for a travel agency. Bobby Guidry owns a river boat casino and is making more money than ever before. After the trial, I ran into Pat one night at Emeril's Restaurant and drunkenly told him that his real victory over me had occurred long ago when he rode out of Donaldsonville with Sarah. Those kinds of wounds never heal.

Twenty-One

The Gay Grail

Kirksey McCord Nix was an enigma. The son of an Oklahoma judge, he came from a middle-class family. Like me, he was educated and pampered. His father expected him to become a lawyer and his mother wanted him to slay dragons for a living. Instead, Kirksey became an outlaw.

Kirksey was a member of the so-called Dixie Mafia and his side-kicks called him "Junior." Junior reputedly participated in the ambush of Sheriff Buford Pusser and his wife, the subject matter of the movie *Walking Tall.* In 1972, he was convicted of murder in New Orleans and sentenced to life imprisonment. At Angola, he rose to the top of the barrel by establishing himself as a kingfish among the prison population. Indeed, Junior achieved his success at Angola by masterminding a nation-wide scam that provided him with the means to buy a Mercedes and a house on the Mississippi Gulf Coast, all the while behind prison walls.

Junior became a millionaire by using the United States mail and the telephone in a scheme directed at homosexuals. He would run ads like the following in gay magazines:

> "Be my summer lover. Cute, slim, seeks sincere, warm relationship. Willing to relocate for the summer or permanently if love blooms. I'm romantic, cuddly, shy and need someone special in my life."

After Cupid struck, Junior would write love letters and enclose, as a picture of himself, a semi-nude photograph of an attractive young lad. Usually the relationship developed into telephone sex, with Junior talking boy-talk. Then, an inevitable disaster would strike. For instance, pretending to be a first offender joy-rider, he might say he needed money for a lawyer, or money for a fine, or money for restitution, or money for clothing, or money for a plane ticket to join the mark upon his release.

Of course, no young lover ever materialized, and Junior ended up with all of the money.

Besides cunning, Junior needed one other thing to make the scheme work: outside help. He needed comrades to receive mail—since he obviously couldn't use Angola as a return address—or to patch in telephone calls to conceal their point of origin. And most importantly, he needed confederates to pick up the money from Western Union. Most of his helpers were former inmates, but the scheme became so complex that he needed assistants who could come and go from Angola freely. Those with the greatest access to a penitentiary, besides prison guards, are criminal defense lawyers. And Junior had a number of them.

One of his lawyers was Pete Halat, whose law partner, Vincent Sherry, was a judge in Biloxi, Mississippi. The law firm of Halat and Sherry employed Junior's girlfriend, LaRa Sharpe, as a paralegal and the firm maintained a trust account where a lot of his money was kept.

On September 14, 1987, Judge Sherry and his wife Margaret were found murdered. It was clearly a professional hit. Four years later, Junior, LaRa, and two others were indicted by a federal grand jury in Mississippi for conspiracy to murder the Sherrys. The government's theory was that Junior had them executed because the Judge had misappropriated some of the scam profits from the trust account. On November 11, 1991, the defendants were convicted. Junior received a fifteen-year sentence to run after his life sentence at Angola was completed.

I never represented Junior, but I did represent another one of his lawyers, Joe Rome, a young black lawyer from New Orleans. A classic example of academic affirmative action, Joe had graduated from Rutgers and Tulane Law School, only to find himself on the streets without a job. So he hustled business as best he could, and in New Orleans the best place for a young lawyer to do that is at Tulane and Broad. Although the vast majority of defendants at Tulane and Broad are indigent and represented by public defenders at trial and on appeal, defendants must hire a private lawyer for post-conviction proceedings such as writs of habeas corpus and parole and pardon board hearings. Focusing on this market, Joe became a post-conviction specialist, which naturally took him frequently to Angola where he met Junior and began to do legal work for him. Junior referred former inmates to him as clients and soon Joe had a thriving practice. However, many of these clients, without his knowledge, were actively assisting Junior in his million dollar scam.

Once the investigation began, some of these clients cut deals with the State and testified before the grand jury that Joe was a knowing participant in the scam. On October 5, 1989, Joe and Junior were indicted in West Feliciana Parish for theft and criminal conspiracy. The indictment charged that Joe knowingly assisted in the scheme by picking up and delivering ill-gotten profits.

The Feliciana parishes are spectacular, with rolling hills, sandy creeks, moss-laden trees, and antebellum homes. It's the place where

Audubon painted some of his famous birds. As a matter of fact, my mother and Aunt Delta claim one of my ancestors, as a young boy, held the turkey while Audubon painted it.

The Felicianas are also the home of the Louisiana State Penitentiary. Angola, a six thousand acre prison farm deep in the Tunica Hills, is surrounded on three sides by the Mississippi River. No one escapes. The grounds are immaculate, as one might expect with six cents an hour labor. But because of Angola, there are more criminals in the Felicianas than anywhere else in the state, and since criminals commit crimes in jail, most prison crime in Louisiana is prosecuted in the Felicianas. Since Angola is the largest employer in the area, most prospective jurors are in some way related to an Angola guard. In other words, the hen is truly tried by the fox in the Felicianas.

If Joe Rome had any chance, it wouldn't be in the Felicianas. He had three strikes against him: he was black, he was from New Orleans, and he was a criminal defense lawyer (in reverse order). And so we filed a motion to change venue. The "Angola scandals," as the case was referred to in the local press, was the hottest topic of conversation in the community. After all, Kirksey McCord Nix had made more money in prison than most people make out of prison. It was precisely the kind of situation a change of venue was designed to alleviate.

The DA, George "Hal" Ware, Jr., a courtly Feliciana aristocrat, handled the case personally. I was shocked when he consented to the change of venue. I don't know why he did, perhaps because it was the right thing to do—although doing the right thing is not in the typical prosecutor's protocol. Actually, at Tulane and Broad, the saying is that it's only fun to prosecute innocent defendants.

The case was transferred to Alexandria, certainly no hot bed of liberalism, but I was ecstatic because it did have a sizable black community and, of course, Bobbie Gail lived there. The case was assigned to Judge Guy Humphries, a John Wayne clone in semi-retirement. Years before, I had served with him as the token liberal on the Louisiana Law Enforcement Commission and, although we seldom saw matters eye to eye, we had a mutual respect for one another.

Although the change of venue was granted on May 9, 1990, the case was not transferred to Alexandria for some time. The original trial date had to be changed because Judge Wicker rescheduled A. P. Marullo's case. Also, Junior's federal case for the conspiracy to murder the Sherrys had to be accommodated and so, on the basis of a joint motion to continue, trial was not set until July 6, 1992.

While preparing for trial, Joe came to my office one day and announced that the delay for bringing him to trial had elapsed. In Louisiana, a defendant charged with a felony must be brought to trial within two years, and while this prescriptive period had been suspended during the pendency of the motions we had filed, it had not been suspended long enough to justify the thirty-three month delay in the case.

On the morning of trial, we filed a motion to dismiss on the grounds that too much time had elapsed. Hal reacted as though he had been holding the Audubon turkey and it had shit on him. The Judge, regaining his composure, granted the motion and the Supreme Court ultimately affirmed and dismissed the case.

I suspect Hal believed I intentionally duped him and that it was me, and not Joe, who was watching the clock all along. I'm sure some people believe a criminal defense lawyer is duty bound to bring his client to the gallows on time. Not I. This was a case where we caught the dragon dozing. And in this business, you take the kill any way you can.

Twenty-Two

The Fallen Priest

Dino Cinel didn't look like a priest. Originally from Italy, he had come to this country in the early 1970s for graduate study. He received a masters degree in American History from New York University and a Ph.D. from Stanford University. He wore longish hair, and a cherubic face framed by owlish glasses made him look more like a college professor than a priest. Indeed, he came to New Orleans in 1979 to teach history at Tulane University. But Dino was, nonetheless, a priest—of sorts. He moved into the rectory at St. Rita's Church, where the Pastor, Father James Tarantino, gave him free room and board in exchange for assisting with pastoral chores. However, most of Dino's time was spent teaching at Tulane, where the academic community didn't even know he was a priest.

Dino also didn't act like a priest, at least not the way we understood in Donaldsonville they were supposed to act. Sexually active, with a homosexual preference, he began a relationship shortly after arriving in New Orleans with two young men, Christopher Fontaine and Ronald Tichenor, both of whom he'd met in an area of the French Quarter frequented by gays. During these torrid relationships, he made videotapes of their sexual activity, including sodomy, buggery, masturbation, and group sex—in other words, the whole nine inches. The filming took place either in his suite of rooms at the rectory or at a separate apartment he kept for that purpose. He also went on fun weekend trips with either Chris or Ron to the Mississippi Gulf Coast, staying in a friend's summer house, and once he and Chris spent a romantic week together in San Francisco.

Dino's sexual interests, however, began to change in the late 1980s because of Linda Pollack, a colleague who had come from Scotland to teach at Tulane. Dino and Linda began to date and eventually they fell in love and decided to marry. He told her about his unpriestly past, and she went with him to some voluntary therapy sessions in order to keep him pointed in the right direction.

On December 28, 1988, Dino left for Italy to tell his family he was leaving the priesthood and getting married. After dropping him at the airport, Linda went shopping and accidentally locked the keys in Dino's car. She called St. Rita's to inquire about an extra set of keys. Father Tarantino went into Dino's suite of rooms to look for the keys and, finding none on the desk top, he began to search the desk drawers and he supposedly stumbled upon a magazine advertising telephone sex. Becoming curious, the Pastor removed the magazine and discovered that it contained a catalog of X-rated videos. He then saw other catalogs and, under them, some manila envelopes. Peeking in, he found photographs and negatives of naked boys with full erections. The Pastor then left Dino's suite, but later that night he sneaked back in, continuing his search for pornography. Rifling through the closet in the study, he found some foreign porno magazines and 8mm films which featured naked boys coupling other naked boys. In the bedroom closet, he found the homemade videos of Dino having sex with Chris and Ron.

The next morning, the Pastor called Archbishop Philip Hannan, the very popular leader of the large Catholic community in New Orleans. A canonical lawyer, a World War II chaplain, and a friend of the Kennedy family of Massachusetts, the Archbishop knew his way around political circles and understood how to handle power. Aunt Delta, on the other hand, referred to him as "Mister" Hannan rather than "Archbishop" or "His Excellency," saying he was the only Roman Catholic she knew.

The Archbishop called Dino to demand an immediate resignation from the priesthood and to strongly suggest he stay in Italy. Agreeing to resign but insisting upon returning to the United States, Dino objected to the removal of the materials from his suite. But in spite of this, the Archbishop directed the Pastor to confiscate the materials and, over the course of the next few days, he removed four boxes of pornographic materials. On the Archbishop's instructions, the Pastor delivered the materials to the Church's attorneys, one of whom was Don Richard, the former AUSA who had prosecuted Dr. Beasley.

When Dino returned from Italy in mid-January, he hired William Campbell to represent him. A former ADA, Bill attempted to retrieve the materials but, after keeping them for three months, Don delivered them instead to Harry Connick. In taking this action, however, the Church made it clear that it didn't want a criminal prosecution. One of Don's law partners wrote to the DA:

> "We therefore wish to make it clear that it was not the intention of the Archdiocese in (turning over the materials) that it would be regarded as seeking to initiate or urge prosecution of Dr. Cinel or anyone else thereby. This action on the part of the Archdiocese should therefore not be considered by your office as in any way seeking the initiation of criminal charges with respect to this material

or any activities of Dr. Cinel in relation thereto."

When the materials had been discovered in Dino's suite, the Archbishop's principal concern had been whether Dino's sex partners in the homemade videos were altar boys or other parishioners who might sue the Church. No one had cared much about the porno magazines and 8mm films that had been commercially produced in a foreign country. Although the Church would eventually determine that altar boys and parishioners were not involved, no one at St. Rita's knew the identities of Chris and Ron. Once in the DA's possession, the prosecutors were also more interested in the homemade videos. In order to prove the commission of certain criminal offenses, the DA would have to prove the young males were underage, and it would be much easier to do this through the testimony of the sex partners in the homemade videos rather than by attempting to prove the ages of the unknown male models in the foreign magazines and 8mm films. But the prosecutors also didn't know the identities of Chris and Ron.

In an effort to avoid criminal prosecution, Bill Campbell spoke directly to his old boss, Harry Connick, who told him that his chief investigator, Sergeant George Tolar, was in charge of the case. Bill and Sergeant Tolar began to negotiate and in early May Campbell was told that Connick had decided not to prosecute. Shortly afterwards, however, Connick's position changed because a television reporter, Joe Giardino, had made inquiries about the case and John Volz, the United States Attorney, had written a letter to Connick expressing an interest in the case: "If you decide that state prosecution is not viable, we would appreciate the use of this material as evidence in support of potential federal prosecution."

In view of these developments, Sergeant Tolar told Campbell that Dino would have to reveal the identities of his sex partners and prove that they were consenting adults in order to avoid prosecution. Sergeant Tolar assured him, however, that once the information was validated, Dino would not be prosecuted for anything, including possession of the commercially produced magazines and 8mm films and that the identities of his sex partners would remain strictly confidential. In the words of Bill Campbell:

> "I was making the negotiation in good faith that either we get charged with whatever they can prove or, if we can prove that there's no crime in here, we don't get charged with anything. And that was—that was clear to me and it was clear to Mr. Tolar. And it was—it was confirmed by the fact that he had always reiterated that the commercially made material was of no interest. And so for him, from his perspective, him giving that up was fine with him and I accepted it."

Operating under this game plan, Campbell provided affidavits from Chris and Ron setting forth their birth dates, stating they were consenting adults at the time the videos were made, and attaching copies of their drivers' licenses. With this information, Sergeant Tolar commenced an investigation by running "rap" sheets on Chris and Ron, interviewing Father Tarantino, and taking a number of taped statements from Chris. In one such session, Chris went into a rage upon being shown a magazine from Denmark titled *Dream Boy* which contained nude photographs of him. Claiming it was the first time he knew anything about the magazine, he nonetheless admitted that he was a consenting adult at the time Dino took the *Dream Boy* photographs.

All in all, the DA's investigation validated the fact that Chris and Ron were consenting adults when the videos were made. In Sergeant Tolar's words: "By September the 12th, Mr. Connick had decided that there were going to be no criminal charges in the case because Bill Campbell had been able to demonstrate that the two (2) young men were consenting." Campbell agreed, saying Sergeant Tolar told him, " . . . that would be the end of it."

Also believing the matter over and that he could go forward with his life as a history professor, Dino and Linda married, bought a home on State Street, and had a baby daughter, Sophia. In 1991, the Cinel family moved to New York, where he became a distinguished professor of history at the City University of New York (CUNY) and she became a visiting professor at Columbia.

Sergeant Tolar, however, had a different plan in mind. His old buddy, Gary Raymond, a former cop and investigator in the DA's office, was now a private investigator. Sergeant Tolar put Raymond onto the case and he located Chris and took him to David Paddison, a personal injury lawyer who had been an ADA in Connick's office. Paddison associated Darryl Tschirn, a well-known personal injury lawyer, and on November 30, 1989, these bounty hunters filed a multimillion dollar lawsuit against Dino and the Church. Of course, the real target of the lawsuit was the Church and its treasures.

After filing the lawsuit, the bounty hunters naturally wanted to get their hands on the evidence that had been removed from Dino's suite, but a Civil District Court judge refused to permit them to view the evidence in the DA's possession. Shortly afterwards, a subpoena duces tecum was issued to Sergeant Tolar, directing him to produce "any and all films, videos, magazines and other items seized from the residence of Dr. Dino Cinel or from the rectory of St. Rita's Church." When Connick learned of the subpoena, he wanted something in his file to "cover" the fact that the evidence would be released to third parties. He directed Sergeant Tolar to prepare a "nonprosecution" memorandum:

"To: Harry Connick
From: George Tolar
Date: February 22, 1990
Re: Former Catholic Priest Dino Cinel

On March 29, 1989, I took possession of several boxes of material, most notably video tapes, from Mr. Charles Denechaud, Jr. Mr. Denechaud is the attorney for the Archdiocese of New Orleans.

The video tapes depicted Dino Cinel, an ex-priest, involved in graphic sex acts with various individuals. Two of these individuals, Ronald Tichenor and Chris Fontaine, were eventually identified.

Statements were obtained from Chris Fontaine that he and Dino Cinel did engage in these acts but that Fontaine was seventeen (17) years of age or older.

The second individual, Ronald Tichenor, was located in Florida and was absolutely hostile and uncooperative.

As a result of our investigation we determined that no violation of law occurred."

With this "cover," the DA's office released the materials to the bounty hunters—under the pretext of a consent judgment in the civil case that named Tschirn and Paddison as custodians—and authorized Raymond to make copies of the materials "upon the request of any parties to this litigation." This consent judgment was in direct violation of a state statute, which provided that the Criminal District Court alone should determine the disposition of evidence no longer needed in a criminal investigation.

Meanwhile, Dino, who was still living in New York, didn't find out about the civil case until after the DA had released the materials to the bounty hunters. After being served with the suit, he hired a civil lawyer to represent him in the case, a lawyer who frankly shouldn't have been practicing law. Disbarred once before for being a convicted felon, the lawyer was an alcoholic and altogether a disgrace to the profession—but he was cheap and, unfortunately, Dino got what he paid for. During Dino's deposition, the lawyer advised him that he couldn't take the Fifth Amendment in civil proceedings, and Tschirn, a crafty trial lawyer, raked him over the coals. Dino admitted his homosexual relationships with Chris and Ron and also admitted possessing the materials that had been found in his suite at St. Rita's. But perhaps more damaging was his demeanor during the deposition. In sum, Dino intellectualized conduct that most people considered perverted and, in doing so, he presented himself as an arrogant, unrepentant sinner, saying, for example, when asked about his relationship with Chris, that " . . . considering the promiscuity in which he was living, I was the best person he could have sex with." To make matters worse, the deposition was videotaped, and Raymond sent a copy of it to Connick with a cover letter stating that Dino was a " . . . dangerous pedophile, an admitted pornographer with international connections in the sordid multi-million dollar child pornography business." Connick did nothing.

Approximately one year later, on March 14, 1991, when the Church refused to pay their exorbitant demands, the bounty hunters decided to try the case in the press and, in direct violation of the consent judgment, Raymond leaked the pornographic materials and a copy of Dino's video deposition to Richard Angelico, a local television reporter. Then, using confidential law enforcement information supplied—I suspect—by Sergeant Tolar, Raymond and Angelico went to Florida where Raymond solicited Ron as a client and his lawsuit against Dino and the Church was filed soon afterwards. Next, the United States Attorney's office was implicated, and on April 25, 1991, Paddison and Raymond staged the delivery of the pornographic materials to the federal grand jury, with Angelico filming them as they carried the boxes into the federal courthouse.

Angelico was now ready to break the story but his employer, WDSU, apparently recognizing that discretion is the better part of valor, refused to broadcast the story. This, however, was a minor obstacle to these old pros and they easily circumvented it by planting the story with Hugh Aynsworth, a free lance reporter in Dallas, whom Raymond and Angelico had known from the days of Garrison's investigation into the Kennedy assassination. And so, on May 14, 1991, Aynsworth broke the story in the *Washington Times*, proclaiming that it was "the most documented case of pedophilia involving a religious figure." A *fait accompli.* Angelico was then able to broadcast his story on the same day and there followed an onslaught of media coverage, including scenes from the homemade videos as well as from the porno magazines and 8mm films—all of which naturally created a lynch mob attitude toward Dino. The story spread like wildfire to New York, and CUNY suspended him from his teaching position.

Dino, however, was not the sole target of the press. Alleging a cover-up, the paparazzi also went after the Archbishop and Harry Connick. It turned out that Connick, a St. Rita's parishioner, had known Dino personally and, according to the *Times-Picayune*:

> "District Attorney Harry Connick, who for two years refused to press child pornography charges against ex-priest Dino Cinel, received Cinel as a guest in his home on two occasions before the pornography came to light, Connick's former wife said this week."

The *coup de grace* came when Connick, confronted on camera by Angelico, admitted that an "absolute consideration" in his decision not to prosecute was to avoid embarrassing "Holy Mother the Church."

Archbishop Hannan was also on the rack and screw, being accused of making a deal with Connick not to have Dino prosecuted as long as he resigned from the priesthood. The Archbishop angrily denied the accusation and, in a television interview on May 17, 1991, His Excellency "targeted Cinel and called for criminal charges to be filed against him." Four days later, Connick obediently charged Dino with criminally possessing the commercially produced foreign magazines and 8mm films, the stuff no one had been concerned with when the materials were first removed from Dino's suite at the rectory.

I had been following the story on the sidelines with delight, seeing that two ancient foes—the Church and king—had been caught in their own web of deceit. Unexpectedly, I received a call from Winn Stoutz, a lawyer and old friend, who asked if I might be interested in representing Dino. Always interested in doing battle with dragons, I agreed to meet him.

Since the warrant for his arrest would have to be executed in New York and since fighting extradition is usually fruitless, I advised Winn that Dino should return voluntarily to New Orleans. Understandably reluctant to return without knowing what was in store for him, he agreed, as a compromise, to meet me at Winn's weekend home on the Mississippi Gulf Coast. I learned later, ironically, that this was the site for some of his trysts.

In the meantime, Linda had completed her visiting professorship at Columbia and was teaching at Tulane and living in New Orleans with Sophia. I met with her at my office. She was small, frail, and unstylishly dressed with a boyish hairdo and no make-up; it didn't take long to realize, however, that she had a coldly analytical mind. She was Scottish, Presbyterian, intellectual and, altogether, one tough lady. I liked her immediately. We agreed on a fee and drove to Mississippi to meet Dino.

He was a cosmopolitan charmer who spoke with a beautiful Italian accent and, as with some priests and all good college lecturers, he had a flair for the dramatic. And very pedagogical—lecturing me, as he did, on the cosmic consequences of sticking one's penis in a young boy's behind. But he was also terrified of going to jail and facing the mob in New Orleans. Fleeing to Italy was discussed as an option, but Linda made it abundantly clear that she and Sophia were not leaving. He decided to face the mob in New Orleans.

Lawsuits and sporting events have much in common, particularly that strange phenomenon known as momentum. Momentum usually begins on the offensive side of the playing field and always ends with the winner. In the context of criminal trials, momentum always begins with the prosecution and, unless it is taken away before trial's end, the defense will surely lose.

In this case, the momentum was against Dino on four different fronts:

first, with the press and public opinion; second, in the civil cases brought by the bounty hunters; third, in the criminal case brought by Connick; and fourth, in the CUNY disciplinary action. Each front, however, was important—and all were interrelated. For example, the CUNY action was important because we needed Dino's salary to wage the battle on the other fronts. Similarly, public opinion was important because of its potential impact on prospective jurors. In short, we needed to reverse the momentum on all fronts.

In the mid-1980s, the public had been shocked and repelled by the conviction in Lafayette of Father Gilbert Gauthe for sexually molesting altar boys. Since then, whenever a priest was connected to sex, the public's perception invariably turned to pedophilia. So it was with Dino. In truth, however, he was no longer a priest, and Chris and Ron, far from being altar boys, were actually consenting adults who had been soliciting a sugar daddy in the French Quarter, not in the sacristy. But sometimes truth can be a hard sell.

Realizing that Dino's arrest would generate a rerun of the inflammatory news coverage already in the copy rooms, we had to create our own media event, so I called a press conference for seven o'clock one morning, promising an important development in the Cinel case. This alone created quite a stir since it was not public knowledge that I would be representing him. At the appointed time, I strolled into my conference room with Dino and Linda, hand-in-hand. It was Linda's first public appearance, and I had prevailed upon her to dress as though on a honeymoon. And, drawing upon my confessional experiences in Donaldsonville, I prepared a statement for Dino to read to the press which made him sound repentant without actually admitting guilt. The press then filmed us walking into the police station where Dino voluntarily surrendered. The strategy worked: the coverage showed the self-surrender of a repentant, married man with a seductive wife—a far cry from a pedophile in priestly garb. Nonetheless, it was just one small step for the defense.

The press and public opinion are an important part of the criminal justice system and are becoming increasingly important with the proliferation of media outlets. It has been suggested, for example, that the O.J. Simpson defense team attempted to inoculate the jury pool by generating favorable pre-trial stories about Mr. Simpson. Much the same way, politicians attempt to spin a particular slant on a story. Dragon slayers must carefully control the kind and the quantity of information available about a defendant.

The criminal case was allotted to Judge Fred Shaw at Tulane and Broad. Judge Shaw was crazy. Now lest I be misunderstood, he had good reason to be crazy and he may not have always been crazy, but crazy he was. His life had been Sophoclean. Although he was married with a family, his true love had been his mistress. After a twenty-year relationship, he finally had left his wife and family to marry the mistress, only to have her suddenly become ill with a rare blood disease. While at her bedside in the hospital, he had suffered a major heart attack and, refusing to stay in Intensive Care, he had been given a bed in her room. She died in his arms. Eventually, Judge Shaw reconciled with his wife and moved back home with his family. Then one night, the house burned to the ground and his wife and only daughter perished in the fire. He was left with only one surviving child, an alcoholic son who had accidentally set the fire in the first place.

Pandemonium reigned in Judge Shaw's courtroom. The alcoholic son had his own desk and minute clerk—located right next to his father's bench and minute clerk—and he functioned as a sort of deputy judge, interrupting and correcting his father at will during the course of judicial proceedings. Now as long as the Judge and the alcoholic son were in sync, things went pretty smoothly but, more often than not, all hell broke loose when, for example, the Judge sustained an objection and the alcoholic son overruled it simultaneously.

The pace was also crazy. Judge Shaw and the alcoholic son took their respective seats at eight o'clock in the morning and it was not uncommon for them to adjourn for the day an hour and a half later. In earlier years, when the Judge was in his prime and the alcoholic son was too young to preside, the Judge had consistently tried as many as three jury trials a day—as one jury deliberated, another was selected. And court usually wouldn't adjourn until three o'clock the following morning. In short, Dino wouldn't stand a chance with Judge Shaw or, for that matter, with the alcoholic son.

I was having lunch one day with Robert Glass, a capable lawyer, and I mentioned this predicament to him. He responded by saying that Judge Shaw habitually recused himself in cases in which Franz Zibilich appeared as defense counsel since Franz was doing some legal work for the Judge. I had taught Franz in law school and his late father had been one of my mentors. I knew that Franz was a good young lawyer, actively practicing at Tulane and Broad and, since I hadn't tried a case there in many years, there would be many benefits to having him on the team. I told this to Dino and he instructed me to hire Franz as co-counsel. Sure enough, with Franz aboard, the case was reallotted to none other than Judge Frank Marullo. It was like striking gold.

Judge Marullo, on the other hand, was not too happy about getting this hot and steamy potato. And having him on the case was not all pluses: Judge Marullo was a Roman Catholic, Italian, and very macho; there was the real danger of Dino being viewed by him as a betrayer of faith, country, and manhood. And naturally, everyone is prejudiced against pedophilia. Moreover, the Judge's wife Jackie exhaled fire at the mere mention of Dino's name. And Jackie didn't stand alone: R.A. and my mother were right there with her.

Many judges have problems with their court reporters because they often get tired from their tedious task of recording trial proceedings.

Consequently, trials frequently have to be halted midstream in order to allow the court reporters to take a break. Fortunately, Judge Marullo didn't have this problem because his court reporter, Miss Alma, never got tired. The reason Miss Alma never got tired was because she slept right through the trial proceedings. Now mind you, even this didn't create a problem because Miss Alma typed while she slept. Instead, Miss Alma's problem was her hearing—but not, as you might expect, because her hearing was bad; rather, it was because her hearing was too good. For instance, when proceedings were held in chambers, Miss Alma, asleep at her machine, would often pick up in the background the "Donahue" show playing softly on the TV next to the Judge's desk. In those cases, the transcripts were always accurate, but the questions and answers would be those of Donahue and his guests.

While Miss Alma heard very well, she didn't always listen very well. Once, during a bad check case, the lawyers and the defendant were in chambers to discuss a plea bargain and the Judge instructed Miss Alma, who also acted as his secretary, not to interrupt him with any telephone calls. A few minutes later, the Judge's intercom buzzed. "Telephone call," Miss Alma announced.

"I thought I told you to hold my calls," the Judge snapped.

Seconds ticked by as we resumed our plea negotiations when, suddenly, the buzzer went off again. "Judge, it's Sears," Miss Alma said solemnly.

"I don't care who it is. I don't want to be disturbed," the Judge said firmly.

After another short pause, the buzzer sounded for the third time. "Judge," Miss Alma whispered, "They say they're going to sue you if you don't pay your bill."

We couldn't stop laughing—especially the defendant—who, I suspect, felt he was in the hands of a kindred spirit.

In preparing Dino's case, we identified five stages of attack: first, prosecutorial misconduct; second, the unconstitutionality of the child pornography statute; third, recusal of the DA; fourth, plea negotiations; and fifth, the trial itself. Because prosecutorial misconduct is an evidentiary matter that could have positive public relations effects, we launched this line of attack first. We filed a motion to dismiss grounded on the claim that Dino had received transactional immunity. A prosecutor has the power to forgive wrongdoing by granting immunity and usually, but not always, this is done in exchange for a defendant's cooperation against another wrongdoer. Another aspect of the motion to dismiss was the inordinate amount of prejudice created by the bounty hunters in releasing the evidence to the public before the trial. Joe Walker had done a survey for us to measure the level of hostility in the community toward Dino. It was staggering. We didn't want to move for a change of venue, however, because New Orleans was by far the best place to try this kind of case. Instead, we argued that the more drastic remedy of dismissal was warranted in order to punish the DA for having violated a state statute by intentionally releasing the evidence to the bounty hunters prior to trial.

When the hearing on the motion to dismiss began, the prosecutors and press corps whispered amongst themselves that the Judge was in my pocket because of our long friendship. Nothing was further from the truth. While the Judge and I remain close friends, he is usually harder on me in the courtroom because of our friendship. Known on the bench as "Frank the Tank," he actually almost put me in jail during the course of the hearing. While Walker was on the witness stand, the prosecutor demanded a full copy of his survey and, knowing that one day it might serve as an invaluable jury selection tool, I strenuously objected. The Judge ruled against me:

> Lemann: "I'm not going to give it to him, Your Honor. You're going to have to put me in jail."
>
> The Court: "Maybe I'll have to do that."
>
> Lemann: "Maybe you will."
>
> The Court: "Okay. Sir, before I—I never indicated anything about putting anybody in jail in reference to an attorney, and before—the attorney is telling the Court now, and I find that somewhat contemptuous, 'You will have to put me in jail.' You're not a witness. You're a learned—you're somebody who knows a lot more about the law. And when we're dealing in this aspect, I make decisions, some are right and some are wrong. . . . But as far as baiting the court, 'You're going to have to put me in jail,' I'm going to do that if I order it and you decide that you don't want to. You brought the subject up and it will happen. It will happen quicker to you than it will happen to that witness, because a witness is a witness. You're an attorney and an officer of this Court. And one of the things about direct contempt is not only the question of my decision but your demeanor before the Court. You have other people out in this audience and I have to protect the integrity of the Court and I won't permit that."

Lemann: "I agree, Your Honor, and I apologize."

The Court: "Well your apology is accepted in the record. . . . "

After further reflection, I gave the prosecutor the Walker survey. I was absolutely wrong in baiting the Court, and I am lucky not to have gone to jail.

This was not the only time I was unable to back down Frank the Tank. Years earlier, I had represented a black defendant accused of brutally murdering a young, white girl in the lakefront area of New Orleans. Although the police had searched the crime scene for fingerprints, they had been unsuccessful in matching any of my client's prints. Midway through the trial, the prosecution realized the police had failed to obtain my client's palm prints. Hoping to match a palm print, the prosecution requested, and Judge Marullo ordered, my client to give his palm prints. I consulted with my client, advising him that the most the Judge could do if he refused would be to hold him in contempt and impose a six-month sentence. Already in jail and facing the death penalty, my client wisely refused, whereupon the Judge ordered us into chambers, further ordering the sheriff to bring forth the two largest deputies in his command. When the two uniformed brutes arrived, my client still steadfastly and insolently refused to give his palm prints. With that, Frank the Tank removed a machete from beneath his desk, handed it to the uniformed brutes, and ordered "Sheriff, cut this man's arm off." Shocked and embarrassed for my friend, I looked over to the court reporter, hoping to find Miss Alma asleep at her machine next to Donahue on TV. Instead, I found Miss Alma wide awake, taking it all down meticulously, her eyes as big as those of my client. Needless to say, my client provided his palm prints.

The materials discovered in Dino's suite were evidence of the following possible crimes: first, crime against nature, because the homemade videos depicted Dino voluntarily engaging in "unnatural sex acts"; second, molestation of a juvenile, because the homemade videos established that Dino had sex with minors—but only if Chris or Ron were under seventeen years of age; third, the manufacturing of child pornography, because the homemade videos constituted child pornography—but, again, only if Chris or Ron were under seventeen; and fourth, the possession of child pornography, because the commercially produced foreign magazines and 8mm films unquestionably involved some prepubescent boys engaging in sexual conduct.

Since the most recent homemade video was dated 1984, the five year prescriptive period for crime against nature had expired by the time the DA received the materials in 1989. Thus, there could be no prosecution for that crime. The sexual molestation offense and the manufacturing of child pornography offense all depended upon the ages of Chris and Ron.

Because the DA's office initially didn't know the identities or ages of Chris and Ron, there could be no prosecution for those offenses. Thus, the theory of our motion to dismiss was that the identities and ages of Chris and Ron were provided to Sergeant Tolar by Bill Campbell in exchange for the promise that, if the information was validated, the DA would not prosecute Dino for any offense, including the possession of the child pornography contained in the foreign magazines and 8mm films. Campbell maintained that this was the oral agreement he had with Sergeant Tolar and, from a practical standpoint, it made sense: why else would Campbell cooperate with the DA's office if Dino, in any event, would be prosecuted for possession of child pornography?

As expected, Campbell testified at the hearing about the immunity agreement and, surprisingly, Sergeant Tolar didn't totally disagree with him, acknowledging that Connick had decided over his objection not to prosecute Dino for possession of child pornography. In contrast, Connick denied that Sergeant Tolar had ever recommended such a prosecution and swore instead that the reason there had been no prosecution was because he had believed the United States Attorney would prosecute. This conflict in the testimony created a defense lawyer's dream. The Judge would have to choose between Campbell's consistent testimony and the inconsistent versions given by Connick and his chief investigator. Judge Marullo agreed with us and dismissed the case.

Obviously, this would not be a one punch fight, and the State appealed. In the meantime, the press kept up its bombardment by covering the civil cases as though they were criminal. Tschirn tried to depose Dino for a second time, but we blocked it with the Fifth Amendment. We then decided on a long shot and sued Connick, Tolar, Tschirn, Paddison, Raymond, and Angelico in federal court, alleging a conspiracy to violate Dino's due process and privacy rights by wrongfully releasing and publishing the materials removed from his suite. After the suit was filed, Raymond sold copies of some of the materials to Geraldo Rivera, who published them over his nationally televised show; and he, too, was added to the suit. The media defendants brought in the big law firms and, although they smothered us with an avalanche of pleadings, the tenor of the news coverage slowly, almost imperceptibly, began to tone down. Even though our federal lawsuit ultimately would be dismissed, it took time—and to a criminal defense lawyer, time is like money in the bank.

After Judge Marullo's decision dismissing the case was reversed, we executed our second line of attack, this one directed at the constitutionality of the child pornography statute. The statute, like those in many states, originally criminalized only the manufacturing or distribution of child pornography and, in doing so, it excluded the defense of lack of knowledge of a child's age. In 1986 the Louisiana Legislature amended the statute to make the simple possession of child pornography a crime, and it did this without providing the defense of lack of knowledge. We argued that the amendment created an unconstitutional burden at odds with the presumption of innocence and the First Amendment. One simply cannot tell by looking at a nude photograph whether a model is sixteen or seventeen years of age, and it is fundamentally unfair to punish the possession of such material without affording the defense of lack of knowledge. The Judge agreed and declared the statute unconstitutional. The State appealed for the second time. The Supreme Court affirmed in part and reversed in part, agreeing that the exclusion of the lack of knowledge defense created an unconstitutional burden, but disagreeing that the entire statute was unconstitutional.

We were also making headway in the civil cases. The courts held that Chris's and Ron's sexual abuse lawsuits were barred by the one year prescriptive period. After all, their relationships with Dino had ended in 1984, and they had waited until 1989 to file their claims. They had tried to overcome the prescriptive period by utilizing a legal doctrine known as *contra non valentem agere nulla currit prescripto*, and I tell you this to illustrate that we dragon slayers sometimes speak in ancient tongues. Under this doctrine, Chris and Ron had argued that since they had been psychologically dominated by Dino, they had not been free to file their lawsuits until 1989. The courts rejected this argument, recognizing that these men, both of whom had married since ending their relationships with Dino, were simply two hustlers looking for another score.

The only civil claim remaining was the one for the publication of Chris's nude photographs in *Dream Boy*, which he first became aware of in 1989. The case went to trial in February 1995, but midway through—and over our objection—the Church settled, no longer able to stand the heat of the battle. In my view, this was a mammoth mistake but, in any event, the settlement removed another source of prejudicial publicity.

Our third pre-trial attack was to disqualify Harry Connick. We argued that Connick had improperly interjected religious beliefs into his prosecutorial decisions. After all, Connick had stated publicly that a primary reason for not prosecuting Dino initially was to spare "Holy Mother the Church." And then after the alleged cover-up had failed, Connick had filed the charge four days after the Archbishop had publicly called for the prosecution. Judge Marullo agreed and disqualified Connick. The State appealed again, and the higher court eventually reversed the Judge for a third time.

Throughout these long pre-trial skirmishes, I sought—I begged—for a plea bargain that would allow Dino to plead guilty to a misdemeanor, thereby safeguarding his CUNY job and sparing him the mandatory two-year sentence required by the child pornography statute. The prosecutors, however, would have no part of such a deal. Their case was air tight: Dino had admitted possessing materials that clearly constituted child pornography. There was no possible defense, and even Slim would tell me, "if you can get this jury past those dirty pictures, I'll know you can do anything!"

Dragon fighting is much like bullfighting. Like the matador, the knight must first wear down the beast. When Dino's case finally went to trial in August 1995, more than four years had elapsed since the charge, and almost seven years had gone by since the alleged offense. While the case was still high-profile, one thing was clear: the momentum was no longer clearly with the prosecution. The passage of time, along with some well-placed banderillas, had taken their toll on the beast. And then, as in bullfighting, a strange thing occurred. Instead of developing self-doubt, the bull in this case, ADA Tim McElroy, wounded and dazed, became even more resolute in the confidence of his charge. It is this phenomenon that gives matadors and dragon slayers the edge. Tim the Bull charged forward, not seeing the blood already flowing from his flared nostrils.

The passage of time had also brought a new Senora to the arena. For some reason—I'm not sure why—R.A. had started to attend my trials. It certainly wasn't due to a lack of nervousness, because she was still as nervous as a death row inmate at Angola. After a trial day, she would go home and, complaining of exhaustion, immediately take to her bed.

When it came time to select a jury in Dino's case, I relied heavily upon the Walker survey, which had revealed that our best jurors would be young to middle-aged African-Americans. While this group is generally considered good for the defense in any criminal trial, the conventional wisdom at Tulane and Broad was that black males, typically very macho and strongly homophobic, made good jurors for the prosecution in cases involving homosexuality. As jury selection progressed, it quickly became apparent to me that Tim the Bull was following the conventional wisdom. I waited in the briar patch.

At one point during the *voir dire* as I walked over to the defense table, I saw Joe Rome in the audience and, believing him to be an observer, I went over to greet him. In the past, when I regularly tried cases at Tulane and Broad, people like lawyers and policemen were exempt from jury duty. A few minutes later, I was thunderstruck to hear the minute clerk call Joe as a prospective juror. During Tim the Bull's questioning of him, Joe said that one of his children went to St. Rita's School and that he attended church there, but nothing was said of our prior relationship. When my turn came, the following exchange occurred:

Lemann: "You and I know one another, is that right?"

Rome: "Yes, sir."

Lemann: "The fact that we know one another—do you believe that would cause you to have any difficulty in either giving the State or the defendant a fair trial?"

Rome: "No, I also know the two prosecutors."

Shortly afterward, Joe requested a side bar with the Judge, and to questions from both Tim the Bull and me responded that, although he had some familiarity with the case, he had not drawn any conclusions about it and could weigh the evidence with an open mind.

Tim the Bull accepted Joe as a juror and, ultimately, Joe became foreman of the jury. Later, I would be criticized by the press and others for not revealing my prior representation. Having disclosed that we knew one another, however, I felt it was up to Tim the Bull to probe further. I find it hard to believe he was unaware of the Rome case, especially since it was a lesson for prosecutors not to sleep on their watch. But at any rate, I'm not aware of any rule against shooting a dragon in the back.

Satisfied with the jury, and after the State's opening statement, I outlined our defense:

> "The first thing that's going to become evident to you is that Dino Cinel is a very, very complex individual. He was born in 1941 during World War II and he was born in Northern Italy in a very small farming village. It was a very small and it was a very poor village. He was the youngest of nine children. His father was a farmer, and you will hear that when Dino was very young, his father was in a farming accident and had to have his leg amputated, and basically this accident incapacitated him and that was a very serious economic and traumatic happening to this very poor family. An older brother, who was in World War II, came back and sort of took over from the father when he became injured and he was cruel to Dino. There was a little school in that village—only had two rooms and only went up to the fourth grade. And in that village when the boys finished the fourth grade, they went to work farming. When the girls finished the fourth grade, they went to work in the silk factory. Dino was, from a very early age, enamored by education. He became fascinated with education. It became something that he wanted very much, and in that little village there were really only two educated men. One was the doctor, the town physician, and the other was the priest. And they were role models for Cinel. His family didn't have the wherewithal to send him to medical school so that didn't happen. Instead, he went to be a priest. He went to a seminary close by and went to this seminary when he was nine—between nine and ten years old. And, when he went to that seminary, that was it. He left his parents. He left his brothers and sisters. And he was only a nine or ten

year old. He didn't come home for holidays. That was his life.

Now that seminary had a rector, a head priest, who was probably in his sixties at the time, and he was a very prominent rector. He was a very strong individual. He was politically well known within the Church and he was a towering figure in Dino Cinel's life. And when Dino Cinel was about twelve years old or so, this rector began to sexually abuse him. He was forced to masturbate the rector. This was a traumatic development in this young boy's life. It had lasting effects. It caused total confusion. Here was a youngster being taught that masturbation was a mortal sin and here was the towering figure in his life making him masturbate him. It was a most traumatic thing that you will hear throughout the testimony that I will introduce to you. It caused an overwhelmingly significant impact in this young boy's life.

Dino Cinel—when he finished that seminary—continued his studies to become a priest and he ended up in another seminary as a novice where he was involved with intense spiritual training and there was another very important person in Dino's life at that time, the Master of Novices—and he was again a very imposing, a very important person in this young man's life. He challenged Dino early on about whether or not there had been any unusual sexuality in his background and he confronted Dino with the relationship that he had had with the first rector. And this Master of Novitiates—I think he's called—he blamed Dino; you see, when this was happening to Dino as a youngster, Dino didn't really feel as though it was his responsibility—when this was going on with the older rector. But this second most important person in his life made Dino feel that all of this was his fault and placed him under complete psychological dominance. Told him that he was going to, or could, end his career as a priest but that he would permit him to continue to study to become a priest only if he obeyed and listened to him totally. So this was an important development in Dino's life.

Eventually in 1966, he was ordained as a priest. What you will find out in the testimony that we're going to put on is that there were two significant tensions in Dino Cinel's life. One was the constant tension between whether he really wanted to be a priest or whether it was really the academic life that he wanted. The priesthood up until this point had provided him the education that he so dearly wanted. The second tension that you will see that went on in this complicated man's life was this constant tension between his sexuality. Was he homosexual? Was he heterosexual? Should he be sexual at all, given the fact that there obviously were vows of celibacy—not only vows of celibacy but of chastity. There's a big difference. A vow of chastity means purity of thought even. So this—these dynamics you will see constantly at play in the development of Dino Cinel as a human being.

Dino comes to the United States for the first time in 1968. Doesn't speak a word of English. And you will hear when he testifies for you during this case—and although he doesn't have to, he will—he speaks with a very heavy Italian accent; and keep in mind that Italian still is his first language. When he speaks in English, at times he may grope for words. He came to this country again pursuing the academic world. He came to New York University in 1968 and went to graduate school there. He got a degree—a Master's Degree in American History from N.Y.U., a very prestigious school. When he finished that, he went back to Rome. His Order, I think it's called the Scalabrini Order, let him come to the United States to advance his academic career, but then they would want him to come back to do priestly chores. But still there was always this great goal of his to advance academically in education. So he came back to this country in the 70s, and he went to Stanford University out in California—you know, it's called the Harvard of the West. And he ultimately got a Ph.D., a Doctorate of Philosophy, from Stanford University, again in the field of American History. He will tell you—and some of you will remember, some don't—but the mid-seventies in California, in the San Francisco area, was a place of great social experimentation. A great place—it was the time of the hippies, it was the time of the Vietnam resistance. In the Church, it was a time of great liberalization. At that time, it wasn't the present Pope, and there was great discussion within the Catholic Church about ending celibacy, about increasing freedom. And while Dino lived there and was studying to become a Ph.D., he was in a very liberal group of Catholics. The priests who were friendly with him essentially felt that celibacy was going to end, that the new movement in the Church would be sexual freedom for priests. And he became sexually free during that time period. And that is when he began to acquire pornographic material. Keep in mind that when he acquired these materials in the mid-seventies in the San Francisco area, it was lawful. It was legal to possess. And you will see from the dates on the material, that the material he acquired during the early seventies was homosexual. That was his sexual interest.

Because of this conflict about whether you're homosexual, whether you're heterosexual, Dino sought psychiatric counsel way back then, in the 1970s, over this. You will hear testimony that will demonstrate to you that when a youngster is trying to define his sexuality and a traumatic thing occurs to him—as in this case, the molestation by the rector—that it is such a severe psychological happening, that one stops to grow sexually. He becomes stunted. That's what happened to Dino Cinel. So that's when—in the seventies—when he began to try to find his sexual identity and explore sexual freedom, he actually went to the homosexual experience that was his first sexual experience and began to identify with that homosexuality.

Around the end of the seventies, in 1979, a number of things happened. He finished his Ph.D. He became a United States citizen. He left his Order, the Scalabrini Brothers. He taught at the University of Texas. And then in 1979, he received an appointment from Tulane University to become a full-time history professor. Dino, at this particular time, was essentially a lay person. He went to Tulane University every day as a professor. He didn't wear a Roman collar. He dressed in lay clothes. He was a full time history professor at Tulane University. He was still, however, not totally ready to break from the Catholic Church. He's a priest, although what he did was he worked out an arrangement with St. Rita's where he could stay there and of course, frankly, the fact that it was free room and board was a factor. It was free room and board in exchange for which he would say a mass once in a while and help out with some priestly functions. But he was essentially a full-time professor at Tulane and what I call a part-time priest. This was in early 1979 and the eighties. Now during this time he continues to acquire pornographic material. But you will see from the material the progression that I'm talking about—the footprints are there. You will see that in the beginning, in the early seventies, some of the material unquestionably involves juveniles. So there is and will be child pornography. When he acquired this, it was lawful, number one. Number two, you will see that it forms a minute part of the overall pornography. As one of you said yesterday, ultimately it became a crime—only if one of the participants was under seventeen. You can't tell, no one can tell, by looking at the overwhelming majority of this material, whether you're talking about a seventeen year old or a sixteen year old. If it's seventeen, it's legal. If it's sixteen, it's not. You can't tell. . . ."

Mr. McElroy: "Excuse me, Your Honor. I hear a, a closing argument at this point now. . . ."

Lemann: " . . . I suggest the evidence. . . ."

Mr. McElroy: "I object to the arguing nature."

The Court: "Objection sustained."

"I suggest—thank you, Your Honor. I suggest that the evidence will be unclear on that point. There is some—the early material—that unquestionably does show juveniles. As we move on in time into the late seventies and to the early eighties, the material becomes homosexual. Older people, adult pornography, but homosexual.

About the middle of '85 into '86, some very important things happened. In July of '86, Dino Cinel begins on his own intensive counseling. Once a week from July of '86 into 1989. Intensive counseling—psychiatric, psychological, therapeutic counseling—trying to resolve this sexuality. You will find that ultimately—from the material you will see—that around the mid-eighties, the material begins to change to heterosexual and by the time you get to the '86, '87, '88, material, it all becomes *Playboy, Playgirl, Hustler*, girly magazines. He is making this transition. He is slowly finding his sexuality and he is—with the help of this intensive counseling—he's moving away from homosexuality into heterosexuality. And then you will see that a significant thing happens to him in September of '88."

I then recounted for the jury the courtship between Dino and Linda, their decision to marry, his trip to Italy to tell his family, the so-called accidental discovery of the pornographic materials by the Pastor, Connick's decision not to prosecute, the release of the materials to the bounty hunters and, finally, Connick's breach of the immunity agreement by bringing the criminal charge.

Tim the Bull learned for the first time during my opening statement that we would not deny that some of the materials contained child pornography. While he had been gloating with bloodshot eyes over the sordid nature of the materials, I had been carefully documenting the publication dates on the porno magazines and 8mm films. The dates were consistent with my theory: the hard core child pornography had been acquired by Dino in the 1970s when its possession was legal, and the gradual shift in the nature of the materials had tracked his sexual growth into a mature heterosexual. In short, the man on trial was not the same man who had possessed the materials in 1988, and he was not the same man who had acquired the child pornography in the 1970s. I ended my opening statement thusly:

> "I will prove to you that Dino Cinel lacked criminal intent. The Judge will explain to you that this is a specific intent crime. It requires a specific intent to violate the law. Dino Cinel—when he bought this material, it was legal. He never, ever understood that it became illegal; but by the time it became illegal in Louisiana, it was something that he was no longer consciously possessing. I will show to you that Dino Cinel, that the very first time that he heard anything about this being illegal was that Bill Campbell told him when he hired Bill Campbell back in '89. And when they were working on this, trying to get this material back, Bill Campbell told him that it was illegal, and he didn't believe Campbell. He went to the library—the evidence will show—and researched the law, and Title 14, the green book, and saw that it didn't punish the possessor of the material. But what he didn't know because he's not a lawyer was that there was a supplemental pocket part in the back of the book that contained the 1986 amendment. But we will show that in August of '90, he testified under oath that as far as he knows, it's not a crime to possess this kind of material in Louisiana. This man did not criminally intend to violate the law. The evidence will show that he's a failed priest. It will show that he suffered from human frailty. It will show that he was a sinner. But it will not show that he's a convict."

The prosecution's case was a simple one. The Pastor was called to establish how the materials were found, and Don Richard was called to relate that he eventually delivered the materials to the DA. Sergeant

Robert Kessell, Tolar's partner, was called to verify receipt of the materials by the DA's office. Interestingly, Tolar was not called as a witness. After he contradicted Connick at the hearing on the motion to dismiss, he lost his cushy job as a DA investigator and, after seventeen years in that capacity, he was abruptly transferred back to uniform as just another cop on the street.

The State ended its case by showing the homosexual materials: hour after hour, frame after frame, picture after picture, penis after penis. We went through this laborious process with Sergeant Kessell on the witness stand reading captions, such as, "Guy sucks big dicks," or, "He takes it all up the ass." Throughout this painful and eventually boring testimony, Winn Stoutz, sitting next to me at counsel's table, kept pulling on my sleeve insisting that we object. But I wouldn't object and, instead, gave Tim the Bull all the rope he wanted.

On cross-examination, I walked up to Sergeant Kessell dragging with me the large boxes of heterosexual materials and, in copycat fashion, I had him read aloud caption after caption, "Girl sucks big dicks," or, "She takes it all up the pussy." The jury started to smile. "It's a matter of taste!" Kessell protested.

"Precisely!" I said, ending my cross-examination.

We began the defense by calling Dr. Max Lubin a psychologist who had done a battery of tests which essentially corroborated our theory: Dino was presently a well-adjusted heterosexual with a severe sexual conflict in his past. We then called a film expert who testified that 8mm films had largely been replaced by videos in the early 1980s. These "silent films," as I would call them to emphasize their antiquity, contained the worst of the child pornography. It was very important to date them before 1986 when it became a crime to possess child pornography in Louisiana.

Of course, Dino was our main witness. We had spent hours with him on video rehearsing his testimony, with me telling him over and over again that he had to project as though he were "going to confession before the jury." There could be no intellectualizing at Tulane and Broad. Owing, no doubt, to my experience as a confessor in Donaldsonville, I must have coached him well because he appeared humble, meek and repentant, like a "lost sheep returning to the flock." When the prosecutor charged in to cross-examine, Dino—upon my instructions—refused to wave the cape at him and Tim the Bull became dazed, disoriented, and pathetic-looking, standing there alone in the ring, kicking and snorting as I prepared the sword.

We ended with Linda. She identified a large, beautiful photograph of Sophia and explained the nightmare of shielding her from the ravages of the case. Linda was tortured and tragic—a real Scottish heroine. In closing argument, I said:

> " . . . Our defense in this case has always been one of lack

of intent. Lack of intent. The Judge will instruct you on the law. He's going to tell you that before we send a person to the penitentiary in this country, you have to be satisfied that he had a criminal intent to violate the law. He will read to you this statute which penalizes and criminalizes the possession of child pornography. The statute doesn't say anyone who possesses 'except policemen.' It says everyone who possesses this material intentionally and with knowledge that there is a participant under seventeen is guilty. Everyone, including policemen. Yet Kessell, a policeman, could intentionally possess this material yesterday in the courtroom. He can know that it's child pornography. He can know that it's against the law. But he doesn't commit a crime because he doesn't intend to violate the law. His intention in possessing it is to enforce the law. I have in my briefcase over there copies of this material that I've been carrying around for a long time. Copies of this material which clearly constitute child pornography. It's mine. I possess it. I possess it intentionally. I know what it is. I know that there's a law against it. But they're not going to come and arrest me. The reason they're not going to come and arrest me is because they know that I'm possessing it not with the intent to violate the law, but I'm possessing it with the intent to defend someone. People can possess things with different intentions. And it's that intention that makes the difference. Kessell could walk out of here with his badge and, if he goes and acquires some of this material knowing that it is someone under seventeen and intentionally brings it to his home and puts it under his bed for his own personal use and gratification (if that's what he likes) then, even though he's a policeman, he of course violates the law. Because then his intent is to violate the law. So the difference is not the badge. The difference is not the fact that we're possessing it in a courtroom instead of some place else. The difference is in one's state of mind. Now that's what the government has to prove to you beyond a reasonable doubt—that in this man's mind, back in December of '88, that he possessed this material intentionally for the purpose of violating the law. Now I believe I have shown you that he didn't even know it was against the law . . . and remember, the material is not on trial, the man is on trial.

. . . He bought this material when it was legal. He ultimately grew out of the material. He ultimately stored it

> away. He never, ever found out that it was illegal. There's an old saying, you know: 'Out of sight, out of mind.' And I believe that he was not consciously possessing this material for the purpose of violating the law and, unless they prove to you otherwise beyond a reasonable doubt, then you would be required to return a verdict of not guilty."

When Dino was in the witness box, I showed him a law book containing the child pornography statute, which he identified as being similar to the one he used to find the law on child pornography. After I demonstrated how the back of the book contained a supplement of amendments, he had testified that he had been unaware of the supplement and, for that reason, hadn't found the 1986 amendment criminalizing the possession of child pornography. Having introduced the law book into evidence as an exhibit, I started to read to the jury during closing argument the section on crime against nature. Tim the Bull objected wildly, galloping around the courtroom, his tongue beginning to hang. However, since the law book was in evidence, the Judge properly overruled the objection and allowed me to read from it and explain to the jury what few people realize: crime against nature applies to heterosexuals as well as to homosexuals. I continued:

> " . . . If a married couple in this city today have oral sex, consensual, in the privacy of their bedroom, they violate this law. Now do you think it would be fair to send somebody to jail for this? With his spouse or her spouse and they didn't even know the law? And how many people know this law? That's the danger of bedroom crime. You know, I have a philosophy: You stay out of my bedroom, I'll stay out of your bedroom. And I don't want legislators from North Louisiana telling me what I can do in my bedroom here in New Orleans. If I can stay out of their bedroom, they ought to stay out of my bedroom."

Deeply religious people—and there appeared to be at least one on the jury—can be very unforgiving when betrayed by one of their leaders. There was the danger then that such a juror would hold a former priest to a higher standard. On the other hand, the blacks on the jury were often judged in everyday life by a different standard and, knowing they would be sensitive to this aspect of the case, I weaved homophobia into the double standard cloth:

> " . . . Another thing that I am very concerned about is the fact that he was a priest. That you somehow will hold him to a higher standard because he was a priest and because he was a failed priest. And I tell you these prosecutors

have subtly been trying to do that. You know, they were asking the man about his vows of celibacy, and chastity, and was he a liar because he betrayed those vows—they are subtly trying to get you to condemn this man because he's a sinner. And I was worried about that. And each of you gave me your word that you wouldn't do that. You wouldn't hold him up to a higher standard.

And another thing that I am very, very, very, very concerned about and still to this day, this moment, very upset and concerned about, is the homosexuality of this material. You know, there's, there's what we call, and I have it, and uh, you know, homo—homophobia. Uh, it, it, it, it frightens heterosexual men. It, it, it does. And, and, and it does me. And I'm, I'm afraid about that, see. Because they are gambling that you all are heterosexual and that you're going to be so turned off by this material that you're going to convict this pervert regardless of whether or not he still is—regardless of whether or not he had criminal intent—but simply because it's homosexual. There is absolutely no doubt in my mind but that if we were dealing with a sailor who lived on Decatur Street and had three boxes of little girly magazines under his bed, and I'm talking about under seventeen, but girly magazines, and he was a sailor and not a priest. You know where we'd be right now? We'd be down at Johnny White's drinking beer together. We wouldn't be here. This man is on trial because he was a priest and because he was gay at the time. That's why he's on trial. That's wrong. That is absolutely wrong."

Johnny White's is a well-known bar in the French Quarter and when I said this, some of the jurors grinned. The crescendo was building and I smelled roses blowing in the wind of the arena:

"You know, let me tell you a little bit about sex. I can't tell you anything about uh, uh, homosexuality because I, I was never a homosexual. But I can tell you a little bit about sex. I can tell you that I grew up in a little small Catholic town fifty some odd years ago where mortal sin was the big thing and under the Catholic Church and all that other stuff. And I had my first sexual encounter . . . ."

Mr. McElroy: "Excuse me, Your Honor, this is outside of the record and I'm objecting to it. We're well out of the evidence now. Where Mr. Lemann

> grew up and what his experiences were is not arguing the case."

The Court: "Overruled."

> "You know, I remember my first sexual encounter with a little thirteen year old and it's, it's, uh, some forty years later, and I still remember it. And you know what? I remember the way she looked back then, and I liked it. And I remember today the way she looked back then, and I still like it. And I remember what she looked like at fourteen and fifteen and sixteen, and I liked it back then and I like it today. And I carry a photograph of that in my heart today—forty some odd years later. And you know what? If I had a photograph of her, I'd carry it in my wallet today. And if that's a crime, take me away, Sheriff. Because I'm not ashamed of it. I'm proud of it. It was a good experience. It was a sin, but it wasn't a crime. Now I've never been a homosexual. But my guess is if a thirteen year old homosexual has a sexual encounter with another thirteen year old homosexual, and it's an enjoyable one, it's their cup of tea. My guess is they liked it and they look upon the other human body with attraction and with sexuality and with lust, and with all the good and passionate emotions that heterosexuals associate with it. But it might be difficult for us to deal with. And that's their gamble. That's their bet. This case would have never been prosecuted if the material involved had been heterosexual. They are gambling on homophobia. That's what they're doing and it's wrong."

As in bullfighting, timing in dragon fighting is critical and, like the matador, the knight must know precisely when to move in for the finale. Of course, the signs are really different and modern day dragon slayers have to sense the moment as much as see it. Whether it's a deathly stillness in the courtroom or a bailiff's wink or a juror's nod or a judge's twitch or a prosecutor's gasp—whatever it may be—I knew in the Dino Cinel case that the time had come for the kill:

> "So I've got to ask you also for mercy. I've got to ask you also for forgiveness. I've got to ask you also to recognize that there is such a thing as redemption. It does happen. And I believe that this man has redeemed himself. I've got to ask you to consider—as any judge before sentencing would—the amount of pain and anguish and suffering that this man has already gone through as a result of

this. He has lost his job. His whole career of fifty-one years working toward academic excellence is over. It's gone. He's been held up to public scorn. What his wife has gone through—to shield this and to continue to shield this from Sophia.

You know, child pornography is an evil thing. And the legislatures historically in Louisiana and elsewhere have had long-standing laws against child pornography. But it was against the manufacturer, the distributor, the creator, the wholesaler, the retailer, the people who made money off of this smut. That has always been against the law in Louisiana. And I think that's a good law. Now in their wisdom, in September of '86 for the first time the legislature decides, well, we also now are going to punish the possessor. And when the judge reads the penalty provision, note that the possessor is treated under the penalty provision exactly the same way as the guy who creates this, manufactures it, and makes money off of it. They both get at least two years. But the theory of the prosecution and of this statute is that, well, if you punish Dino Cinel—this person, this possessor—that may have the effect of deterring another person from possession and purchase. And if we deter another person from purchasing, then that's one less dollar of profit that the retailer will make and then the wholesaler and then the distributor and the manufacturer and, ultimately, to the creator of all of this. And so the notion is that if you punish this possessor, it will deter other possessors with the hope that eventually some guy in Denmark won't be paying some teenagers to jerk off in front a camera. That's the theory. And it may be a valid theory. But it's all built on maybes—maybes—maybes. If you convict Dino Cinel in this case, I can tell you one thing that won't be a maybe. This is the child that will be punished (displaying the photograph of Sophia). This is the child that will be punished. This little five year old who will for the rest of her life have to live with the stigma that her father is a convict. Now I ask you ladies and gentlemen to return a verdict of not guilty in this case. And I ask you to do it not for Dino Cinel because his life—he may not know it—but his life is over with. I ask you not to do it for Linda Pollack because, after all, she was an adult and she had a choice and she chose. But the person who never had a choice is Sophia. And she's the one. It's her life that I leave with you."

The long wait began. R.A. was mortified over the revelation of my sexual exploits in Donaldsonville. Rachel and Amy wanted to know if it was "Mom or Bobbie Gail or Ann Goette?" Reflecting on my 3-M syndrome, I took the Fifth.

The jury deliberated for forty-five minutes before returning a verdict of not guilty. It was unanimous. Afterwards, Joe Rome told me one of the jurors had asked in jest whether they could add to the verdict the words, "but with continued therapy." Dino was lucky to have been tried in New Orleans. A Los Angeles jury might have acquitted him out of anger; a San Francisco jury might have acquitted him out of sympathy; but only a New Orleans jury would do it with a grin!

TWENTY-THREE

KNIGHTHOOD

After the Dino Cinel verdict, as I walked out of Tulane and Broad under the glare of television lights, Richard Angelico thrust the microphone in front of me asking for my reaction, and I said, "Just another dragon at my feet." A short time later, I received a piece of hate mail which ended in these words:

> "I guess everyone in this crummy U.S.A. has to have an attorney—no matter how low he has to stoop. Hail to the dragon slayer."

So you see, not everyone likes dragon slayers. In fact, most people hate dragon slayers. *Vanity Fair* commissioned a story about the Dino Cinel case and the writer interviewed me. She asked me the following question: "If Father Cinel were not dealing in pornography, how could he afford the Lincoln Continental, the Lake Pontchartrain residence and all the other elements of his affluent lifestyle?" My answer was simple and direct: "Manna from heaven!"

After reading the article in *Vanity Fair*, a woman from England wrote to the editor, "I don't know who is more despicable, Father Cinel, the local archdiocese, or Cinel's lawyer, Arthur 'Buddy' Lemann." It was bad enough to have been stereotyped in the article as "a sleek, portly man who favors three-piece white linen suits, saddle shoes, Panama hats, and fat cigars," and who "drawls, mouthing his frayed cigar." I had to hide the magazine from R.A. and my mother and—after all—not all of my three-piece suits are white linen.

Like a damsel in distress, the public's need for a dragon slayer is fickle. Dragons don't come along every day and, therefore, it's not unusual for long periods of time to go by with nothing to do but shine one's armor and sharpen one's lance. During these lulls, I reflect upon my life as a dragon slayer. Has it been worth it? Is society better off with the likes of Candy Smith, Stephen Rosiere, and Dino Cinel walking the streets?

Should I have been a tax lawyer with Monroe & Lemann, a real estate lawyer with Polack, Rosenberg & Rittenberg, a farmer, a cook, or a tree surgeon—any one of which would have been far more pleasing to my father? I reckon I'll never know the answers to these questions. Perhaps some people are just born to be dragon slayers. And, of course, the real question should be: do you suppose dragons step a little more cautiously around these parts these days because of my bloody lance? What makes all of this even more confusing is the fact that not all dragon slayers are criminal defense lawyers, and not all criminal defense lawyers are dragon slayers. Take Don Quixote and Robert Shapiro as examples.

Donaldsonville continues to be wrong. It's now the cancer capital of the world. The toxic smog from the petrochemical plants is so bad that the little pine trees planted around the Riverdale Country Club forty years ago are still the same size. King Industrio doesn't roll anymore and the Sisters of Charity have gone. After my father died, Andrew Capone became the town historian. I remember him when he was just a kid. There was nothing particularly scholarly about him. I'm not even sure he went to college.

I still ponder what archeologists will say two thousand years from now about the custom of people building second homes across the street from their houses. However, after much reflection, I have identified a number of practical advantages to this custom. For example, a person in Donaldsonville with a second home across the street from his house doesn't have to worry about packing or about the kids forgetting something before going on vacation. More importantly, one can start drinking before leaving and arrive drunk without worrying about a DUI—one only need be careful in crossing the street. And then, just when I thought I had it all figured out, my brother-in-law broke with tradition and built his second home in his backyard. He doesn't even have to worry about crossing the street.

I've also solved Miss Francis' case. She was obviously innocent and framed by the Monsignor. The proof is that no one, not even the Monsignor, could be so stupid as to believe that someone on a housekeeper's salary could afford a weekend home on the coast and a brand new car. No, I'm now convinced that it was the Monsignor who was stealing the money from the Church and that Miss Francis took the fall for him. I must admit, however, I can't figure out who blew the whistle. You know, for sure, it wasn't the Monsignor and I know for sure it wasn't Charlou, the police chief. You see, Charlou didn't mess with white collar crime, especially the Roman collar kind. So who fingered Miss Francis? Even Uncle can't figure that one out. And don't believe for a moment that simply because I'm trying to set the record straight about Miss Francis I'm following in the footsteps of Aunt Delta. There is a fundamental difference between me and Aunt Delta. I revise history; she forges history.

Naturally, the Jesuits are still around, but in smaller numbers—and not as smart. In fact, Uncle says there are now more former Jesuits at

Loyola than Jesuits. Mo went back to being dean of the Law School—and is still as haggard as ever. Fleta now looks like Demi Moore.

Through the grapevine, I heard that O'Grady has married again—his third, but the first time to someone other than Maddie. The stump must be better. Lil' Frankie is back on Grand Isle "stayin' by his mama's." Judge Sear is still holding court, which is where I must go momentarily. And Miss Alma, bless her heart, is now taking dictation from the Big Judge in the sky, asleep, no doubt, at her machine on a cloud.

Mother and Aunt Delta are trying to recover from two crushing blows. According to a recent book, my great, great, great, great, grandfather, Don Carlos Percy, was not a descendent of the Earl of Northumberland after all but, rather, an Irish impostor! On top of that, we have the problem of Meriwether Lewis. My mother and Aunt Delta always laid claim to him in their lineage. My father, on the other hand, being more the skeptic, used to postulate that the line ran from either Lewis or Clark. Now, Stephen Ambrose, the renowned historian, asserts in a new book that Meriwether never married. I suspect Mother and Aunt Delta will be attending the next Clark family reunion.

R.A. is still nervous. When she found out I was writing this book, she asked, "Is it something for law students to read?"

"No, it's something to be nervous about," I replied, as she immediately took to her bed.

Whenever I finish a big case, I always plant a garden. I like to dig deep into the ground and get dirt under my fingernails. It's my way of remembering that all of glory is fleeting and that hell (and Monsignor Gubler) are just a little farther down.

I was wrong about one thing. I no longer fight dragons alone. Arthur IV has joined Slim and me at the outfit, and Jonathan begins law school in the fall. And, of course, there will always be "MiMi, MaMa, MoMo."

THE END

Author's Note:

The cases and clients in this book are real. While it is autobiographical in essence, it is not intended as a suicide note. Accordingly, I have changed the names of certain characters in order to protect the guilty. After all, I am a criminal defense lawyer.

Text is set in Bookman Light.
Titles are set in Mason Alternate.
Drop Caps are set in Amedicus Caps.

Hail to the Dragon Slayer is available as an audio book, read by the author.